SELECTED REPORTS
in
ETHNOMUSICOLOGY
VOLUME III, No. 2

SELECTED REPORTS in ETHNOMUSICOLOGY
VOLUME III, No. 2

Editor of this Issue:
Charlotte Heth

Editorial Board:
Peter Crossley-Holland
Charlotte Heth
Nazir Jairazbhoy
J. H. Kwabena Nketia
Chairman, Council on Ethnomusicology
James Porter
Robert Stevenson

Assistant Editor:
Živilė Gimbutas

Illustrator:
Richard Keeling

Program in Ethnomusicology
Department of Music
University of California, Los Angeles
1980

Cover Illustration:

Standing male figure blowing conch, 5 7/8" by 2 1/4" ceramic. Mexico, Nayarit.
From the collection of the Museum of Cultural History, UCLA.

Copyright © 1980 by the Regents of the University of California

Library of Congress Catalog Card Number: 76-640181

ISBN: 0-88287-000-9 — entire series
ISBN: 0-88287-012-2 — this issue

Preface

Continuing the precedent established in Volume III, Number 1 of **Selected Reports in Ethnomusicology** *of presenting traditional music in the Americas, this issue focuses on the oldest music in the Americas, that of the American Indians. I am grateful to the Subcommittee on Publications and the Council on Ethnomusicology for allowing me to bring together this collection of articles on American Indian music. It is the first time a work on the subject has covered such widely differing geographical and theoretical orientations.*

For advice on assembling the issue, I must thank James Porter for laying the groundwork. For reading, commenting on, and sometimes providing editorial help, I must thank Abraham Schwadron, Robert Winter, Kenneth Lincoln, Velma Salabiye, Raymond J. De Mallie, and Raymond D. Fogelson; for research and bibliographic help, Cynthia Schmidt and Yvonne Ashley.

Živilė Gimbutas and Richard Keeling deserve praise for their work in preparing the copy and the illustrations.

University of California *Charlotte Heth*
Los Angeles
November, 1979

CONTENTS: SELECTED REPORTS IN ETHNOMUSICOLOGY

Charlotte Heth	ix	Introduction
David P. McAllester	1	"The War God's Horse Song" — An Exegesis in Native American Humanities
William K. Powers	23	Oglala Song Terminology
Thomas Vennum, Jr.	43	A History of Ojibwa Song Form
Maria La Vigna	77	Okushare, Music for a Winter Ceremony: The Turtle Dance Songs of San Juan Pueblo
Nora Yeh	101	The Pogonshare Ceremony of the Tewa San Juan, New Mexico
David E. Draper	147	Occasions for the Performance of Native Choctaw Music
Marcia Herndon	175	Fox, Owl, and Raven
Charlotte Heth	193	Selected Bibliography and Discography

INTRODUCTION:

THE TRADITIONAL MUSIC OF NORTH AMERICAN INDIANS.

American Indian music in the twentieth century is still integral to almost every Indian activity. Whether it be an ancient ceremony, a social dance, an Indian conference, a tourist attraction, a fair, a graduation exercise, or a political rally in "Indian country," there will be Indian music to accompany the proceedings. The music used by Indians today spans a continuum from the most sacred or magical (and restricted) to popular rock and country-western, with traditional sacred and social songs found in between. Indian musical expressions vary from area to area, tribe to tribe, and even from singer to singer, creating an overwhelming diversity of genres and styles.

Unlike the music discussed in the first issue of this volume on America, Indian music has not been transplanted — it is indigenous. The dislocation that has affected music has been a result of Indian migrations, both forced and voluntary. In what is now the United States, there are over two hundred fifty Indian tribal groups speaking different aboriginal languages and dialects, and living in every part of the country. Many of these people now do not live in their aboriginal homelands for a variety of reasons. United States government policy in the first part of the nineteenth century sought to remove all Eastern Indians from their homes to places west of the Mississippi River and created Indian Territory, now the state of Oklahoma, to accommodate them. After 1850, treaties with the plains-dwelling tribes brought them either to Indian Territory or confined them to reservations near their homelands. The Navajos and Apaches in the Southwest suffered military removals and forced marches away from their homes. The West Coast tribes fared no better.

In the mid-twentieth century another government policy, relocation, brought Indians to cities for job training. This recent removal resulted in dislocation and alienation for many people. Despite all these migrations of Indian people, hundreds of Indians participate regularly in their own tribes' musical lives; thousands of other Indians attend these activities whenever they can. These religious and social events enrich and unify Indian life, and, in most cases, they cannot be carried on if the music has been forgotten.

INTRODUCTION

Aboriginal Music.

Indian music cultures should not be viewed as monolithic. Cultural pluralism exists to as great a degree among Indians as it does among the general population of North America. Practitioners of music may be highly trained specialists such as Navajo ceremonial singers, or they may be secular members of the community such as Cherokee Stomp dancers. Some music, like the San Juan Turtle Dance, is tightly structured and rehearsed while other music, like the Cahuilla Bird Dance, is performed in a loose cyclical form with a leader and volunteer chorus.

Traditional musical activities among the Indians living on or near reservations or in rural areas are still practiced and retain a high value in accordance with their origins in the aboriginal societies. Music was sometimes given to Indian singers by the Creator, a lesser deity, a guardian spirit, a slain monster, or an animal. Although many songs have identifiable composers, others have religious or mystical origins not identified with people living today. These traditional activities are regionally or tribally specific; they are performed, for the most part, in native languages, and are tied to ancient calendars and belief systems.

Categories of Indian music would include music for public ceremonies and social occasions as well as for private and semi-public activities such as curing, prayer, initiation, hunting, influencing nature, putting children to sleep, storytelling, performing magic, playing games, and courting. While one tribal or community group would have music for some of the above activities, it would not necessarily have music for the others. If the function involving the music has disappeared, the music is usually retained only in a fragmentary form.

The articles in this issue deal with aboriginal forms of Indian music and not with revivals, pan-tribal music, or Indian innovations based on Western music. A balance between anthropology and musicology appears to have been achieved here with Powers' linguistic model at one end of the gamut and Yeh's musical/symbolic analysis at the other. The essays are presented, as nearly as possible, as the authors wished, and any mistakes in presentation lie with the editor.

David McAllester's article on the Navajo "War God's Horse Song" gives a publication history of the poem and outlines its various treatments by scholars and anthologists. McAllester carefully points out that *the poem is not the song* and then proceeds to provide us with a model for translating and studying Native American songs, especially Navajo songs. The idea of using indigenous philosophies and esthetics to understand a song according to its original meaning in context is welcome here. Further, the ethical and comparative reservations voiced in the article are problematic to all researchers in ethnomusicology, not just to those studying Native Americans. The translation model that McAllester presents for study and publication of such material has been needed for some time. Especially important to those of us who are singers is the full Navajo text with vocables and repetitions. McAllester's "ideal" is important for all of us to consider.

William K. Powers' "Oglala Song Terminology" also presents a new model for considering Native categories. Powers' concern with "how people structure their perception of reality and the manner in which they verbalize about it" leads him to suggest alternatives to the "questionnaire-type" approach to information gathering.

After observing that the Western notion of language compartmentalization (exclusive and specialist music vocabulary) may not obtain in other cultures, Powers goes on to explain that the analytical model derived from such technical vocabularies is limiting in application to cross-cultural phenomena in music. Indeed, Powers suggests that all people in the world might *not* consider music a cultural category, and, as the Oglala model suggests, might consider song as an extension of the human body.

The synthetic model constructed by Powers to show how the Oglala verbalize about song is a structural and linguistic approach to the subject. He compares the total number of morphemes found in Lakota lexemic units related to song with the same morphemes as they appear in other domains.

As in McAllester's article in this issue, the key to understanding lies in the native language. These two articles, expressing Native American concepts in their own languages, are a substantial contribution to knowledge.

Thomas Vennum, Jr. presents Ojibwa song form in a historical perspective (1899-1971) and effectively highlights the problems which the scholar encounters in doing historical research in ethnomusicology. In comparing early recordings and monographs with current Ojibwa musical practice, Vennum identifies certain gaps and attempts to rectify them. His retranscription of Densmore's Chippewa recordings in order to use the selective criteria and notational system of his contemporary transcriptions points out the value of using this primary source material. Additionally, the advantages of current recording techniques over the early cylinder recordings become evident in the freedom the scholar has to record longer and more culturally valid selections. Finally, Vennum's musical analysis outlines the evolutions of Ojibwa song form, and places the past squarely in the future.

Maria La Vigna's article on the San Juan Turtle Dance should be studied together with Nora Yeh's article, which follows it, and with the newly released *Oku Shareh: Turtle Dance Songs of San Juan Pueblo* (Heth and Ortiz 1979, NW 301). La Vigna's study outlines the musical repertoire at San Juan Pueblo and focuses on the ceremonies for which new music must be composed on each occasion of performance. La Vigna's attention to the compositional process and the concepts underlying the idea of composition adds more depth to our knowledge of Indian views of their own music. The article goes on to describe the performance of the Turtle Dance and gives a comparative analysis of songs from different years. The fixed and variable musical elements and cueing devices emerge with clarity and definition.

Nora Yeh's work, "The Pogonshare Ceremony of the Tewa," differs from La Vigna's in several important ways. While La Vigna discusses overall concepts, Yeh gives us a detailed analysis of several versions of the *Pogonshare*, or Cloud Dance. The Pogonshare, although composed anew each year, has many more fixed phrase units than the Turtle Dance. The composers' art emerges in the variable phrase units where manipulation of limited musical materials creates a new composition. Yeh also includes minute details of choreography, phrase length, repetition, and color symbolism. This micro-analysis of the Pogonshare complements La Vigna's macro-analysis of the *Okushare*.

David E. Draper's "Occasions for the Performance of Native Choctaw Music" increases our knowledge of Choctaw music by giving an overview of the existing categories of musical performance. Along with aboriginal music, Draper describes

INTRODUCTION

fiddle-guitar and Christian church music. Draper, like Vennum, has compared his work with Densmore's, enabling him to update her work and add to the quality of current material available on the Choctaw.

The aboriginal *hitla tuluwa*, or social dance song, repertoire forms the bulk of the paper. The analysis of the variants of the Jump Dance and Draper's subsequent conclusions hold promise for application to other tribal song categories.

Marcia Herndon's "Fox, Owl, and Raven" deals with an esoteric and restricted category of music: conjuring or magic songs. The integration here of cosmic view and music places the reader in another world. The function and form of music become integrated with life itself and, more importantly, with the spirit world.

The papers presented in this issue reflect current scholarship trends, tempered by historical comparison. Although the focus is on aboriginal music, the music described still exists in the twentieth century. Indian music has not disappeared as a result of conquest, intermarriage, relocation, and urbanization. The 1970's see many Indians retaining their unique cultures while others adopt Pan-Indian or Western ways. Although Indians have composed music to fit the times, they have also performed their oldest songs again and again.

Charlotte Heth

# "THE WAR GOD'S HORSE SONG,"

AN EXEGESIS IN NATIVE AMERICAN HUMANITIES[1]

David P. McAllester

One of the most widely published Native American song texts is "The War God's Horse Song." The most frequently reproduced version was first printed in 1930 in *The Navajo Indians* by Dane and Mary Roberts Coolidge. The text faces the first page of Chapter One, "Legend and History," the frontispiece, as it were, for the whole book, and is presented without explication. It stands as a piece of Native American Humanities, sufficient unto itself:

The War God's Horse Song

(Words by Tall Kia ah'ni. Interpreted by Louis Watchman)

I am the Turquoise Woman's son.
On top of Belted Mountain
Beautiful horses — slim like a weasel!
My horse has a foot like striped agate;
His fetlock is like a fine eagle plume;
His legs are like quick lightning.
My horse's body is like an eagle-plumed arrow;
My horse has a tail like a trailing black cloud.
I put flexible goods on my horse's back;
The Little Holy Wind blows through his hair.

His mane is made of short rainbows.
My horse's ears are made of round corn.
My horse's eyes are made of big stars.
My horse's head is made of mixed waters
(From the holy springs — he never knows thirst)

> My horse's teeth are made of white shell.
> The long rainbow is in his mouth for a bridle,
> And with it I guide him.
> When my horse neighs, different-colored horses follow.
> When my horse neighs, different-colored sheep follow.
> I am wealthy, because of him.
>
> Before me peaceful,
> Behind me peaceful,
> Under me peaceful,
> Over me peaceful,
> All around me peaceful —
> Peaceful voices when he neighs.
> I am Everlasting and Peaceful.
> I stand for my horse.

Since 1930, this version of the text has been reprinted by Astrov, 1946, Clark, 1966, Rothenberg, 1968, and Brandon, 1971. Other translations have been published by O'Bryan, 1956, Link, 1956, McAllester (in Rothenberg), 1968, and Wyman, 1970.

In her anthology, *The Winged Serpent*, Margot Astrov felt the need for an explanatory note:

> Living now in the semi-arid desert regions of the southwest, the Navajo are mainly herdsmen, skillful blanket weavers and unexcelled silversmiths. Their unusually poetical cycles of songs breathe the infiniteness of the sky, and their melodies are carried by the soft warm smell of the unbroken soil. The resemblance of certain traits of Navajo myth and song with epic and song of the south Siberian tribes is striking (Astrov 1962: 183).

The extended, sometimes cosmic, similes in the poem are unusual in Native American song texts and do, indeed, make this one "unusually poetical" to the non-Indian ear. In *Technicians of the Sacred*, Jerome Rothenberg accompanies the Coolidge version, "slightly revised," with a more extended rendition of the same text from a set of seventeen Horse Songs recorded by Frank Mitchell in Chinle, Arizona, in 1963. The two poems are included in a section of the book entitled "Origins and Namings," along with "To the God of Fire As A Horse," from the Rig Veda. In the commentaries, page 422, he cites a text from the Brhad Aranyaka Upanishad, "which equates various parts of the sacrificial-horse with elements of the cosmos, much as the Navajo does . . . ." Although more circumstantial, this is like Astrov's comparison with Siberian epic. Rothenberg also invites the reader to compare the Horse Songs with three African praise poems in the same volume.

William Brandon presents the poem in *The Magic World*, without comment except to indicate that it is "adapted" from the Coolidges' version. The spacing is quite different, lines are rearranged, and phrases are altered. His license to do this is asserted in the book's Introduction:

> I have used the word with the same freedom I would use with Sappho or Gottschalk or any poetry in translation. My sole aim has been to remember that these are living words, not quaint transliterations from an inaccessibly "primitive world." My only criterion has been, do the lines feel good, moving? I have tried to pay no attention whatsoever to the value of a given piece as ethnological information. I have tried to approach each line exactly as I might approach a line of Sappho's, only as literature (Brandon 1971: xiii-xiv).

This is standard Humanities treatment, in the tradition of Euro-American scholarship (to a slight extent) and esthetics. In the former case there is an impulse to compare the material to similar poems from other traditions for the humane lesson of our common motives and perceptions around the world. In the latter, Brandon, apparently like the Coolidges, treats the poem in the tradition of *l'art pour l'art*, although he does volunteer the ethnological information that the work is Navajo.

My contention is that if we are studying Native American Humanities, our effort must be to get as close as possible to the original meaning of the expressions of these humanities, rather than to reinterpret them in terms of the poetic intuitions of outside cultures, whether these be in Africa, ancient India, south Siberia, or the United States. In Native American Humanities it is an error to consider a text such as that of the "Horse Song" out of its cultural context, for the context is what gives it its Native American meaning. We must be prepared for the connotative excursion into the indigenous philosophy, mythology, art, music, religion, medicine — ethnography, in short — with every poem.

As the text stands in Coolidge, Astrov, Rothenberg, and Brandon, there are fatal opacities as to what it is all about that no poetic intuition can remedy. All we know about the "War God" is that he is Turquoise Woman's son. Is that enough for us to know in order to appreciate the poem? Who is Turquoise Woman? Another deity, one supposes, but would it not help to know that this is one of the several names of Changing Woman, the principal creator in the Navajo pantheon? In fact, this song is a celebration of her creation of horses after Enemy Slayer (one of the "War God's" real names; the Navajos do not call him a war god) earned this gift through arduous travels and difficult learning.

It deepens the cosmic connotations of the poem to know that Belted Mountain (perhaps better translated as Black Belted Mountain; see Haile 1950, I: 225) is the sacred mountain of the East, one of the four that bound the Navajo country, and that mountains have symbolic significance in Navajo thinking as the homes of deities, winds, and spirit horses. To go a little further, "slim like a weasel" is probably derived from a mistranslation of "dlǫ́ǫ́'" (any four-footed creature; here 'horse'), which is a homonym for "dlǫ́ǫ́'," meaning prairie dog or weasel (see comment no. 14, page 12 below, and Haile 1950, I: 332), and the line about flexible goods is probably a mistranslation of "their bodies are made of fabrics of all kinds." What are "mixed waters"? Is the parenthesis about holy springs part of the poem or an explanation by Louis Watchman, the Coolidges' translator? Rothenberg judged, apparently correctly, that the latter was the case and dropped the parenthesis from his revised version.

What is the "Little Holy Wind"? Brandon's intuition about the living word prompts him to drop the "Little," but it is precisely this adjective which identifies the wind as part of the Navajo soul concept (Haile 1943: 79-80). Why are "Everlasting" and "Peaceful" in the penultimate line capitalized? Brandon and Rothenberg feel better with the case lowered and so lose any indication that there is something special about these two words. They are, in fact, an attempt to render the most potent phrases in the Navajo language, Sq'ahnaaghéi, Bik'ehózhǫ́ǫ́. The first means to live the perfect life into old age, again and again, as does Changing Woman herself. The second means that having achieved this ultimate goal of Navajo philosophy, one is accordingly in a state of transcendant peace, harmony, beauty, and blessedness (Witherspoon 1974: 41-59). These two phrases occur again and again throughout Navajo sacred texts, and their connotations are as important to an understanding of Navajo thought as are such concepts as "salvation" and "charity" to Western thought.

There is a temptation to adopt a posture of mystification when dealing with exotic languages. In the case of unwritten languages, outsiders used to insist that the "ignorant savages were unintelligible." Now the pendulum has swung the other way and we are likely to hear that Whole Earth Man speaks in concepts too subtle for stodgy Indo-European languages to express. I suggest that the former view was colonial obtuseness and that the latter might be termed colonial chic. Neither has a place in Native American Humanities. As Dell Hymes points out in a famous article (1965), Native American poems deserve many translations as poetic fashions and transcultural perceptions change, but they must be retranslations of the original native text. In reworkings and adaptations at second and third hand, errors in basic meaning are compounded and opacities grow even dimmer.

There is a brighter chapter in the literary history of the Horse Song. In 1956 Aileen O'Bryan published a translation made with the help of Sam Ahkeah, noted interpreter and Navajo leader. She recorded it from an old friend, Sandoval Hastin Tlótsi hee, in 1928. O'Bryan's monograph *The Diné: Origin Myths of the Navajo Indians* puts the song squarely in its mythic context. In this version of the origin myth, horses came to mankind by two avenues. First, Changing Woman bestowed them on the world from where she had been keeping them in her house of jewel rooms. Then Enemy Slayer went to the house of his father, the Sun, and was given the power to create horses when he returned to the earth. The second process seems to complement and even ratify the first. Several horse songs are given, among them a variant of the one under discussion here. The Navajo connotations of the song text are largely explained in the myth narrative. Although the phrases "Everlasting" and "Peaceful" do not appear in this version of what might be called for our purposes "Horse Song 1930," they do in one of the others and are translated by Mr. Ahkeah: "Most High Power Whose Ways Are Beautiful" (O'Bryan 1956: 181). Though this account is basically a recording in narrative form of the Navajo origin myth as told by one man, there are also valuable linguistic and ethnographic notes and references to much of the relevant literature available at that time.

LaVerne Harrell Clark's *They Sang for Horses* is a scholarly search of the literature, originally undertaken for her M.A. degree at the University of Arizona. Its wide-ranging purpose was explained in the sub-title when it appeared as a book in 1966: *The Impact of the Horse on Navajo and Apache Folklore*. She makes the point that the folklore of all Southern Athapascan peoples should be studied as a unit and as a result, in this study, the wealth of contextual material surrounding the Horse Songs is unmatched in the literature. The basic story is like that in O'Bryan, but the many variations on it add immeasurably to the richness of the associations one can bring to an understanding of the Horse Songs. Part of "Horse Song 1930" appears on the dust jacket (inside) and on page 11, and all but four lines of the O'Bryan version appear on page 29.

In the near half-century since the Horse Song first appeared in print no text in the Navajo language has been published. However, Fr. Berard Haile had recorded it in Navajo as early as 1932 from Slim Curly of Crystal, New Mexico. It is part of the myth of the origin of the Blessingway ceremony, given in such full detail that the story and related songs filled 840 pages of Fr. Berard's notebooks. It was not until 1970, nine years after his death, that this rich material was published under the editorial hand of Leland C. Wyman. With the appearance of *Blessingway* it was possible to see that the Coolidges had made available merely a fragment, albeit a beautiful one that has caught the anthologizing imagination ever since. The Coolidges may have chosen to publish only what they thought was the most beautiful part. More likely, Tall Kia ah'ni may have held back most of the material because of the sacredness of the Blessingway ceremony. In the words of Frank Mitchell, Blessingway is the "backbone of Navajo religion"; when this ceremony is no longer performed there will be no more Navajo people (Interview with David P. McAllester, 1957). He, too, recorded his version of the origin myth of Blessingway for Fr. Berard but he did not reveal more than a sketch of the songs and prayers, even though he was a close friend of the sympathetic priest-scholar. He finally recorded this material only at the request of his family in the last years of his life. His Horse Songs were seventeen in number compared with Slim Curly's twenty-one.

The Haile/Wyman work is comparable to that of Clark in richness, although it is focussed on the myth of a single ceremony. The Blessingway origin story is given as collected by Fr. Berard from three different ceremonial practitioners: Slim Curly, Frank Mitchell, and River Junction Curly, who, like Frank Mitchell, was from Chinle, Arizona. Although the Navajo texts were not presented in the published version, Wyman (1970: xxvii) cites four repositories where they can be consulted, one of them a private collection. Since 1970 it has been possible to study the Horse Songs in the original and, to some extent, assess the translation presented in Horse Song 1930. Fr. Berard's translation of Slim Curly's version is on pages 260-62 of *Blessingway*. My translation of Frank Mitchell's version is on pages 41-43 of *Technicians of the Sacred*. With a span of different versions of the same song extending over a period of forty-one years, we begin to have a situation approaching what Dell Hymes hoped for. However, we still do not have more than one translation from the original of any given text of Horse Song 1930, and information as to the whereabouts of a version of the text in Navajo has only been available to the public at the end of that period.

In most of the discussion above, the Horse Song has been treated as if it were a poem in the Euro-American sense but actually, of course, it is a song, as are most Native American "poems" from the traditional period. I would like to summarize the objections, strictures, and exhortations above in a set of suggestions as to how songs such as these might be studied in a course on Native American Humanities.

The first question to be resolved is whether material which is often secret and sacred should be studied by outsiders at all. Most archives of Native American music contain songs with various degrees of restriction as to their use imposed by the Native donors. Let us assume that we have a body of song material for which permission has been granted for serious, responsible study. The next question in my mind is whether it is reasonable to gather a body of songs from all over North America and hope to obtain a coverage that is worth studying. It is analogous to assembling poems from all over Europe in one volume: the result is a *potpourri* with the slight value and the many frustrations of every superficial survey. Little is gained from looking over a host of uncomprehended snippets. Let us assume the ideal: that our body of song material is coherent and comprehensive. Now let me list my suggestions for how such songs might be presented and studied.

1. Each song would be available in a sound recording on disc or tape, sung by Native performers with appropriate accompaniment.

2. For each recording there would be a written transcription into musical notation with the Native text written under the appropriate notes in the melody.

3. For each text there should be an interlinear translation which would show a) the text as sung, b) the text as it would be spoken in ordinary speech, c) the literal translation of the words, as far as possible. Finally, a free translation should give the meaning in colloquial English to clarify the ambiguities often present in literal translations. I will illustrate with the first line of Horse Song 1930.

a)	Dotł'iji	'isdzaŋa	biyazhe,	shinishlinago...[2]
b)	Dootł'izhii	'isdzáán	biyáázh	shi nishłį́įgo...
c)	Turquoise	Woman	her son	I I-am-being...

Free translation: Since I am the son of Turquoise Woman...

4. There should be copious notes explaining esoteric references and putting the song into its cultural context. This would include the relevant mythic material and all other explanations offered by the original singer.

If we had all of this for, say, Horse Song 1930, the material would be at hand with which to achieve a significant comprehension of what the poem signifies and how it is part of the Blessingway origin story, which, in turn, is a component of the Navajo Creation Story. The study of textual subtleties and the relations between text and melody could be legitimately pursued. If there were the will and the talent in the class there would be the resources available to conduct exercises in translation, asking each student to create his or her own. This could be as rewarding to Navajo students as to those who approach the material from outside the original culture.

In support of my argument I quote William Bevis' statement on the need for this seemingly laborious kind of documentation.

Is it preferable in translation to preserve the strangeness of an alien culture, or to offer easy entry into a strange world? The second is illusory, for strange worlds are not easily entered and there are no shortcuts to aesthetic experiences. Therefore extensive changes of the original in order to "totally translate" the "feeling" or "hidden meanings" should be practiced as little as possible. Extensive notes on a literal text are definitely preferable to rewriting if the intent is to give one a sense of Indian art forms, and if the Indians repeated themselves we should learn how to listen to repetition. Words should be translated by words, and what is understood by means other than words should be explained as the context of the utterance. Form and genre are integral parts of "spirit" and "meaning" and must be respected. Of course it may not sell as well, but when the literal version of the Pawnee dawn song begins to live the reader has enlarged his imagination. We won't get Indian culture as cheaply as we got Manhattan (Bevis 1975: 321).

In the same vein I would like to explain why, in my ideal presentation, I would go beyond Bevis and insist on a sound recording. Without it one can have no notion of the indigenous meter, sound quality and, of course, melody. Navajo music is almost entirely limited to two note values, one twice the length of the other. This is a feature of the phonemically long and short Navajo vowels, as well. If we are to immerse ourselves in Navajo Humanities we must expose ourself to this rule system so remote from linguistic and musical experience of most other cultures. Nasality is also characteristic of Navajo singing and is phonemic in the language. Is there any way we can learn to see this as another interesting vocal possibility rather than an aberration?

A dominant feature in most Native American song texts is the extensive use of vocables, or non-lexical syllables. Many songs are made up entirely of vocables. Very few of such songs have made it into the anthologies, of course. In those songs that are partially vocabalic these syllables are usually considered as "nonsense syllables" and are dropped from the translation. Another reason for their omission is that vocables are easy to sing but awkward to the ear in ordinary speech. Yet they may comprise as much as half the original text; they are integral to its structure and they are essential in identifying the song genre. A sound recording will ensure that the vocables are retained and can be identified (with the help of the interlinear translation) by the listener/reader. It is then possible to consider them as an aspect of the particular quality of Native American poetry.

Repetition is another stylistic element to be considered. There is a great deal of it both in the vocables and in the lexical texts of Native American poetry. As Bevis says, readers who want to understand a tradition that features repetition must learn to listen to it. To the Navajos, for example, repetition increases power. Its use serves purposes of both form and function, and the serious listener/reader must be concerned with how these are interrelated in Navajo thought.

It seems clear that Horse Song 1930 suffered some deficiencies in its presentation to the English-speaking world as an item from Native American Humanities. It was separated from its cultural context, transmogrified from song into spoken poetry, stripped of its vocables and repetition, rendered in fragmentary form, and denied the possibility of correction. In this essay I have tried to repair some of these inadequacies and suggest how they can be avoided. I would like to conclude by presenting the Native text of the same song in the version recorded by Frank Mitchell, with his comments and my current ideas as to how it might be translated. The reader can compare this with how I did it in 1968. Underlinings are explained in Note 3, page 20.

Horse Song No. 5

(of 17 recorded by Frank Mitchell for David P. McAllester, Chinle, Arizona, 1963)[3]

Introduction: He neye yaŋa

Chorus:

Ye shika 'ani ye shika 'ani, ye shihika 'aniye ye shihika 'ani
Yee shíká 'ání yee shíká 'ání   etc.   etc.

With me-for they call   etc.   etc.   etc.

Burden:

Ye shihika 'ani, ye shihika 'ani ya'e, neye yaŋa
Yee shíká   'ání   etc.

With me-for they call   etc.

Ye shika 'aniyi ye shika 'ani, ye shihika 'ani, ye shihika 'ani
Yee shíká 'ání   etc.   etc.   etc.

With me-for they call   etc.   etc.   etc.

Burden:

Ye shihika 'ani, ye shihika 'ani ya'e, neye yaŋa
Yee shíká   'ání   etc.

With me-for they call   etc.

1. K'a yołgai 'isdzaŋa biyazhe, shinishlinago,   (Burden)
   K'ad yołgai 'isdzáán biyáázh shinishlįįgo

   Now shell-white woman her-child I-I-am-being.

2. K'a   jihona'aiye   bighe'e,   shinishl<u>i</u>nago,   (Burden)
   K'ad   johonaa'áí   bighe'   shinishłį́įgo

   Now   Day-disc-carrier his-son   I-I-am-being

3. Dotł'iji   'ishkii,   shinishl<u>i</u>nago,   (Burden)
   Dootł'izhii 'ishkii   shinishłį́įgo

   Turquoise Boy   I-I-am-being

4. Na'atsiyilidi<u>ye</u>, dotł'izhg<u>owo</u> 'ekinanidi'<u>iye</u>, k'a'ahyi<u>yi</u>lai,
   Ná átsi'íílid   dootł'izhgo 'ak'inańt'i   k'ad 'ahyiila

   Rainbow   blue-being   it-on-they-are now-arched-over

   k'a   nihehilaiyi   <u>ye</u>yoshchi'eshdo, [1)]   (Burden)
   k'ad   ni'nihyinlá   woshch'ishídoo

   now   earth-coming-down-to this-way-will

5. K'a   jihona'ai, <u>ye</u>yi'yisizini 'eshki<u>ye</u> bili'<u>i'e</u> (Burden)
   K'ad   jíhonaa'áí yii'sizini   'eshkii   bilį́į́

   Now   Day-disc-carrier (from) him-came-forth boy his-horses [2)]

1) This means "From where the rainbow arches over, edged with blue, a little way from the end, they are calling me." His mother told him that sound was a horse. He had asked, "What is that sound? Is that anything bad from battles I have been through lately?" She said, "No, that is the sound of horses, up where your father lives." He was going to his father's house. The rainbow road went clear up to the place where the Sun's house was. Before he reached the end is probably where he heard the horses.

2) "Sun-standing-within-Boy, his horses." It is speaking of the other brother, the Sun's son who lived up there. Since horses came from up there, it is his horses that Enemy Slayer hears. The Sun's boy's horses are calling me. The son of the Sun: his horses are calling. "Standing within" refers to his mother. Sun's boy, descended from the Sun, his horses are calling me.

6. Dotł'ijiyi   łį́į́'   inishili'i'e,   (Burden)
    Dootł'ishii   łį́į́'   éí shilį́į́'
    Turquoise horses those   my-horses

7. To'osa'   diłhiłiye   bike'ego,   (Burden)
    Tó'ósaa'   diłhił   bikéego
    Water-jars 3)   dark   their-feet-being

8. Besist'ogiye,   biketł'a   sikadego   (Burden)
    Bésist'ogi   bikétł'ááh sikaadgo,
    Arrow-heads 4)   their-soles it-is-spread-out

9. Hadahiniye 'ihiye, bike be nodǫs 'ego   (Burden)
    Hadahoniiye'   biké bee noodǫ́ǫ́zgo
    Mirage   their-feet with striped-being

10. Ka niłch'i diłhiłiye bigalego,   (Burden)
    K'ad níłch'i diłhił   bigaango
    Now wind   dark   their-forelegs-being 5)

11. Yanajiniye   bitse'ego   (Burden)
    Yánaajin   bitsee'go
    Sky-down-dark 6) their-tails-being

12. Yodi 'iłtase'e, ye bitsiis'ego   (Burden)
    Yodi 'iłtas'éi yee bitsíísgo
    Fabrics all-kinds of their-bodies-being

3) The little water jar is the horses' feet. It refers to their hooves.
4) This refers to the arrowhead-shaped part of the hoof, underneath.
5) "Dark wind his legs" means "in motion, running hard."
6) This means the black shadows in the sky, coming down from the clouds.

13. K'os diłhiłi ye bich'i'dego   (Burden)
    K'os diłhił yee bich'idigo
    Cloud dark with them-on-being [7]

14. Shabitłajiłch'ijiye, bitsis ka nazlai yego,   (Burden)
    Shábitł'ajiłchii   bits'íís káá' naazláígo
    Sun-flare-red [8] their-bodies-over-the-surface around-being [9]

15. K'a jihona'aiyeye, 'eye bidashdesilayego   (Burden)
    K'ad jíhonaa'áí   bidááh déé' siláago
    Now Day-disc-carrier them-facing-from it-lies-being [10]

16. Shayitaŋiye   bikeshde   silayego   (Burden)
    Sháyitą́   bikeshdę́ę́' siláago
    New-moon [11] behind-from (on-his-back) it-lies-being

17. Shabitł'ooliye bits'a 'ayost'i'ego   (Burden)
    Shábitł'óól   bitsą́'aat'íigo
    Sun-his-rays   their-back-straps-being [12]

18. Na'a tsiyilidiye, k'a bichoyoshtł'olego   (Burden)
    Nááts'íílid   k'ad bich'oshtł'óolgo
    Rainbow   now their-stomach-strap-being

7) This means their skin.
8) This means little bits of rainbow.
9) The sparks that you can see at night in a horse's hair.
10) The Sun comes up in front of them, way over there, and shines on their hair.
11) "New moon" refers to his saddle.
12) A leather strap that goes around behind, under the tail. You used to see that on saddles in the old days.

19. Na'atsiyilidiye, yiki dasizinigo (Burden)
    Nááts'íílid   yiki dasizíigo

    Rainbow   on-it they-are-standing [13]

20. Nałtso dloo' dołhił diye, k'a bik'oyostilego (Burden)
    Niłtsą dlǫ́ǫ́' diłhił   k'ad bik'ostiiliigo

    Rain horses [14] dark now their-necks hanging-down-which-
                                                    are-being [15]

21. Nanije'iye bija'ago (Burden)
    Nanise'   bijaa'go

    Plants [16] their-ears-being

22. K'a sǫ'tso diłhiłiye bina'ago (Burden)
    K'ad sǫ'tsoh diłhił   bináá'go

    Now stars-big dark   their-eyes-being [17]

23. To'ołanashchiniye   bini'ego, (Burden)
    Tołah náshchíín   binii'go

    Water-together-produced [18] their-faces-being

13) "Standing on it" means the rainbow is its means of power, like electricity in a car. They can start up fast, as when you turn the key in a car.

14) "Dlǫ́ǫ́'," anything that travels on four legs. It means "horse" here; "niłtsą dlǫ́ǫ́'" means "rain horses."

15) This refers to hair hanging down in a line along the neck, the mane.

16) "Nanise'," "it grows up," means his ears grow up like plants.

17) Since stars are always shining so bright at night, horses can see in the dark to where their home is.

18) Water from springs and brooks, out of the ground. Some is sweet, some is salty; it is all colors, too. "Łanáschíín" means "all mixed together." Horses anywhere will drink any kind of water and it won't hurt them unless it is poisoned. Any natural kind of water won't hurt them. Sometimes it gets a coating of dust and horses blow it off. It's the same way they blow out to clean off the grass they are going to eat,

24. Yow̱o   tso   wheye   bida'a̱go   (Burden)
    Yo   tsoh   bidaa'go

    Shell-big [19] their-lips-being

25. Yołgaiye   bighoo'o̱go   (Burden)
    Yołgai   bighoo'go

    Shell-white their-teeth-being

26. K'a   hatso'ilghał   ye   bizade̱go   (Burden)
    K'ad hatsoo'olghał   yee bizaadgo

    Now flash-lightning [20] of their-sound-being

27. Łi'dilni'   diłhiłiye,   biza̱ŋa   hoko̱si̱go   (Burden)
    Łįį'dilni'   diłhił   bizaa'ná hoko̱sgo

    Horses-sound [21] dark their-mouths around place-around-being

28. Hayołkałiye,   bitahgo,   ye'enadi'nishogo,   (Burden)
    Hayołkáál   bitahgo   yee 'enádí'nishogo

    Daybreak it-amongst-being with sound they-will-make (be making)

29. Bizhi'he   diłhiłgola,   k'a   shihinila̱yago,   (Burden)
    Bizhí   diłhiłgolá   k'ad shihińláago

    Their voices dark-being-it-seems now me-it-reaches-then

so as not to swallow dirt or anything else that might be harmful. The marking on a horse's face, the whorl of hair, is a sign of that. It is the guiding point of a horse's whole being. The bridle is there. They can eat weeds with thorns and it doesn't hurt them, or poison insects and it doesn't hurt them.

19) Refers to the big kind of sea shell that has a lip and little points like teeth.

20) Lightning was put in their mouths to bite with. Horse's bite will hurt.

21) "Dilį́" refers to any sound of a musical instrument. When you are going to make music you put the instrument to your mouth. When horses were first made, dark sound-makers were put in their mouths.

30. Hayołkał   bihadidiniya,   biza   heyelayehego,   (Burden)
    Hayołkááł bitádídíín   bizaa'   híílaago
    Daybreak[22]) its-pollen their-mouths lying-within-being

31. Ch'ilatah   hozhoniye, hadidiniye, bidato'oye
    Ch'ilátah   hozhóní   tádídíín   bidató
    Plant-tips pretty   pollen   their-dew

    biza   dahazlaha yehago,   (Burden)
    bizaa'   dahaazláago
    their-mouths lying-within-being [23])

32. Shabitł'oliye, k'a   bizanat'i'ego,   (Burden)
    Shábitł'ool   k'ad bizaat'i'igo
    Sun-rays   now   their-bridles-being

33. Shigane dishnashila, hozhogo, yehe shilak'e'e yayego, (Burden)
    Shigaan níshn'ááji   hózhǫǫgo yee shilá k'ééyáago
    My-arm right-side beautifully with my-hand into-being

34. Deye shiye   shilį   'esili'dego,   (Burden)
    Díishjį   shilį́į' selįigo
    This-day   my-horses they-became-then

22) In the early dawn, everything new is coming up with it. The horse will receive new air into its mouth to breathe and sound forth, with dawn pollen. It is like when you learn something, then it is in your head and then you are using it and teaching others with it. A horse does not know when it is tired or sleepy — they are not made like us. Whatever it was that was put in its mouth is what makes it not feel tired. It is put in its mouth and goes up in his mind so he cannot forget it.

23) It is like certain food we like: we all eat plenty of that. The horses will always have flowers, pollen, dew, plenty of vegetation to eat. It means they will always have plants and waters, and so they will always be lively.

35. Ke'anadilzhish k'a do'nidilnishigo,   (Burden)
    Ke'ańdiljish   k'ad doońdíídįįłgo
    Increasing   now   not-diminishing-then

36. K'ase'ahnaghei,   k'abik'ehozhoni
    K'ad są'ahnaaghéí   k'ad bik'ehózhǫǫ
    Now old-age-again-returning   now it-according-blessing

    neshili'e'ei,   (Burden)
    shilį́į́' 'éí
    my-horses those [24]

37. K'ase'ahnaghei,   k'abik'ehozhone
    K'ad sa'ahnaaghéí   k'ad bik'ehózhǫǫ
    Now old-age-again-returning   now it-according-blessing

    'eshkiye, shinishłiyehego,   (Burden)
    'eshkii   shinishłį́įgo
    boy   I-I-am-being

Chorus:

Ye shika'aniyi yeshika'ani, ye shihika'aniye yehe shihika'ani
Yee shíká 'ání   etc.   etc.   etc.
With-me-for they call etc.   etc.   etc.

Burden:

Ye shihika 'ani, ye shihika'ani ya'e- ne'eya!
Yee shíká 'ání   etc.
With-me-for they call   etc.

[24] This means the horses will not be harmed in the future in any way. They will stay well. It means the same for me in the next line.

Horse Song No. 5: Free Translation.[4]

He- neye yaŋa,

With their voices, for me they are calling,
With their voices, for me they are calling,
With their voices, for me they are calling,
With their voices, for me they are calling,
With their voices, for me they are calling,
With their voices, for me they are calling, *ya'e, neye yaŋa,*

With their voices, for me they are calling,
With their voices, for me they are calling,
With their voices, for me they are calling,
With their voices, for me they are calling,
With their voices, for me they are calling,
With their voices, for me they are calling, *ya'e, neye yaŋa,*

1. Now White Shell Woman, *ŋa*, her child, since that is who I am, *na*,
    With their voices, for me they are calling,
    With their voices, for me they are calling, *ya'e, neye yaŋa,*

2. Now Day Disc Carrier, *ye*, his son, *'e*, since that is who I am, *na*
    With their voices, for me they are calling,
    With their voices, for me they are calling, *ya'e, neye yaŋa,*

3. Turquoise Boy, since that is who I am, *na*,
    With their voices, for me they are calling,
    With their voices, for me they are calling, *ya'e, neye yaŋa,*

4. The rainbow, *iye*, where it is blue, *wo*, they are on it there, *iye*,
    Now, where it arches over, now, where it reaches the earth, *yiye*,
    Just this way, they will be,
    With their voices, for me they are calling,
    With their voices, for me they are calling, *ya'e, neye yaŋa,*

5. Now Boy Descended From Day Disc Carrier, *ye*, his horses, *i'e*,
    With their voices, for me they are calling,
    With their voices, for me they are calling, *ya'e, neye yaŋa,*

6. The turquoise horses, those are my horses, *i'e*,
    With their voices, for me they are calling,
    With their voices, for me they are calling, *ya'e, neye yaŋa,*

7. Dark water-jars, *iye*, being their hoofs,
    With their voices, for me they are calling,
    With their voices, for me they are calling, *ya'e, neye yaŋa,*

8. Arrowheads, *ye*, being the frogs of their under-hoofs,
    With their voices, for me they are calling,
    With their voices, for me they are calling, *ya'e, neye yaŋa,*

9. Mirage-stone, *ihiye*, being their striped hoofs,
    With their voices, for me they are calling,
    With their voices, for me they are calling, *ya'e, neye yaŋa,*

10. Now dark wind, *iye*, being their forelegs,
    With their voices, for me they are calling,
    With their voices, for me they are calling, *ya'e, neye yaŋa,*

11. Dark cloud shadow, *iye*, being their tails,
    With their voices, for me they are calling,
    With their voices, for me they are calling, *ya'e, neye yaŋa,*

12. Fabrics of all kinds being their bodies,
    With their voices, for me they are calling,
    With their voices, for me they are calling, *ya'e, neye yaŋa,*

13. Dark clouds, *i*, with these being covered,
    With their voices, for me they are calling,
    With their voices, for me they are calling, *ya'e, neye yaŋa,*

14. Red sun sparks, *jiye*, being scattered over their bodies,
    With their voices, for me they are calling,
    With their voices, for me they are calling, *ya'e, neye yaŋa,*

15. Now Day Disc Carrier, *yeye, 'eye,* from before them is gleaming in them,
    With their voices, for me they are calling,
    With their voices, for me they are calling, *ya'e, neye yaŋa,*

16. New moons, *iye*, being their cantles,
    With their voices, for me they are calling,
    With their voices, for me they are calling, *ya'e, neye yaŋa,*

17. Sunrays, *iye*, being their backstraps,
    With their voices, for me they are calling,
    With their voices, for me they are calling, *ya'e, neye yaŋa,*

18. Rainbow, *iye*, now being their girths,
    With their voices, for me they are calling,
    With their voices, for me they are calling, *ya'e, neye yaŋa,*

19. Rainbow, *iye*, since they are standing on it,
    With their voices, for me they are calling,
    With their voices, for me they are calling, *ya'e, neye yaŋa,*

20. Dark rain-horses, *diye*, now with their manes streaming down,
    With their voices, for me they are calling,
    With their voices, for me they are calling, *ya'e, neye yaŋa,*

21. Sprouting plants, *iye*, being their ears,
    With their voices, for me they are calling,
    With their voices, for me they are calling, *ya'e, neye yaŋa,*

22. Now great dark stars, *iye*, being their eyes,
    With their voices, for me they are calling,
    With their voices, for me they are calling, *ya'e, neye yaŋa,*

23. Waters of all kinds, *iye*, being their faces,
    With their voices, for me they are calling,
    With their voices, for me they are calling, *ya'e, neye yaŋa,*

24. Great shell, *wheye*, being their lips,
    With their voices, for me they are calling,
    With their voices, for me they are calling, *ya'e, neye yaŋa,*

25. White shell, *ye*, being their teeth,
    With their voices, for me they are calling,
    With their voices, for me they are calling, *ya'e, neye yaŋa,*

26. Now flash-lightning being their neighing,
    With their voices, for me they are calling,
    With their voices, for me they are calling, *ya'e, neye yaŋa,*

27. Dark music, *iye*, sounding from their mouths,
    With their voices, for me they are calling,
    With their voices, for me they are calling, *ya'e, neye yaŋa,*

28. Dawn, *iye*, filling it with their sounds,
    With their voices, for me they are calling,
    With their voices, for me they are calling, *ya'e, neye yaŋa,*

29. Their voices, *he*, dark-seeming, now reach me,
    With their voices, for me they are calling,
    With their voices, for me they are calling, *ya'e, neye yaŋa,*

30. Dawn pollen, *iya*, lying within their mouths,
    With their voices, for me they are calling,
    With their voices, for me they are calling, *ya'e, neye yaŋa,*

31. Pretty flowers, *ye*, their pollen and dew lying within their mouths,
    With their voices, for me they are calling,
    With their voices, for me they are calling, *ya'e, neye yaŋa,*

32. Sunrays, *iye*, now being their bridles,
    With their voices, for me they are calling,
    With their voices, for me they are calling, *ya'e, neye yaŋa,*

33. To my right arm, *e*, beautifully to my hand they come,
    With their voices, for me they are calling,
    With their voices, for me they are calling, *ya'e, neye yaŋa,*

34. This day, *ye*, becoming my horses,
    With their voices, for me they are calling,
    With their voices, for me they are calling, *ya'e, neye yaŋa,*

35. Increasing, now, not diminishing,
    With their voices, for me they are calling,
    With their voices, for me they are calling, *ya'e, neye yaŋa,*

36. Now ever returning to long life and therefore blessed, my horses,
    With their voices, for me they are calling,
    With their voices, for me they are calling, *ya'e, neye yaŋa,*

37. Now, since I, myself, am the Boy of Ever Returning to Long Life, and
    Therefore Blessed,
    With their voices, for me they are calling,
    With their voices, for me they are calling, *ya'e, neye yaŋa,*

    With their voices, for me they are calling,
    With their voices, for me they are calling,
    With their voices, for me they are calling, *yehe,*
    With their voices, for me they are calling,
    With their voices, for me they are calling,
    With their voices, for me they are calling, *ya'e, ne'eya!*[5]

NOTES

1. Parts of this paper were included in my essay "A Different Drum: A Consideration of Music in the Native American Humanities," presented April 16, 1977, at the conference "The Religious Character of Native American Humanities," at Arizona State University, Tempe, Arizona. I would like to thank Dr. Sam D. Gill, convenor of the conference, for permission to use this material here.

2. Pronunciation Key: Vowels have "Continental" values. Single vowels are short, double vowels are long. " ´ " indicates high tone: in long vowels a single " ´ " indicates rising or falling tone according to placement, for example, "oó" is rising; "óo" is falling. " ̦ " under vowels indicates nasality.

Consonants are roughly as in English, except for the following:

- ʼ   glottal stop as between the syllables of "oh-oh."
- gh   soft version of uvular "r" as in French "murailles."
- h   final "h" is pronounced: a distinguishable aspiration.
- ł   is voiceless "l" as in Welsh "Flloyd."
- tłʼ   can be made by putting the tongue in position for the click we use to start a horse moving, but then force the air *out* instead of sucking it in.
- ŋ   soft "ng" (used in songs only).

For a much more detailed key to pronunciation, see Morgan and Young 1958: i-vi.

3. Non-lexical syllables are underlined to help the reader separate them from the rest of the text. Some of those indicated are dubious. The "ŋa" in " ʼisdaŋa" may be a way of indicating the entirely lexical long "a" of " ʼisdzáán," in verse 1. Similarly, " ʼahyiyilai" may indicate in song the spoken " ʼahyiila." The numerals in half-parentheses in the text refer to Frank Mitchell's comments on the song.

4. I have been moving toward keeping the Native word order as much as seems possible. This enables the translation to keep more of the original sequence of the words intact. I have also retained the repetitions and many of the vocables that were lost in the 1968 translation.

5. For an effort to "translate" vocables and deal with non-lexical elements that are incorporated into lexical words, see Rothenberg 1969. The reader who is interested in this problem will note that I have not yet found a way to include "internal" vocables (like hi in shihika) in my free translation.

REFERENCES CITED

Astrov, Margot
    1962 *American Indian Prose and Poetry.* New York: Capricorn Books. Originally published as *The Winged Serpent*, 1946.

Bevis, William
    1975   "American Indian Verse Translations." In *Literature of the American Indians*. Edited by Abraham Chapman. New York: New American Library, Meridian Books. Reprinted from *College English* 35: 6 (March 1974).

Brandon, William
    1971   *The Magic World, American Indian Songs and Poems.* New York: William Morrow and Company, Inc.

Clark, LaVerne H.
    1966   *They Sang for Horses, The Impact of the Horse on Navajo and Apache Folklore.* Tucson: University of Arizona Press.

Coolidge, Dane and Mary Roberts Coolidge
    1930   *The Navajo Indians.* Boston and New York: Houghton Mifflin Company.

Haile, Berard, O.F.M.
    1943   "Soul Concepts of the Navajo." *Annali Lateranensi* 7. Citta del Vaticano: Vatican Polyglot Press; reprint ed., 1963.
    1950   *A Stem Vocabulary of the Navajo Language.* 2 vols. St. Michael's, Arizona: St. Michael's Press.

Hymes, Dell
    1965   "Some North Pacific Coast Poems." *American Anthropologist* 67: 2 (April 1965).

Link, Margaret S.
    1956   *The Pollen Path, A Collection of Navajo Myths.* Stanford, California: Stanford University Press.

McAllester, David P.
    1968   "War God's Horse Song II." In *Technicians of the Sacred: A Range of Poetries from Africa, America, Asia & Oceania.* Edited by Jerome Rothenberg. New York: Doubleday.

Morgan, William and Robert W. Young
    1958   *The Navajo Language.* Salt Lake City, Utah: Deseret Book Company.

O'Bryan, Aileen
    1956   *The Diné: Origin Myths of the Navajo Indians.* Bulletin 163. Bureau of American Ethnology, Washington, D.C.

Rothenberg, Jerome
    1968   Editor. *Technicians of the Sacred: A Range of Poetries from Africa, America, Asia & Oceania.* New York: Doubleday.
    1969   "Total Translation, An Experiment in the Presentation of American Indian Poetry." *Stony Brook* 3/4.

Witherspoon, Gary
    1974   "The Central Concepts of the Navajo World View (I)." *Linguistics* 119 (January 1974).

Wyman, Leland C.
    1970   *Blessingway.* Tucson: University of Arizona Press.

OGLALA SONG TERMINOLOGY

William K. Powers

> Everyone of us believes that he knows exactly what constitutes his personal individuality, and where he would consider that it ended. My feelings, thought, recollections, are myself. My head, arms, legs, internal organs, etc., are still myself. All the rest that I perceive is not I. Thus my individuality is grasped by my consciousness and circumscribed by my bodily exterior, and I believe that my neighbour's is precisely so too.
> Lucien Lévy-Bruhl (1966: 114).

Introduction. Adequate exegeses, if not apologia, for Lévy-Bruhl, the eminent French sociologist, have appeared in all recent references to his works (notably, Cazeneuve 1972, Douglas 1970, Evans-Pritchard 1965, Needham 1972) and readers interested in the argument over the significance of the terms 'pre-logical,' 'mystical,' 'law of participation,' etc., all terms associated with perceived constructs of the "primitive" mind, should consult these authors. My point here is that once stripped of the evolutionistic parlance of the turn of the century, the substance of Lévy-Bruhl's thesis is enlightening without being demeaning to non-Western peoples. He provides, sometimes obscurely, an interesting theoretical frame within which one can interpret how people structure their perception of reality, in this case, music, and the manner in which they verbalize about it.

Historically, ethnomusicologists have expressed interest in the same problem. Merriam, in speaking generally about how songs are acquired, states that:

> Some standards must be held by all people if there is to be a music style or even a music system at all, and ... enough examples are available to indicate that some, at least, of these standards are verbalized. It is also to be expected

that cultures differ in the extent of such verbalization, but at the same time it is very doubtful that any people have nothing whatsoever to say about their musical style (Merriam 1964: 169-70).

Recognizing that people do in fact have something to say about their musical styles and standards, we are are not so much led to the inevitable question: what do they say? Rather, given that ethnomusicology, like anthropology, is still primarily a product of Euro-American tradition whose theories and methods are essentially proffered for Euro-American consumption, we are more properly concerned with asking: do people verbalize about their music in a manner similar to or different from our own? This, of course, is a question not easily answered without some frustration.

For example, in discussing the techniques of conscious composition among Native Americans, Nettl has written that "it is difficult to do research ... because the natives do not ordinarily discuss such matters among themselves. Consequently native informants have trouble explaining techniques" (Nettl 1956: 16). But the "trouble" here has nothing necessarily to do with native informants. Since the 1960's it has been a well established fact in anthropology that ethnographies, in this case musical ethnographies, are largely sets of questions and answers which are collected by an investigator and ultimately described, analyzed, and published. But as Frake has succinctly pointed out, "The problem is not simply to find answers to questions the ethnographer brings to the field, but also to find the questions that go with the responses he observes after his arrival" (Frake 1964: 132).

I single out these statements because I think they are relevant points of departure for a paper which deals with how one group of non-Western people, the Oglala of the Pine Ridge Sioux Indian Reservation in South Dakota, verbalize about their music style and standards. I would agree with Merriam that verbalizations about music differ because cultures differ, but I am more concerned with the *manner* in which people verbalize rather than the *extent* to which they do so. As I shall demonstrate, there is an important analytical difference between these two perspectives. I also agree with Nettl that it is difficult to elicit explanations for some types of musical behavior, but I feel that it is not so much a problem with the respondent's inability to verbalize as it is with the methods traditionally employed by ethnomusicologists to elicit such verbalizations.

These methods are in turn influenced by the Euro-American musical tradition, which seeks to compartmentalize vocabularies employed to analyze corresponding cultural domains. Although the terms used in these vocabularies are ultimately derived from the folk idiom, the process of compartmentalization renders them, in Western tradition, technical language. This technical language then becomes exclusively associated with the domain, in this case music, and is perceived to be isolable from other cultural domains which are in part defined in terms of the vocabularies themselves.

Euro-American technical language is very much analogous to culture itself — in the evolutionary sense. As incipient *Homo sapiens* we sought to create culture but, once created, we became forever subservient to our creation. As ethnomusicologists we spend most of our academic evolution creating and refining means of analyzing and comparing musics of the world. But once our theories, methods, techniques, and terminologies are established, we are forever chained to the products of our scholarly energies. Like culture, we are flexible: when our means of technical musical communication require changing, we can alter our earlier constructs. But rarely do we change our general conceptual model of music.

The technical language of the Euro-American tradition is indeed complex, but for purposes of this paper, I would simply characterize it as *analytical* in the linguistic sense, i.e., displaying a tendency to divide into component parts. I would then follow by characterizing the model of the musical universe as seen through the eyes of Euro-American ethnomusicologists as an *analytical model* of music. One of the most significant diagnostic features of this model is that it is presumed that all music is a cultural phenomenon which should be analyzed and described in purely cultural terms. Now one of my objectives is to demonstrate that it is more often the nature of the model rather than the competency of the native that renders cross-cultural interpretations of musical behavior difficult. Using our own analytical model as a basis for investigating the music of small societies, or even for segments of Euro-American cultures, presupposes that the native's model is somewhat akin to our own. Methodologically, we attempt to elicit glosses for what we perceive to be meaningful components of the native's musical domain, but which, cross-culturally, may not be. It is in this spirit that I seek an alternate means of interpreting Oglala song terminology.

Towards an Alternate Musical Model. All models begin somewhere, and I agree with Lévi-Strauss's notion that an anthropologist's model must be built up from what the native tells him (Lévi-Strauss 1962: 322 *et passim*). This is to say that new models are constructed from raw ethnographic data, not from the old models an anthropologist brings to the field. Here I would suggest an alternate model for music, in this case built up from ethnographic data I have collected from the Oglala over the past 25 years. I require a different kind of model for two important reasons.

First, in the past, one of the initial problems that have confronted Western musicologists and anthropologists investigating music verbalization was that our own preconceptions about technical languages presuppose that these vocabularies are exclusive. We fully recognize that the technical language of music in Western society is in the purview of specialists. In small societies, however, what musicians or others say about their music is not necessarily a part of any exclusive domain. Not only the specialists, but people at large understand what is being said about their musical culture, and all may freely participate in musical discourse despite their lack of specialization. But this in itself does not demonstrate that what they have to say about their music is any less "technical" or meaningful. In the spirit of cultural relativism it is safe to say that all people speak of their music in its cultural context, and they maintain a vocabulary which enables them to communicate their musical culture freely, totally, and clearly, relative to the cultural matrix in which their music is created and performed. Technical language in fact is very much like the incest taboo: although it is universal, or near universal, the way it manifests itself is often quite unique.

The second reason for an alternate model is that in Western society, music is perceived to be an aspect of culture, as Herskovits would say, "the man made part of the environment" (Herskovits 1948: 17). However, there is no reason to believe that all peoples of the world, given that they distinguish at all between natural and cultural domains, consider music as a cultural category. Lévi-Strauss's illuminating idea that places humans in a dialectical relationship between nature and culture (Lévi-Strauss 1949) perhaps may be modified to suggest that at least some people, including the non-specialist in our own society, may classify music as part of the *natural* order. If this is the case, then we would expect to find music, and what people have to say about it, analogically related to other domains likewise perceived to be natural rather than cultural. In fact, music may be represented as a "natural symbol" (Douglas 1970) expressed in the metaphors of human bodily functions, as well as others. Here I am inspired by Lévy-Bruhl's ideal of "appurtenances," first discussed in *The "Soul" of the Primitive*, in which he writes:

> First of all the primitive's idea of individuality comprises, in addition to his own body, all that grows upon it, all that comes from it, its secretions and its excretions: hair of the head and body, nails, tears, urine, excreta, seminal fluid, perspiration, etc. . . . The hair and secretions, etc., of the individual are his very self, just as his feet or his hands, his heart or his head, are. They "belong" to him in the fullest sense of the word. Henceforth I shall speak of them as his "appurtenances" (Lévy-Bruhl 1966: 115).

Lévy-Bruhl's notion of "appurtenances" is critical to his ideas of "pre-logical mentality" and forms a fundamental part of his "law of participation," i.e., "primitive" man considers his appurtenances as an integral part of himself, but nowhere does Lévy-Bruhl suggest that so-called primitive mentality is inferior to "civilized mentality" (on this point see Cazeneuve 1972: 1-23); it is simply a different kind of logic. That this logic is to be found among all peoples is demonstrable, and if we were to substitute, in the above quoted passage, the term 'a person' for 'primitive,' it would not be difficult to show that all of us "participate" in our "appurtenances" or those of others in varying degree. Each of us is aware of culturally relevant appurtenances which we may or may not share with other cultures, for example, our emotional or sentimental attachments to a lock of hair, baby shoes; our preoccupation with coiffures, deodorants, make-up, false eyelashes and nails; our dedication to cleanliness complete with soaps, powders, oils, douches, and scented bathroom tissue, all demonstrate quite adequately that what once might have been the purview of "primitive" mentality and "pre-logical" thought are quite *civilized*. Thus Lévy-Bruhl's theories, taken out of their evolutionistic context, are quite appealing and applicable to contemporary peoples, Euro-American or otherwise.

Lévy-Bruhl's theories, particularly the law of participation, were intended to explain a wide range of phenomena otherwise treated under the more usual rubric of "primitive" religion: mana, taboo, magic, witchcraft, sorcery, etc. In further modifying his ideas, I wish to add to his list of appurtenances music itself or, perhaps more appropriately, *song*, because the latter would seem to have a wider degree of application to peoples of the world than the more limited (to Euro-American tradition) *music*. This addition, upon which I will elaborate, seems particularly appealing when attempting to analyze the music vocabulary of the Oglala, which, like that of other Native Americans, is almost entirely vocal. As I shall demonstrate, song is consciously or unconsciously conceived to be an extension of the human body rather than something external to it.

I am suggesting the following contrast between Oglala conceptualization of music and the more traditional Euro-American concepts: where Euro-American music is conceived to be cultural and employs an analytical model for purposes of description and analysis, the Oglala perceive their music to be natural and employ a synthetic model to describe and analyze it. Here I use *synthetic* in the linguist's sense, i.e., displaying a tendency to combine two or more elements to form a unit. The two models may not be mutually exclusive, as Lévy-Bruhl suggested for the distinction between pre-logical and logical mentality. Thus we may find "specialists" among the Oglala, who are more analytical, and non-specialists among Euro-Americans, who are more synthetic. The model is primarily intended to be useful in understanding how people speak about their musical tradition.

Methodological Consideration. In viewing how the Oglala verbalize about song, my approach is essentially structuralist and linguistic; the essential unit of analysis is the morpheme. In the past, ethnomusicologists have attempted to elicit information about verbalization using as the basis of their analysis the lexeme. But this presupposes that the music terminology under investigation somehow corresponds with the native language of the investigator. The result is an accumulation of lexical items which in fact do correspond, for example, song, drum, drum stick, flageolet, etc. But ideas which do not translate easily, or at all, are not elicitable at this level.

At the morphemic level, given that a synthetic model will produce a vocabulary that relates music to other natural order, and in this case bodily functions, I am concerned with identifying morphemes employed to discuss music, and compare them with the same morphemes in other natural domains, i.e., functions of the human body. This approach, of course, requires sensitivity to Lakota, the native language of the Oglala, and my own competency, part of which I regard as raw ethnographic data, led me to initial identifications of morphemes.

In addition to native language competency, as a starting point for analysis I find Lévi-Strauss's analysis of myth inspiring, and perhaps some analogue may be drawn between Lévi-Strauss's minimal unit of myth, the "mytheme," and my minimal unit of analysis, the morpheme. The structuralist approach to myth requires that one of the operations include rearranging the myth in terms of recurring themes. These "bundles of such relations" (Lévi-Strauss 1963: 207) then say something not always clear in the myths themselves. For Lévi-Strauss, all myths serve to work out fundamental contradictions in the social order, most of which deal with basic problems of subsistence: food, clothing, shelter; and sexual relations, etc.

Regarding morphemes as bundles of constituent units (since, like mythemes, they are minimal units of meaning), I arrange the total number of morphemes found in Lakota lexemic units related to song and compare them with the same morphemes as they appear in other domains. Just as Lévi-Strauss regards much of mythical thought as being unconscious, I regard the formulation of most words employed to discuss music (or any other domain) similarly, although this may not always be the case. The resultant model is then a logical one based on ethnographic data and the native language, but as is true of all models of social structure, it may not necessarily be identical with the native model of music (see particularly Lévi-Strauss 1962: 323-24, "Consciousness and Unconsciousness").

This synthetic model not only explains how and why certain lexical units are selected over other possibilities, but it gives some indication of the history of such selections and offers as well a modicum of predictability.

To illustrate the nature of the synthetic model and how the Oglala verbalize about their musical culture, I will focus on four aspects of music: 1) the concept of song; 2) performance standards; 3) composition and learning; and 4) classification of musical instruments. Throughout I will demonstrate how the synthetic model reveals a persistence in employing "natural" terms for recent musical adaptations, for example, newly introduced musical instruments from Euro-American culture.

The Concept of Song.

In Lakota, there are seven morphemes called by linguists "instrumental prefixes" (Beuchel 1939, 1970; Swanton 1911) which, when prefixed to verb stems, modify the mode of action. One such morpheme, *ya*, when prefixed to verbs and adjectives, indicates that the action is performed by means of the mouth. Also, *ya* appears with two inseparable prepositions to form *iya* 'to speak' and *eya* 'to say.' This morpheme may refer to actions performed literally or figuratively, for example, *yaka* 'to tell, mean'; *yatkan* 'to drink'; *yata* 'to chew'; *yahtaka* 'to bite'; or *yahwa* 'to bore by speaking' (from *ya* + *hwa* 'sleepy'); *yaignuni* 'to confuse by interrupting the conversation' (from *ya* + *ignuni* 'to lose with'); *yaiha* 'to make laugh by talking' (from *ya* + *iha* 'to laugh'); *yainila* 'to silence one by speaking' (from *ya* + *inila* 'silent'); etc.*

Given that *ya* always refers to actions performed by means of the mouth, it serves as the basis for describing and evaluating a wide range of musical events, sounds, and standards. For example:

Yatun 'to sing out' (from *ya* + *tun* 'to give birth to'; the same radical also means 'to bear children, to be born').

Yaotanin 'to make public in song' (from *ya* + *otanin* 'public, manifest, visible').

---

* **Note on Pronunciation**: Vowels are continental. Consonants are pronounced approximately as in English, except:

    c = ch

    g is guttural before vowels.

    ȟ is guttural.

    j = zh

    n after vowel indicates preceding vowel is nasalized.

    š = sh.

Stress falls on the second syllable, except where noted. For further reference to orthography, cf. Buechel 1939, 1970; Powers 1977.

Yabu 'to growl as one sings (from *ya* + *bu*, a radical element which suggests a rapid succession of sounds, e.g., *nabubu* 'to tap one's feet in time,' *kabubu* 'to clap one's hands in time'; the latter is used to indicate a type of bread in which the dough is shaped by flattening it with the hands).

Yahogita 'to become hoarse from singing' (from *ya* + *hogita* 'hoarse').

Yahmun 'to hum' (from *ya* + *hmun* 'to buzz,' as bees buzz).

Yaiyowaza 'to trail the voice' (from *ya* + *iyowaza* 'echo').

Yašna 'to sing incorrectly, blunder in song' (from *ya* + *šna*, an enclitic which suggests that an action or state of being was somehow interrupted, or prevented from successful completion). Compare *wošna* 'to blow out a candle'; *yušna* 'to extinguish a light.'

Yaštan 'to finish singing, end the song' (from *ya* + *štan* 'corked, plugged up'). Compare with *waposˇtan* 'hat,' literally, "something into which the head is 'plugged'."

Yatokca 'to alter, modify, change the song' (from *ya* + *tokca* 'different, unusual').

Yajo 'to play a wind instrument' (from *ya* + *jo* 'to whistle, or to sing like birds').

Yawankicu 'to begin or lead a song' (from *ya* + *wank(a)* 'upwards' and *icu* 'to cause to, to take').

Yaptan 'to change the tune, song' (from *ya* + *ptan* 'change').

Yazilya 'to sing slowly, drawl' (from *ya* + *zica* 'to stretch like rubber').

Yahla 'to make the voice rattle' (from *ya* + *hla* 'rattle'). Compare with *sintehla* 'rattle snake,' i.e., 'rattletail'; also metaphorically, a 'death rattle.'

Obviously the use of the morpheme *ya* enables the Oglala to criticize or otherwise evaluate songs and singers infinitely. What is important is that the modality of song is not distinguished from other oral functions of the body, *except by context*.

Another morpheme (also used as a lexeme), *ho*, means 'voice' or, by extension, 'sound.' It is used in a number of ways to verbalize musical concepts:

Hotanin 'to raise one's voice in song' (from *ho* + *otanin* 'public, manifest, visible').

Hotun 'to sing out' (from *ho* + *tun* 'to give birth to').

Olowan kin ho 'melody' (from *olowan* 'song,' *kin*, definite article, and *ho*; literally, 'voice of the song').

Wicaho hukuciyela 'low tones, notes' (from *wica*, generic noun marker; *ho*, and *hukuciyela* 'down below').

Wicaho wankatuya 'high tones, notes' (from *wicaho* and *wankatuya* 'up above').

Wicaho oegnake 'scale' (from *wicaho* and *oegnake* 'to place in a container,' i.e., a voice that is delineated).

Wicaho oyuspe 'tape recorder' (from *wicaho* and *oyuspe* 'to catch'). Interestingly, to record is *nagoya* 'to scratch automatically,' which refers to the making of a disc.

Hokapsanpsan 'to whine' (from *ho* + *psanpsan* 'swaying back and forth,' as a swing).

Hoiyohpeya 'to tire the voice from singing' (from *ho* + *iyohpeya* 'to cast out,' as a fisherman casts a line).

Hoyeya 'to sing, send a voice' (from *ho* + *yeya* 'to cause to go').
Houkiye 'to receive, learn a song' (from *ho* + *ukiye* 'to cause to come,' said of songs learned in a vision).
Hotanka 'loud-voiced' (from *ho* + *tanka* 'large, great,' said of both the voice in singing and the sound of an instrument).

Still another term, *jo* 'to whistle,' appears in *jolowan* 'to whistle a tune' (from *jo* + *olowan* 'song') and *jahotun* 'to whistle up a tune' (from *jo* + *hotun* 'to give birth to a song'). Later I shall return to this term because it figures prominently in classifying native and modern musical instruments.

The generic term for song is *olowan*, which is formed from the noun marker *(w)o* and *lowan*. In the past *lowan* has been translated simply as 'to sing' (Beuchel 1970) but, given the infinite range of verbalizing about various modes of vocality using the prefix *ya*, it is more profitable to gloss *lowan* as 'to sing a song.' Actually, *lowan* delineates the parameters of "song." It is interesting to compare this idea with the ethnomusicologist's concept of song, particularly the notion of *incomplete repetition*, which has been widely regarded as a diagnostic feature of Plains Indian music (Nettl 1956: 111). As I shall show, the analytic and synthetic models of "song" conflict to some degree, making this contrast instructive to future classifications of Native American music.

In the past 'incomplete repetition' has been used as a technical term to identify a particular type of song structure which is only partially repeated. This structure is normally written ABCBC. *A* stands as the introduction, or non-repeated portion of the song; *B* as the theme; and *C* as the cadential formula. Thus in songs of the 'incomplete repetition' type, the theme and cadential formula are repeated in one rendition of a song, but the introduction is not; hence the name.

The Oglala concept *olowan* 'song,' however, corresponds with the ethnomusicological statement *BB*, which is to say (and this can be tested empirically) that a song is "equal" to two renditions of the theme. Since the cadential formula *C* is conceived to be an integral part of the theme, the Oglala do not distinguish between theme and cadence. This contrasts with the ethnomusicological notion of incomplete repetition in an interesting way, for partial repetition does not, in fact, adequately describe the structure of song; rather it describes *performance* of the song. Just how concepts related to performance are discussed will be treated below, but first I would like to make some comments on the relationship between *olowan*, 'song,' and other bodily functions, since the relationship is not obvious at the lexemic level.

The morpheme *lo* is found in very few Lakota words and is relatively easy to isolate. The use of *lo* in domains other than 'song' is instructive:

lolo 'soft, tender, moist, flabby, fleshy.'
locin 'to be hungry,' literally 'to want meat.'
talo 'meat of a hoofed animal' (e.g., *tatanka* 'buffalo bull'; *tahča* 'deer').
logute 'hollow of the flank of man or animal.'
lohe 'the flabby part of the cheeks or throat.'
lote 'throat proper.'
lotku 'flesh below the center of the mandibular region' (the "second chin").

All other forms of *lo* are found in words pertaining to food and cooking, for example:

loigni 'to hunt food.'
lolicupi 'rations.'
loliȟ'an 'to prepare food.'
lolobya 'to boil until tender.'
lol'opetun 'to buy groceries.'
lolopiye 'bag for storing meat.'
lowitaya 'fresh, raw' (as meat).
loyake 'fresh' (as opposed to dried meat, etc.).

What I am suggesting here (perhaps on less firm grounds than my case for the morpheme *ya*, and morpheme/lexeme *ho* and *jo*, is that the radical element (*lo*) found in the term for song (*olowan*) is the same radical element found in lexemes associated with human anatomy (the face and throat), and with food and methods of preparing food. In all cases it is the function of the human body that generates a synthetic model of Oglala musical verbalization with respect to concepts of song and singing. Stated another way, the manner in which the Oglala verbalize about song is analogous to the manner in which they verbalize about other bodily functions such as eating, as well as human anatomy involved in food ingestion.

Performance.

As stated earlier, analytical and synthetic models of music culture need not be mutually exclusive. Nowhere else is this clearer than in Lakota terms associated with the performance of music. When speaking of performance, at least part of the Oglala conceptual model coincides with the ethnomusicologist's notion of incomplete repetition. But again it should be reiterated that incomplete repetition is a function of performance and not an adequate description of song structure.

Elsewhere (Powers 1970: 358-69), I have suggested that the performance model for Plains music should be refined and represented by AA^1BCBC. A corresponds with the introductory phrase sung by the leader of the song group; A^1 corresponds with a repeat of the introductory phrase by an individual or the entire chorus (known in English as the "second"); B corresponds with the theme of the song; and C, with the cadential formula. In actual performance, as noted before, the Oglala do not distinguish between B and C; they are both regarded as the song proper (*olowan*). However, for purposes of performance, the Oglala identify both the introduction (A) and the second (A^1) in their native language.

The introduction is called *yawankicu* 'to take the voice upwards'; while the second is referred to as *pawankiye* 'to push the voice upwards' (from *pa*, instrumental prefix, 'to push or press'; *wank(a)* 'upwards'; and *iye* 'to cause to'). Since approximately 1974, the Oglala have begun to call in English this particular seconding effect "push ups." The term is used to determine the number of renditions of a war dance song each group will sing, one 'push up' being equivalent to one rendition. The term *pawankiye* carries the connotation of raising the pitch. In normal practice the leader starts the song on one tone and is seconded by a singer who slightly raises the pitch. The conscious raising of pitch is considered good singing technique.

In addition to these "technical" terms for the parts of a performance, there are some idioms. Thus the proper way to sing the introduction is *pan* 'to whine, cry'; the second should be sung *akiš'a*, a general term relating to both human and animal cries of a piercing nature, best translated into English as 'yelping.' Both the introduction and the second may also be sung *yuš'a*, which is the squeaking sound produced by rubbing one's finger around the rim of good crystal. Still another idiom, *yupesto*, is used to indicate excellent attack in the introduction or second. It means 'to sharpen,' as one would sharpen a pencil or stick. It is partially derived from *pa*, meaning an animal or human head.

The morpheme *ka*, when prefixed to verb stems, indicates that action is accomplished by means of striking with the arm and hand. Not surprisingly, this morpheme enables the Oglala to describe or evaluate the act of drumming almost to the same extent that *ya* can be employed to verbalize about singing. A partial list of words related to drumming is:

kabubu 'to drum' (from *ka* + *bubu*, reduplicative of *bu*, a radical element suggesting a succession of rapid sounds); it also means 'hand clapping,' although in all Oglala drumming a drumstick is used.

icabu 'drumstick' (from *i* 'by means of,' *ca* [*k* preceded by *i* changes to *c*], and *bu*).

kat'inze 'to drum in steady beats' (from *ka* + *t'inze* 'firm, tight').

kašna 'to miss a beat' (from *ka* + *šna*, an enclitic which indicates that an action or state of being was interrupted).

kaijena 'to drum out of time' (from *ka* + *ijena* 'to mix, to mix up,' as apples with oranges).

The adverb *kpankpanyela*, when used with verbs meaning 'to drum,' translates as "tremolo" or "thunder drumming." The word refers to anything "abundant" or "countless." The expression *sam iyeic'iye*, when used in conjunction with verbs signifying 'to drum' (and also 'to dance'), means that the singer has played too many beats, i.e., all the others have stopped drumming, but he continues. The expression means literally "to cause oneself to 'go over' or 'do more than required'."

During a performance of group singing, one song (*olowan*) is repeated anywhere from four to perhaps, nowadays, twenty-five times. The act of repeating a song is called *piyalowan* (from *piya* 'to renew' and *lowan* 'to sing a song'). Curiously, the Oglala regard repeating a song metaphorically the same as curing a patient, i.e., both are "renewed." (A medicine man is called *wapiye* 'someone who renews.')

When the last complete song is finished, the singers pause and sing the *sinte* 'tail' (compare with *coda*). The *sinte* is comprised of BC, i.e., the theme and cadential formula without the introduction and lead.

Not all verbalization related to performance is necessarily constructed from instrumental prefixes and other morphemes. For example, tempo is classified into *hʸanhi* 'slow'; *ohʸankoya* 'fast'; and *iwaštegla* 'easy, casual,' the latter identifying a preferred dance temp intermediate between slow and fast. The pitch of the song may be classified as *wankata* 'high' or *kuta* 'low,' a relatively higher pitch being preferred. The length of a song or performance of song may be classified as *hanska* 'long' or *ptecela* 'short,' a higher value being placed on songs which are short (i.e., with fewer vocables or words to the strophe), than renditions which are long.

Often before beginning a series of songs in a normal voice (*hotanka* 'loud-voiced'), a singer may practice a song to himself by whistling, *jolowan* 'to whistle a song.' If all the singers are not sure of a new song, they may begin singing *jiyahan* 'lowly, softly' for one or two renditions until they become confident. The Oglala also contrast the volume of the song in terms of it being *iyonihan* 'just audible' or *iyoja* 'amplified.'

Finally, the members comprising the performance group are known as *lowan-s'a wicaša* 'male singer' (from *lowan* 'to sing a song'; *s'a*, an enclitic indicating frequency, regularity, i.e., one who normally does something; and *wicaša* 'man'). Female singers are called *wicaglata* 'responders' (from *wica*, third person plural, and *aglata* 'to answer, respond') from the fact that their voices slightly trail behind the men's at the end of each song. The entire group of singers is called *h"oka* (etymology unknown; it may be a foreign word, possibly deriving from Omaha or Ponca). When song groups perform, the verb *ahiyaya* 'to pass around' (as a pipe in a council) is a metaphor for group singing. The term stems from the earlier custom of each man at the drum taking turns beginning a new song, thus "passing around the songs."

Composition and Learning.

With respect to the process of composition, Nettl has written that "Among North American Indians there are two important ways in which new songs can be acquired: conscious composition, a process akin to that of Western composers; and learning songs in visions or dreams" (Nettl 1956: 14). If by "acquire" Nettl means "compose," then his statement corresponds perhaps with all musical compositional process of the world. A synthetic model of music will not settle the real or putative distinction over conscious versus unconscious composition because the process of composition is universally synthetic by definition, i.e., a bringing together of parts whether they be musical, graphic, plastic, or otherwise. If by "acquire," however, Nettl means to "obtain" or otherwise "learn," the analytical model contrasts with the synthetic. It is difficult to separate compositional from learning processes among the Oglala; they are bound conceptually by a model that serves to explain "how new songs are brought into being" (Merriam 1964: 165), as well as how old songs are retained in the tribal repertoire.

Given that music is part of the natural order, it is *there*, occupying a niche in the natural universe, with a human-like capacity to be born and to die, to undergo changes, to be renewed — "cured" if you will (as the language suggests). Music is not so much composed from whole cloth as it is, metaphorically, reincarnated, just as is true, so the Oglala believe, with humans. The term *yatun* 'to give birth to a song' is perhaps the closest gloss to 'to compose,' but the connotation of *tun* is 'to give rise to something *that has already existed in another form* (on this point see Powers 1977).

Looking then at how new songs are brought into being, it is impossible, given their reincarnative nature, to determine which songs are "consciously" composed and which have evolved through other means, such as visions or rearrangements of existing songs: these "compositional" processes are all aspects of the same phenomenon. For example, the noun *wounspe* means 'lesson' or 'teaching.' A song "learned" in a vision may be referred to as *olowan unspeic'iye* and the process of "teaching" a song to another is *olowan unspekiya*. All these linguistic forms are derived from the verb *unspe*, which under different contexts means 'to know (have learned)'; 'to teach' (with the suffix *kiya* 'to cause to'); or 'to learn' (with the reflexive suffix *ic'iye* 'to cause oneself to'). Thus the Oglala consciously or unconsciously merge three concepts, which we as academics attempt to separate consciously or unconsciously, based on a simple axiom that that which is taught is learned, and that which is learned is known, that which is known is taught, etc.

This is not to say that music is somehow an absolute form; once a song has been *unspe* (taught, learned, known), it may be altered, transmitted, studied, or casually "caught." The Oglala verbalize all of these operations. For example, what has been traditionally regarded as "conscious" composition by the analytical model is verbalized by the Oglala in the term *olowan kaga* 'to make a song.' Songs which are made are by definition those sung in a secular context, but the original components of the song may have been sung in another context, e.g., a religious context, and thus ultimately were refashioned from a song which was originally *unspeic'iye*, 'learned in a vision.' The act of reshaping a song to fit a new context, i.e., transfer from a religious context to a secular one, is called *yatokca* 'to change by means of the mouth.' Of course, in the transformation of one type of song to another, the song structure is changed by the song-maker, but the original song on which the alteration is based remains in the tribal repertoire. The term *yatokca* may also be used to indicate changing a song of one genre to fit the structure of another genre, for example, making a Rabbit dance song into an Omaha dance song. But the term would never be used to suggest a transformation of a song used in one religious context to another religious context, because this kind of change would decrease the power of the song or perhaps antagonize the supernaturals. This is not to say that such transformations do not occur in practice. But they are regarded as inauspicious or done in bad taste.

The process of learning songs in a secular context is called *olowan oyuspe* 'to catch a song,' and it would be improper to speak of "catching" a song in, for example, a vision. The fundamental distinctions between religious and secular contexts on the one hand, and composing and learning on the other may be illustrated:

Yatun
('to give birth to a song')

	"Compose"	"Learn"
Religious	*unspekiye* ('to teach')	*unspeic'iye* ('to learn')
Secular	*olowan kage* ('to make a song')	*olowan oyuspe* ('to catch a song').

Although in everyday usage one might hear *unspekiye* 'to teach' employed in a secular sense, the proper word for "teaching" another a song is *akiyapi* 'to practice, give mind to, try, test.'

Whereas components of song performance are categorized (cf. *yawankicu, pawankiye*, etc., above), the components of the structure of a song are not. For example, there is no Lakota counterpart for the "vocable" or burden syllable. I attribute this to the notion that the vocable is a structural feature of *olowan* 'song,' i.e., of the theme and cadence, which are not distinguished from each other. Songs are made or learned with a set of vocables which remain intact, and unless the song is changed (in part by altering the vocables as well as thematic music), the vocables partly distinguish one song from another. Although there is no space to elucidate the problems of vocables in this paper, it should be stated that while vocables do not have meaning in a semantic sense, they do have a grammar which tends to render the range of song syllables finite. I wish to pursue the notion of grammaticality of vocables in a future paper.

It is probably safe to say that words in songs sung in a secular context are classifiable; such songs are said to be *wocaje* 'name' songs. Those songs with words sung in a religious context, however, are not so distinguished, and I speculate that the logic is that "supernatural" words are a structural feature of "supernatural" songs and cannot be further distinguished.

Finally, with reference to "the extent" to which the Oglala verbalize about musical composition as we try to understand it in Western tradition, it should be understood that questions like "Under what conditions did you compose (or learn) this song?" or "Where did this song come into being?" etc., will elicit an infinite variety of responses that may not necessarily be further analyzed. Even if it were possible to categorize the "conditions" of composition, it is unlikely that there would be very much contrast cross-culturally. Densmore has pointed out that "the Indian isolated himself by going away from the camp, while the white musician or poet locks his door, but both realize the necessity of freedom from distraction" (Densmore 1918: 59). While it is unlikely that all creative people require freedom from distraction, Densmore's statement does reflect that the creative condition is more properly the subject of psychophysical processes and is not necessarily restricted to the domain of musical inquiry.

My own inquiry as to the conditions under which songs come into being led to a number of standard responses which are not or do not seem to be culturally unique to the Oglala. Among some of the responses about the composition of a song, singers told me: "I was just sitting there tapping two rocks together, when this song came to me"; "I was sitting in the back of the pick-up listening to the hum of the tires on the road, when . . . "; "I was standing there in the dance arbor and all of a sudden I began to sing this [new] song"; "All of a sudden I heard this song and began to sing it"; "I was taking my boy to the train station (to go to the army) when I sang this song"; "When he heard President Kennedy was dead, he began singing this song . . . ." Although the need to sing or compose a song under duress or emotional state (rather than doing something else, for example) may be more Oglala than not, the situations or conditions themselves reveal nothing particularly unique.

As to a preference of composing one part of a new song prior to another part, e.g., introduction before theme, or vocables before words, etc., again there seems to be no standard practice. Most genres of songs are marked in part by strophic and final cadences; thus once the function of the song is determined, this part of the song remains standard. There is perhaps a logical argument that vocables hold primacy over texts (since there is no word for vocable), but this cannot be empirically verified. Texts may be added or dropped in the process of changing songs. In some genres — Rabbit dance songs, Love songs — the introduction as well as the final cadences are standardized. In the Omaha dance song, the introduction is derived from the theme, thus the latter is logically composed first. In songs emanating from supernatural origins, the texts are regarded as the most important; however, there are some songs sung in a religious context that are comprised of vocables only.

The time required to compose a song also varies. Some songs are said to have been composed spontaneously at a dance or other kind of gathering, while others, partially completed, have been "carried around in my head," as one singer told me, "for more than a year."

Classification of Musical Instruments.

Returning for a moment to Lévy-Bruhl's notion of "appurtenance," and regarding music as one of those qualities or states perceived to be part of human bodily functions rather than something exterior to it, it is quite simple to demonstrate that vocal music is a prime candidate for such "natural" considerations. In speaking of Oglala terminology specifically, although this would apply to all Native American music in varying degrees, their music is essentially and pre-eminently vocal. However, musical instruments are important as accompaniment and obviously must be considered with respect to what the Oglala have to say about their total musical system.

In discussing musical instruments, I want to focus on three considerations: 1) Vocal music is logically an extension of the human body, and is expressed thusly, as I have shown above, but musical instruments are clearly *things* external to the human body; they are "manufactured." 2) Given the limited number of musical instruments for the Oglala, viz., drum, rattle, flageolet, and minimal variations, is it really appropriate to talk about how the Oglala *classify* their instruments, or might we not merely investigate how they distinguish among instruments? 3) How do the Oglala incorporate Euro-American instruments into their own "natural" model of musical terminology, i.e., do newly-introduced instruments become truly "classified" according to an existing scheme of musical instrument nomenclature?

In Western society it is presumed that music is a bounded domain, and the analytical model reflects this. In the past ethnosemanticists have had, out of necessity, to focus their studies on similar bounded domains such as kinship, plants, disease, and color because these domains are perceived to be finite categories and thus subject to taxonomic classification. As I have demonstrated above, however, Oglala musical behavior and the means of verbalizing about it are theoretically infinite and thus not readily subject to taxonomic considerations except in those cases where the analytical and synthetic models coincide.

What may be regarded as the traditional inventory of Oglala musical instruments, one which existed prior to European contact and one which continues to be associated with the traditional music, is comprised of the following:

cancega 'drum' (from *can* 'wood' and *cega* 'earthen pot');
wagmuha 'rattle' (from *wagmu* 'gourd' and *ha* 'skin, hide');
šiyotanka 'flageolet, "flute," whistle' (from *šiyo* 'prairie chicken' and *tanka* 'great, large').

The drum and rattle always serve as accompaniment to vocal music, while flageolet music is interchangable with vocal music. Thus, in the case of the latter, a class restricted to Love songs, a melody played on a flageolet may have been originally composed for vocal performance. In theory, every song played on a flageolet has a vocal counterpart with important song texts, but in practice this may not always be the case.

The manner in which these respective instruments are played is described as:

apa 'to strike with the hand,' i.e., 'to drum';
yucancan 'to shake with the hand,' i.e., 'to rattle' (from *yu*, instrumental prefix signifying that an action is performed by means of the hands, and *cancan* 'to shake');
yajo 'to whistle by means of the mouth.'

It should be noted here that all native instruments are made from organic materials: wood, clay, gourd, skin, etc. *Šiyotanka*, "big prairie chicken," is derived from the association between the mating ritual of the prairie chicken and human courting rituals. *Šiyo* is an onomatopoeic word perceived to be the sound of the prairie chicken during mating rituals. The analogy may not be obvious: both prairie chicken and humans inflate their cheeks to produce the appropriate mating sounds. The analogy is significant structurally on at least two levels, sound and performance.

The Oglala not only distinguish between the type of instrument based on structural features and analogies and the manner in which it is played based on the part of the body used to produce the sound, but they also distinguish between the latter and the resultant effect of the playing, thus:

apa 'to drum,' but *kabubu* 'the sound of drumming' (from *ka*, instrumental prefix signifying that the action was performed by striking with the arm, and *bubu*, reduplication of *bu*, a radical element suggesting a rapid succession of sounds).
yucancan 'to rattle,' but *yuh'lah'la* 'the sound of rattling' (from *yu*, instrumental prefix signifying that the action was performed by means of the hands, and *h'lah'la*, reduplicated form of *h'la*, a radical element suggesting the sound of elements reverberating in a container,' e.g., *sinteh'la* 'rattlesnake').
yajo 'to whistle, play a flageolet,' but *yajoho* 'the sound of a flageolet, whistle' (from *ya*, instrumental prefix signifying that an action was performed by means of the mouth; *jo* 'to whistle,' as birds; and *ho* 'voice').

Here I think the idea of instrument taxonomy is inappropriate, given that each instrument is the sole member of its own class. Although there are some minimal variations of drums (large bass types and smaller tambourine types), rattles (though even rawhide rattles are still called "gourd" rattles), and sizes of whistles, the native system regards all variations as simply drums, rattles, and flageolets. What is more interesting is the relationship between means of playing and resultant sounds of instruments (they are all derived from external bodily functions, i.e., actions performed by means of the hands, arms, and mouth, and are thus not isolable from other parts of the synthetic model).

Here I might summarize by stating that although musical instruments are manufactured and "exist" outside the human body, the way they are conceptualized integrates them into the synthetic model by emphasizing the manner in which an instrument is played and its resultant sound as analogues of human bodily functions. Although the names of the instruments themselves are comprised of "natural" categories — wood, clay, etc. — they can only be operationalized by means of bodily contact or manipulation, and this is what the native Oglala system emphasizes.

Turning to my final point, I wish to examine how the Oglala verbalize about modern Euro-American musical instruments. As is true in any kind of technological exchange, there are a number of ways that one society may linguistically incorporate new technologies of other societies. One way is to simply incorporate a loan word or corruption of the original word used to designate the technology. Another is to invent a new word in the native language, or conjure up an archaic word which has new-found relevance. Between borrowing in total and inventing anew, there are of course various permutations, and although the Oglala deal with all of them easily (although there is a near absence of loan words from English) when speaking of song, the synthetic model persists.

Of particular note with respect to non-musical domains is the Oglala tendency to describe the material out of which new technologies are made, as well as how new things function. As one example of the former, the Oglala were impressed upon seeing objects manufactured from metal and appropriately enunciated the sophisticated manufacturing process in a number of words: *mazawakan* 'gun' (" 'holy' metal"); *mazacanku* 'railroad' ("iron road"); *masopiye* 'store' (i.e., "iron box [safe]"); *mazaska* 'money' ("silver metal"), etc. As an example of the latter, a boat was called *petawata* 'fire boat'; motorcycle, *napopela* ('an automatic explosion'); a side car was *patujela* ('a bending over,' indicating the manner in which the side car was pumped by two operators), etc.

Despite the sophisticated manufacture of musical instruments, the technological features have never much impressed the Oglala, as the following examples will demonstrate.

Three categories of European musical instruments (which interestingly correspond with the ethnomusicological classification of musical instruments) are:

waapapi 'things struck with the hands,' i.e., "membranophones";
wayuȟlaȟlapi 'things rattled with the hands,' i.e., "idiophones" (*naȟlaȟla* 'to jingle one's bells' is derived from *na*, instrumental prefix signifying that the action takes place by means of the feet, and *ȟlaȟla* 'bells');
wayajopi 'things played by blowing,' i.e., "aerophones."

Chordophones were not known by the Oglala prior to European contact, but once introduced they were called generically *wayukize* 'things played on strings,' literally "things which squeak by means of the hands"; *kiza* is an onomatopoeic word attributed to the sound of a mouse's voice. The Oglala further distinguish between two kinds of stringed instruments: those which are bowed and those which are strummed. The former is called *canyukize* 'to produce the sound of a squeak on wood'; the latter, *cankahotun* 'to strike wood and give birth to a voice.' The instrumental prefix *ka* is the same that we find in *kabubu* 'the sound of a drum.'

While all modern brass and wind instruments are considered *wayajopi* 'things played by blowing,' some brass instruments such as trombones and tubas are called *wayabupi* 'things that produce the sound of a growl.' Lastly, a mouth organ is regarded as being in a class of its own and is called *yapizapi*. *Piza* is an onomatopoeic word perceived to be the sound of a prairie dog which is called *pispiza*. Thus *yapizapi* means 'to produce the sound of a prairie dog by means of the mouth.'

Although a larger inventory of Western instruments and their Lakota equivalents is yet to be collected, I believe that the above examples demonstrate that the underlying means of classifying recently-introduced instruments is consonant with the manner of verbalizing about native instruments and song, both of which are perceived to be "appurtenances" of the human body.

Summary and Conclusions. By way of summary and conclusion, I would like to emphasize the following points:

1. It is unlikely that part of any society's musical system does not include some means of verbalizing about it. And it is postulated that cultural differences are at least partly manifested on the basis of how such verbalizations are conceptualized and formulated, as Merriam has suggested.

2. Throughout the long history of music in the Western tradition, such means of verbalization have been codified and transformed from the folk idiom into a technical language which serves to describe and analyze music through what I have labeled an *analytical model*, one characterized by a tendency constantly to divide musical concepts into their component parts. I have suggested that the preconceptions of what music should be, based on the analytical model, have created problems in understanding not so much the extent to which non-Western peoples verbalize about their musical system, but the manner in which they do so.

3. Based on ethnographic data collected from the Oglala of the Pine Ridge Indian Reservation, South Dakota, I have suggested another model, here called the *synthetic model*, which provides another means of interpreting to an English-speaking audience how one non-Western society conceptualizes its music system. The synthetic model may be characterized by a tendency towards combining units which are analogous to other cultural domains. Here I have made reference to the seminal ideas of Lévy-Bruhl with hopes of demonstrating that among the Oglala the synthetic model of music is one consistent with what the Oglala perceive to be human bodily functions; vocal music is perceived to be an "appurtenance" of the human body classifiable along with other bodily functions, particularly speech. The analogies between music and other functions, however, are not always obvious at the surface level, and my methodology requires that I compare not lexical units of speech, but morphemes.

4. The synthetic/analytic contrast is not intended to be an evolutionary model

per se; however, it should be recognized that even the technical music of Western society is derived from a folk idiom. This is another way of saying categorically that the synthetic model does not go hand in hand with "primitive" society and the analytical model with "civilized" societies.

It is more profitable to view the two models as standing in a dialectical relationship with each other. I would also state unequivocally that I do not believe that the synthetic model as employed for the Oglala is necessarily the only other kind of model that may be contrasted with the analytical. In fact, I suggest that there are many other kinds of models waiting to be constructed from raw ethnographic data from all parts of the world, including segments of Western societies. Perhaps our first step is to investigate more fully the phenomenon of synesthesia, which deals with the interpretation of one sensory modality in terms of another. Merriam has already introduced this idea and its potential usefulness to ethnomusicology (Merriam 1964: 85-101), but to date little or nothing has been done about it. Our own folk ideas about music suggest that within Western society as well as other societies of the world there are an infinite number of ways to verbalize about music — music which is hot, cool, blue, bouncy, funky, catchy; or music which jumps, moves, wails, rocks, or otherwise contorts itself as if indeed it were an "appurtenance" of our own "primitive" mentality.

REFERENCES CITED

Beuchel, Eugene
    1939 *Grammar of Lakota*. St. Louis: Jonathan Swift and Company.
    1970 *Lakota-English Dictionary*. Pine Ridge, South Dakota: Red Cloud Indian School.

Cazeneuve, Jean
    1972 *Lucien Lévy-Bruhl*. Translated by Peter Rivière. New York: Harper and Row. Originally published as *Lucien Lévy-Bruhl, sa vie, son oeuvre avec un exposé de sa philosophie* (1963).

Densmore, Frances
    1918 *Teton Sioux Music*. Bulletin of the Bureau of American Ethnology, No. 61. Washington D. C.

Douglas, Mary
    1970 *Natural Symbols*. New York: Pantheon Books.

Evans-Pritchard, E. E.
    1965 *Theories of Primitive Religion*. London: Oxford University Press.

Frake, Charles O.
    1964 *Notes on Queries in Ethnography*. Special publication, *American Anthropologist* 66 (3), pt. 2: 132-45.

Herskovits, M. J.
    1948 *Man and his Works*. New York: Alfred A. Knopf.

Lévi-Strauss, Claude
    1949   *The Elementary Structures of Kinship*. Boston: Beacon Press.
    1962   "Social Structure." In *Anthropology Today*. International Symposium on Anthropology. Edited by Sol Tax. Chicago: University of Chicago Press.
    1963   "The Structural Study of Myth." In *Structural Anthropology*. New York: Anchor Books.

Lévy-Bruhl, Lucien
    1966   *The "Soul" of the Primitive*. Translated by Lilian A. Clare. Chicago: Henry Regnery Company. Originally published as *L'âme primitive* (1927).

Merriam, Alan P.
    1964   *The Anthropology of Music*. Evanston: Northwestern University Press.

Needham, Rodney
    1972   *Belief, Language and Experience*. Chicago: University of Chicago Press.

Nettl, Bruno
    1956   *Music in Primitive Culture*. Cambridge: Harvard University Press.

Powers, William K.
    1970   "Songs of the Red Man." Discographic review essay. *Ethnomusicology* 14 (2): 358-69.
    1977   *Oglala Religion*. Lincoln: University of Nebraska Press.

Swanton, John
    1911   "Siouan." In *Handbook of North American Indian Languages*. Bulletin of the Bureau of American Ethnology, No. 40, pt. 1. Washington D. C.

Ĕ′niwûb′e of Lac du Flambeau, who recorded thirty-three songs for Frances Densmore in 1911.
(Photo Smithsonian Institution National Anthropological Archives; Frances Densmore, *Chippewa Music – II*, 1913, Plate 26).

A HISTORY OF OJIBWA SONG FORM[1]

Thomas Vennum, Jr.

The scientific study of any music is dependent upon some permanent record of it, either in notational form or sound recordings, to permit detailed and repeated observation. As such notations and recordings accumulate through time, a history of the musical style becomes possible. Thus we are able to discern stylistic development in a music based primarily on written tradition by studying its published and manuscript compositions — for instance, the evolution of rounded binary (sonata) form in the late 18th century art music of Western Europe. Tracing stylistic innovations in an orally transmitted music, however, is virtually impossible without historical sound recordings.

Before the advent of the phonograph, Native American music, for the most part, went unrecorded and uncollected. Most information prior to the invention of the phonograph is limited to verbal accounts. These are mostly negative reactions to the music or descriptions using musical terminology imprecisely; neither tell us much about the style of the music. A few ethnographers were sufficiently trained in musical dictation to take down by ear what they heard in the field, but without sound recordings to verify their accuracy, the published notations often raise more questions than they answer.

Lacking the scientific evidence provided by recordings, reconstructions of musical styles from past oral tradition are at best speculative and even misleading. For example, Alan Merriam (1967), finding that contemporary Flathead music shows few Salish traits but conforms instead to the general Plains style, argues that "enough information can be gleaned to support the conclusion that at the time of contact with Lewis and Clark in 1805 the Flathead already had a well established Plains musical style" (Merriam 1967: 149). In such a contention, however, Merriam is totally dependent upon published reports in historical sources supplemented by the verbal accounts of his informants. Although these sources may have described the cultural *context* of the music, they can tell us little if anything about the Flathead musical *style* prior to ca. 1930, because no recordings of Flathead music are known to have been made before that time. Nor is there evidence of what constituted the Plains style before recordings in the 1890's gave us our first samples.

Fortunately, because such pioneers in the study of Native American music as Alice C. Fletcher and Frances Densmore collected when they did, we now have recordings of songs spanning nearly a century for many North American tribes. This time depth should enable us to begin to write histories of their music, however tentative they must remain due to the comparatively small sample from the early years and the limitations of the photograph recordings from that period.

The present paper describes the history, as far as we can perceive it, of one aspect of the Ojibwa musical style — song form. Ojibwa music offers a particularly rare opportunity for such a study, for its songs received considerable attention at an early date. The sample of Ojibwa recordings from the turn of the century is larger by far than that of any other tribe, and no less than three monographs based on those recordings were published by 1913.

Our present knowledge of the Ojibwa style begins on January 24, 1899, when Fletcher recorded six songs from a Leech Lake (Minnesota) warrior, Swift Flying Feather, who was visiting Washington on tribal business. In the decade which followed, Frederick Burton recorded some 180 songs of the eastern Ojibwa near Desbarets, Ontario. His transcriptions were published in *American Primitive Music* (1909), but unfortunately the cylinders on which they were based appear to have been lost. From 1907 to 1911 Frances Densmore, the most prolific collector of American Indian music, recorded nearly five hundred songs of the southwestern Ojibwa, from forty-five singers on six reservations in Minnesota and Wisconsin. The results of her study were published by the Bureau of American Ethnology, her sponsor, in the landmark two-volume *Chippewa Music* (1910, 1913). About the same time recordings were made by Albert B. Reagan at Nett Lake, Minnesota, and William Jones at Leech Lake. Thus the early sample of Ojibwa music is extensive both in the number of recordings made and their geographic representation.

In spite of this early flurry of interest in Ojibwa music, until recently little has been collected, studied, or published since Densmore's time. Therefore a historical survey of the style, such as the present one, is restricted to comparing the state of the music at two points, separated by more than half a century.

The fieldwork undertaken to record the contemporary sample for this study began in 1968 and was restricted to the southwestern sector of the large geographic area in which the Ojibwa are found. (Hereinafter, the reader should assume "Ojibwa" to mean the southwestern bands of the tribe.) This was the area of Densmore's research, and collecting took place in many of the same communities where she had recorded some sixty years earlier, sometimes even at the same events — the Red Lake Fourth of July celebration, for example. Although Densmore recorded exclusively solo singers, most of the five hundred songs selected for comparison with the historical material were group performances. To balance this somewhat, the sample also included a sizeable number of solo performances by William Bineshi Baker, Sr., the foremost singer on the Lac Court Oreilles Reservation in Wisconsin and the principal informant during the research.[2]

The study focuses on mainstream Ojibwa tribal music only and thus excludes from consideration certain song types which were exceptional ca. 1910 and remain so today. Meriting special studies of their own, these include unaccompanied love songs, songs for the entertainment of children, songs of the *mitewiwin* (Grand Medicine Society), peyote songs, and Christian hymns with Ojibwa texts.[3]

Part of Leech Lake (Minnesota) delegation to Washington, D.C. in 1899 to air treaty grievances. During this visit, Swift Flying Feather (front row, far right) recorded three cylinders for Alice C. Fletcher. A decade later, Frances Densmore recorded Gegwe'djiwe'bīnŭñ' (front row, second from right) and Ge'miwûnac' (back row, fourth from right) on their reservation. (Photo Smithsonian Institution National Anthropological Archives)

Waiting for other singers to join him, William Bineshi Baker, Sr., lead singer at the weekly summer "Indian Bowl" performances at Lac du Flambeau, Wisconsin. (Photo M. Herter, 1974)

Young Ojibwa from Ponemah, Minnesota (Red Lake Reservation) at the drum. Performing as lead singer is Vernon Kingbird; his brother Albert is at his left. (Photo C. Brill, 1969)

In order to compare Densmore's material with the songs collected for the study, it was necessary to retranscribe all her songs from taped copies of the original cylinders, for her published transcriptions contain many inaccuracies (see Vennum 1973: vii-ix; 1975: 24-25). Only in this way, using the same criteria and notational system adopted for the contemporary sample, could the historical sample be brought into line with it for comparison.

* * *

Early chroniclers of Ojibwa culture make it clear that they found the music to be essentially formless, though little can be culled from their verbal reports. In his study of the *mitewiwin*, for instance, Walter J. Hoffman omits transcriptions for many of the songs he collected, dismissing them as "monotonous repetition[s] of four or five notes in a minor key" (Hoffman 1891: 192). His impression was that *mite* music consisted of melodic fragments performed "ad libitum in direct proportion to the degree of inspiration which the singer imagines himself to have attained." Even such a musically trained individual as Frederick Burton found Ojibwa singers to be "deficient in sense of proportion" (1909: 92), as he attempted in vain to discover eight-measure periodic structure in their songs. Burton's ethnocentrism in matters of form is reflected in passages such as the following, in which he discusses an older and newer version of one song:

> Musically the song is far better in the modern version because there are fewer repetitions of the leading phrase. It appears that the Indian singers felt the tendency to monotony in the older version, and as they were not educated in music and knew nothing of thematic development, they solved the art problem by discarding some of the repetitions, thus evolving at last a perfectly made tune that happens also to be exquisitely beautiful (Burton 1909: 99).

The early cylinder recordings enlarge somewhat our knowledge of Ojibwa song, but more in other matters of style than form, due to their limitations. With the advent of more sophisticated recording means it has been possible to capture Ojibwa song more fully. We can now study the whole of a singer's performance, note how he regulates the flow of his melody with cadential formulae, repeats phrases to attain structural balances, etc.

The Form of Contemporary Ojibwa Song.

Today nearly all Ojibwa songs are in the so-called "incomplete repetition" form. This form has been used by several Plains Indian tribes in the past and currently has its widest diffusion in the music of the northern and eastern edges of the Plains.[4]

A typical song is begun by the lead singer of a group, who prefaces the opening phrase of the melody by several drum beats, to identify the type of song he has chosen and establish its tempo. The duration of this introductory drumming varies with the singer and the circumstance. In group performances a few beats suffice to

Woman's Dance Song.

Singer: William Bineshi Baker, Sr.
Place: South Hamilton, Massachusetts **Collector:** Thomas Vennum, Jr.
Date: May 28, 1971 **Catalog No.:** 71CO31[b]

(translation: Your bed is too small
[or] I would come over to sleep
with you.)

S1: transcribed
S2: ABC/BC

identify the song type for the other singers and the dancers. Only four or five unaccented 8th-notes, for example, are needed to "announce" a standard War Dance song. Sometimes, however, a long period of drumming can occur while a singer searches his memory for a song. (In solo performances for a recording session, the singer may omit introductory drumming altogether, presumably because it is unnecessary.) The drumming is then taken up by the group and continues uninterruptedly until the beginning of the coda.

After the preliminary drum beats, the lead man sings the first phrase (A), ending in a brief downward portamento followed by a pause. The other singers then repeat, or "second," the opening phrase, perhaps slightly varied (A^1), the lead singer joining them part way through the phrase or waiting until the beginning of the second phrase (B):

This double introductory phrase is a standard part of the song. Even in performing a song alone, a singer will automatically take on the role of the group and sing a complete repetition of the (A) phrase, although in doing so he may omit the portamento, the pause, and sometimes both, at the end of the first phrase. Therefore, although the double introduction has been described as an antiphonal structure in Plains Indian music (see Merriam 1967: 250), in Ojibwa music the description properly fits only group performances.[5]

After this double introduction, the main body of the melody follows, hereinafter to be called 'the development.' Although other terms have been used to describe this part of the melody — the 'chorus,' for example — the term 'development' seems appropriate, for the melody at this point, more often than not, is composed of phrases closely related to the introduction — (A^2), (A^3) — and/or new phrases — (B), (C), (D), etc. — which develop material from the introduction. Such development may consist of a continuation of rhythmic patterns, dynamic stresses, or melodic contours appearing in the introduction (see the discussion of "Motivic Composition" in Vennum 1975: 131-39).[6] The development section is concluded with a cadential formula, which may be an extension of the final phrase of the development or detached from it (X). This cadence ends with a portamento and pause, similar to that which ended the (A) phrase:

The group then performs the incomplete repetition, which is a restatement of the development section of its cadence.[7] It is termed 'incomplete' because it omits the introductory phrases (AA^1). In the transcriptions and formal schemata, a virgule precedes the first phrase of the incomplete repetition: [AABC/BC], etc.:

The final cadence of the incomplete repetition concludes one complete statement of the melody, after which the lead singer returns to the (A) phrase and begins the repetition of the entire melody.

The number of statements making up a song varies: a religious song may have only four — this number having sacred associations[8] — unless it is sung during some ritual act, such as food consecration, when it is repeated until the actions have been completed (see Barrett 1911: 281, 291).[9] Secular songs contain from one to as many as twenty statements, the number being determined by the leader before or during the performance of the song, or by the dancers.

The lead singer usually decides when to conclude a secular song. He may provide verbal instructions to the group before beginning the song. For instance, "Four slow ones and six fast ones" would mean ten continuous statements of the melody with an abrupt change in tempo after the fourth. Or, he might give hand signals during the performance. Although such signals vary with the singer, their meaning is readily grasped by those at the drum, even strangers. The forefinger drawn across the throat indicates that a "cut-off" is desired and that the singers should end the song with the statement they are performing at the time; the forefinger held in the air usually means that an additional statement should be sung.[10]

The mood of the dancers can also affect the length of a song. If a few dancers are present, which is typical of the beginning of a pow-wow, the songs tend to include only three or four statements. By late evening or early morning at a celebration, with as many as ten singers at a drum and more than a hundred enthusiastic dancers present, a song may extend to twenty statements or more. Nowadays dancers may request additional statements of the melody by blowing on bone whistles, a custom recently borrowed from the Sioux.[11]

While most contemporary religious songs end with a final statement of the melody, secular songs customarily end with a coda, called "the tail."[12] The coda is nothing more than the incomplete repetition of the melody performed as a "tail" to the song. It is separated from the main body of the song by a brief pause in both singing and accompaniment.

In preparation for the singing of the coda, the end of the final full statement of the melody is altered: the downward portamento is omitted,[13] slight accents are given to the final weak beats of the melody and accompaniment, and these are followed by rests. The differences may be summarized as follows:

	Between Statements	Between the Final Statement and Coda
Voice:	♫♩♪𝄾 𝄽	♫♩♪𝄾.
Drum:	♫♫♫ etc.	♩𝄾

Although the singing of the coda is like that of the incomplete repetition that precedes it, the drumming is distinctive. The beginning of the coda is always signalled by a sharp tap on the drum, usually by the lead singer. (Either the break in the drumming or the tap may be the "signal," which Densmore [1910: 86] mentions as imperceptible to outsiders but understood by the dancers.) This tap serves as an accented upbeat for the coda.[14] The volume of drumming after this sharp accent is reduced immediately, and the singers begin a gradual crescendo on the drum, which lasts to the end of the song.[15]

As the final cadence nears, the weak drum beats become increasingly accented until, in the final few beats, the unaccented (strong) beats may be omitted altogether:

Contemporary Ojibwa song form can be summarized, thus:

Double Introduction	Development	Incomplete Repetition	Coda
‖: AA¹	BCD...X/	BCD...X :‖	BCD...X

The pervasiveness of this form enables singers to learn new songs with ease. Often at dances, a lead singer may be seen at a drum beating softly on its edge while quietly teaching a new song to the others. Because, in general, the melodies are motivically cohesive and the standard song form is so familiar to the singers, they can anticipate to a large extent the overall pattern of a new song. Consequently, only one or two statements (at normal tempo) are required to familiarize them with the melody, provided that it is not tonally or rhythmically abnormal. From this brief rehearsal the group proceeds directly to a performance of the song at normal volume. Ease in learning songs explains why singers at pow-wows move without hesitation from one drum to another, often performing entirely unfamiliar repertoires with complete strangers, even from other tribes. It also accounts for the rapid diffusion of contemporary songs.[16]

Modifications of the Contemporary Song Form.

Although standard song form as described above characterizes nearly all Ojibwa song today, it is modified somewhat by the performance practices of different singers and regions. The double introduction and the coda are the two component parts most susceptible to modification.

The Double Introduction. In most songs, the double introduction (as described above) consists of two complete phrases,[17] separated by a brief rest; nearly identical, the phrases balance each other. In other songs, however, the formal proportions of the double introduction may be altered by performance practices which destroy this balance; as a result, the two (A) phrases may be disjunct, continuous, or even overlapping.

A singer's age or his familiarity with the song may affect the point at which he begins the second phrase of the double introduction. Older singers, particularly in Wisconsin, strictly observe a brief but clear articulation between the two (A) phrases. The group is not expected to begin the repetition of the (A) phrase until the lead singer has completed his portamento. Ideally, the other singers then enter after a slight pause (in the transcriptions, a quarter-note or less in duration).

Younger singers, especially in Minnesota, tend not to observe a clear separation of the two introductory phrases. They will interrupt the lead singer's phrase, beginning the second phrase (A^1) "somewhere along the line" — to use Baker's expression. This interruption occurs most often in the final statements of songs sung at fast tempos. The group may enter after the lead singer has performed for only two or three beats, thereby abbreviating his (A) phrase. Furthermore, the place at which they interrupt him can vary from one statement to the next. The resultant overlapping of lead singer's and group's phrases produces momentary two-part singing. (A similar overlap occurs when the lead begins another statement of the melody before the group has completed the final cadence of the preceding statement. Such overlaps are the only instances of "polyphony" in Ojibwa music and were noted early in the century as well [see Burton 1909: 85-86].) Older and more conservative singers (mostly in Wisconsin) generally resent these interruptions and consider that the group is "butting in."[18]

Disjunct phrases result when singers are unfamiliar with the song and hesitant to repeat the introductory (A) phrase. An unusually long pause will indicate this reluctance to the lead singer, and he will sing all or at least the beginning of the second phrase as well. He may have to do this for several statements before the other singers have learned the melody.

William Bineshi Baker, Sr., cutting fat and membrane from the inner side of cowhide used for drumhead.
(Photo M. Herter, 1974)

left:
For his homemade drumstick, Baker sews buckskin covering over plastic fishing rod padded with cloth at the beater end.

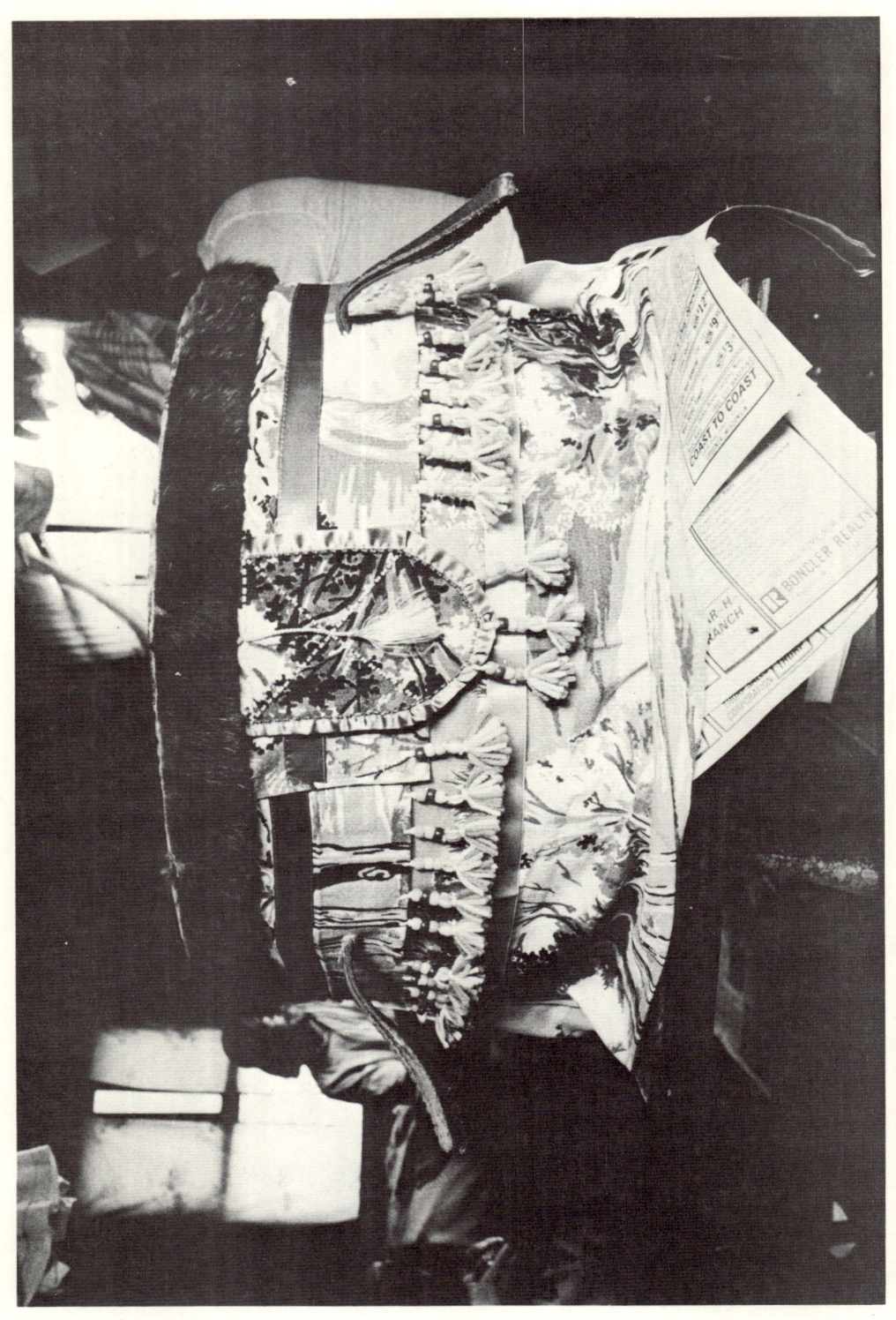

Baker's secular version of the Woman's Dance Drum (*ikkwetewe'ikan*), constructed in June, 1974. (Photo M. Herter)

Among the Minnesota Ojibwa, the role of lead singer in providing the first (A) phrase for each repetition of the melody can be usurped by another singer near the end of a song. This usually occurs when a member of the group wishes to extend the song past the point at which it would end, the interloper assuming the lead singer's function and beginning another double introduction before the group has finished the song.

The Coda. Until recently, at least, the coda was such a standard feature of the secular dance song that the Ojibwa considered a song incomplete without it. When Baker once returned from a pow-wow in Calgary, Alberta, he reported with some amazement that only two songs he had heard during the entire festival had been given "tails."[19]

Not all Ojibwa songs have codas, as has already been mentioned. Sacred songs for the ceremonial Drum Dance are without them.[20] A singer may mistakenly add a "tail" to a Drum Dance song because the coda is such a standard feature of the secular song. When this happens during a ceremony, the Drum-heater must rise and dance to atone for the error (see Barrett 1911: 279, Plate 11; Fig. 2). Only under these circumstances today may a sacred song be extended deliberately, according to Baker. As the Drum-heater is dancing for another's error, he can gain amends by laying his drumstick on the drum; this act requires the man who committed the error to continue singing until the Drum-heater decides to remove his stick from the drum.

When codas are missing from secular songs, the reason is usually obvious. Songs used to accompany show-dancing may end after only one or two statements of the melody, at which time an announcer may request the audience to applaud. Codas may also be omitted from songs during interviews when the singer, to demonstrate some point, may sing only part of a song or, when recording a number of songs in succession, he performs only one or two statements of each melody.

The use of the coda is at present so susceptible to change that its original function — concluding a song — may soon be lost. For instance, sometimes more than one coda will be added to a song. Although older singers customarily sing only one, younger singers, particularly those in northern Minnesota, may sing two or more.[21] When they perform songs with an abrupt change to a faster tempo after several slower statements, younger singers use two: one to terminate the slow section and signal the change in tempo; the other to round out the song.[22] If the performance has become especially lively towards the end of a song (i.e., higher in pitch, faster and more excited in delivery) and the dancers seem to wish to continue, as many as four codas may be sung, often by someone other than the lead singer.[23]

Ojibwa Song Form ca. 1910.

Despite individual and regional variations, song form today is marked by a high degree of homogeneity and fixity. By contrast, song form at the beginning of the century appears to have been heterogeneous and transitional.

The exact state of song form ca. 1910 is unclear. The extant recordings of complete song performances from that period are far outnumbered by those of song fragments, each "a sample rather than a complete structure," as Curt Sachs (1965: 131) describes such musical shards; and while an incomplete performance of a song may suffice to give us an idea of its text, melodic range, its tonal and rhythmic patterns, it provides little information concerning its total form. Because the available evidence is so scanty, observations concerning Ojibwa song form ca. 1910 can only be in large part conjectural and based on what are presumably similar features in contemporary song form.

Densmore's published study does little to clarify for us the form of the music she heard. Furthermore, she uses the term 'form' to cover nearly everything in a song *except* its structure. Thus she states of an old song that its "continuous use under semi-civilized conditions may have modified the form of the melody to its present regularity of time and intervals" (Densmore 1910: 151; see also 1910: v). In another place she cites as evidence of the programmatic connection between "the motive which prompts the singing of a song and the form [= contour] assumed by the song" (1913: 34) the continuous outlining of the tones of one chord. The form of the melody, she feels, "suggests the close attention with which one follows moving objects" (1910: 130). The distinctiveness of the four-measure "rhythmic unit" in a hunting song (Densmore catalog no. 60) she thought provided great "regularity of musical form" (1910: 86).

Densmore's imprecise use of terms is matched by the superficial attention to song form in her analyses and transcriptions. Her overriding interest was in "tonality," rhythm, and "the psychology of Indian song." Such references as she makes to structural detail suggest that she never made a thorough comparative study of the songs she collected. For example, despite the frequent presence of incomplete repetition in her sample, she seems to have been only slightly aware of any formal principle involved. For instance, she notes that Ga'gandac'sang "Manido Listens to Me" (cat. no. 212) "twice [in succession]"; in his repetition, he abbreviated the melody, "suggesting that the first measures are an introduction" (1910: 132). Similarly, she mentions in passing that the opening measures of two Dream songs (cat. 325, 327) "were not included in the repetitions of the song" (1913: 257, 260; see also 1910: 19, 30).

Having paid little or no attention to the general form of the songs she collected, Densmore was forced to assume that internal repetitions represented unimportant "liberties" taken by the singer in performance. This becomes apparent if we compare her published transcriptions with the cylinder recordings from which she made them. Thus, in A'gwitûwigi'cĭg's "The Shifting Clouds" the incomplete repetition is omitted from the transcription, although in his performance it carries the text. She published only the incomplete repetition of Gi'nawigi'cĭg's War Dance song (cat. 172), omitting the long introductory phrase and thereby misrepresenting the range of the melody as well. Because she believed that Gi'wita'binĕs "embellished" his song in the repetitions — "clearly for effect" — she transcribed only "that portion of the record ... on which the song was evidently sung through once in a direct way" (1910: 173; see also 1910: 179).[24]

Many of the inadequacies of Densmore's transcriptions must ultimately be attributed to the recording conditions she faced. Such factors as the nervousness of the Indian singer in a "studio" for the first time, the collector's need to control the recording session, and the limited recording space on the wax cylinder as well as

Densmore's desire not to waste it, determined what went onto a recording. Because of such factors, inevitably Densmore encountered media intrusion problems similar to those facing the ethnographic film maker,[25] for any one of the factors would have sufficed to distort the singer's natural mode of performance. Consequently, the fragmentary nature of many of the performances she collected must have affected her understanding of Ojibwa song just as today it limits the uses to which we can put the material she collected.

Many of her cylinders contain interrupted performances. A singer may start and stop several times and at various places during the course of a song; thus we can only guess what the complete form of the song was. William Prentiss began to record a Begging dance song (cat. 149). Densmore interrupted him after only two phrases, presumably because he was too close to the recording horn (his volume blurs the higher tones). He began again, although for a time he was still closer to the horn. After one complete statement of the melody and part of a second, the singer paused. The recording machine appears to have been stopped at this point. (A sudden cut-off of background noise followed by a slight change in the pitch of the melody I take to be such an interruption.) When recording was resumed, Prentiss continued the melody at the point at which he left off and continued with two more statements of the melody, each lacking the incomplete repetition. Obviously, the form of this entire song remains conjectural.[26]

What appear to be instructions from Densmore during pauses in the singing seem also to have affected the form of the song as recorded. These directions to the singer, or to him through the interpreter, are audible on several recordings. Although much of what Densmore says in these instances cannot be made out, she seems usually to have been inducing her singers to continue.[27] For example, after Gi'wita'bineš had sung the coda to a Woman's Dance song (cat. 135), Densmore's voice can be heard in the background, whereupon the singer repeats the coda. At the conclusion of Wa'bezic's Moccasin Game song (cat. 171), one hears Densmore's voice, whereupon the singer performs the incomplete repetition twice more.

A logical explanation for these interrupted performances is that Densmore did not wish to waste valuable cylinder space. This is at least suggested by a number of cylinders which have one or two brief Love songs "squeezed" between other songs, possibly as fillers. The Love songs were not published, nor do they appear to have been catalogued by Densmore. If a singer came to the end of his song before the cylinder was used up, Densmore may have urged him to continue, repeating part of what he already had recorded, which might explain why singers performed the incomplete repetition several times successively (see cat. 153, 182, 224).

The limited recording space on a cylinder might also be the reason singers sometimes ended performances at unpredictable (and often unlikely) places in a song. They might have wished to complete the song before the cylinder reached its end. Densmore's informants, unaccustomed to timing their songs, were nevertheless sometimes aware of the limits imposed by the wax cylinder. Her *mite* singers, for instance, requested that she signal them before a cylinder ran out, so that they could include the ritually required ejaculation, "we ho ho ho," on the recording, even if it meant interrupting a song (Densmore 1910: 15).

The desire to complete a song before the cylinder ran out could explain why Ĕ'niwûb'e briefly interrupted a War Dance song (cat. 412) at an unusual place. In the penultimate phrase of the development section of statement two, he stops and performs the brief drum tremolo with which he customarily ends his songs. Then, suddenly, he begins again at the incomplete repetition. Possibly Ĕ́niwûb'e was under the impression that the cylinder was about filled and so stopped abruptly in order to conclude the song; discovering that there was more room on the cylinder (hand signals from Densmore?), he then resumed the song (see also cat. 419).

The fact that a number of songs end with the development section may also be attributed to the limited space available on a cylinder. Because the cadential formula is the same at the end of the development as it is at the end of a statement, the singer would find the earlier cadence a convenient point to break off a performance, were the cylinder about to run out.

Despite the incomplete state of some of the songs Densmore collected, a large number appear to be recorded fully enough to enable us to determine the song's general form. These are the performances in which neither Densmore nor her interpreter interfere, and the song is performed straight through.

Fletcher's recordings of Swift Flying Feather and Reagan's Nett Lake recordings are a useful supplement to Densmore's material, for among them are uninterrupted performances of song, which evidence a minimum of control over their performance. Furthermore, Reagan's songs appear to have been recorded in context rather than in a studio and as such could be considered "events with high energy level," the phrase Karl G. Heider uses to describe events in which the performers are so totally absorbed in what they are doing that the media intrusion is minimal.[28] The Nett Lake recordings also enlarge the geographic perspective of song form at the beginning of the century. As the only extant Ojibwa *group* performances recorded ca. 1910, they illustrate an aspect of song form notably absent from the songs collected by Densmore and Fletcher.

Older and Newer Song Forms ca. 1910.

The songs recorded early in the century include a variety of forms, ranging from the simple to the complex. The more complex forms are those which use one or more of the component parts found consistently in today's songs. Thus the formal aspects of contemporary Ojibwa song — in particular, the incomplete repetition and coda — are already to be found incipiently in the older repertoire.

The presence or absence of an incomplete repetition in a melody appears to be the principal means of determining its relative age. Descriptions of earlier performance practice include no mention of this type of repetition. One Red Lake informant, for instance, drew attention to the absence of incomplete repetitions in some older songs on his reservation. In speaking of "the ten songs" performed in succession at the Red Lake Feast of the Seasons sometime prior to 1900, William Dudley (b. 1887) observed that "they only sang the first verse, though each Indian pow-wow song has two verses [today]" (Rynkiewich 1968: 87). 'Verse' is one English term used today by Ojibwa singers to stipulate the form of their songs; 'two verses' refers to a melody divided into two parts. The first "verse" is that part of the song through the development section; the second "verse" is the incomplete repetition.[29]

Because the fragmentary nature of early recordings makes it difficult to determine what made up a complete song ca. 1910, it seems expedient to categorize each song from the historical sample on the basis of a single statement of its melody. In the discussion which follows, it is necessary to distinguish between two formal types at the turn of the century. Any melody in which the incomplete repetition is present will be considered to exhibit a closed form; any melody lacking it, an open form. Codas were missing from all songs whose melodies showed open forms.

Two principle types of open forms are found in melodies from ca. 1910. The first type is a melody consisting of several phrases (ABCD) and concluding in the cadential formula found in today's song — a sustained, final tone, often followed by a downward portamento:

Song of Thanks for Food.

Begging Dance song (cat. 441) recorded by Mec′kawiga′bau
at Lac du Flambeau, Wisconsin, October 1910.

(see also cat. 131, 133, 146, 154, 299, 410, 425).

This form characterizes the transcriptions of Ojibwa songs published prior to the first recordings, such as the Scalp Dance melody given by Keating (1825: 456) or the "War Song of the Chippewas" by Schoolcraft (1855: 562). Because these melodies exhibit the first type of open form, at least some credibility is lent to the reliability of their transcription. The form is also the one found in five of the six songs Swift Flying Feather recorded in 1899. Only rarely and in the repertoires of older singers does it survive today. Where it is found, there is frequently a text insertion introduced from time to time commencing with the (A) phrase. In the historical sample, a variation of this type is the melody whose (A) phrase is repeated — (AABCD) — in which case the melody may be said to resemble the development section of the contemporary song (see cat. 174, 314, 423).

Melodies of the first type of open form occur most frequently in the Dream songs which Densmore collected. This type also characterizes the melodies of Ga′gandac′ and Ga′tcitcigi′cig from several genres, of Ĕ́niwûb′e's War songs, and of about half of the Moccasin Game songs.[30] The variation of this form, which has the repeated (A) phrase, is present in seventeen of Odjĭb′we's songs; usually their melodies have texts and follow the form (AABC) (see cat. 329, 337, 387; also 207, 210, 211).

60 SELECTED REPORTS

Love song belonging to John Livingston
(Fond du Lac Reservation, Minnesota).

Singer: William Bineshi Baker, Sr. **Collector:** Thomas Vennum, Jr.
Place: Concord, New Hampshire **Catalog No.:** 70CO6
Date: June 2, 1970

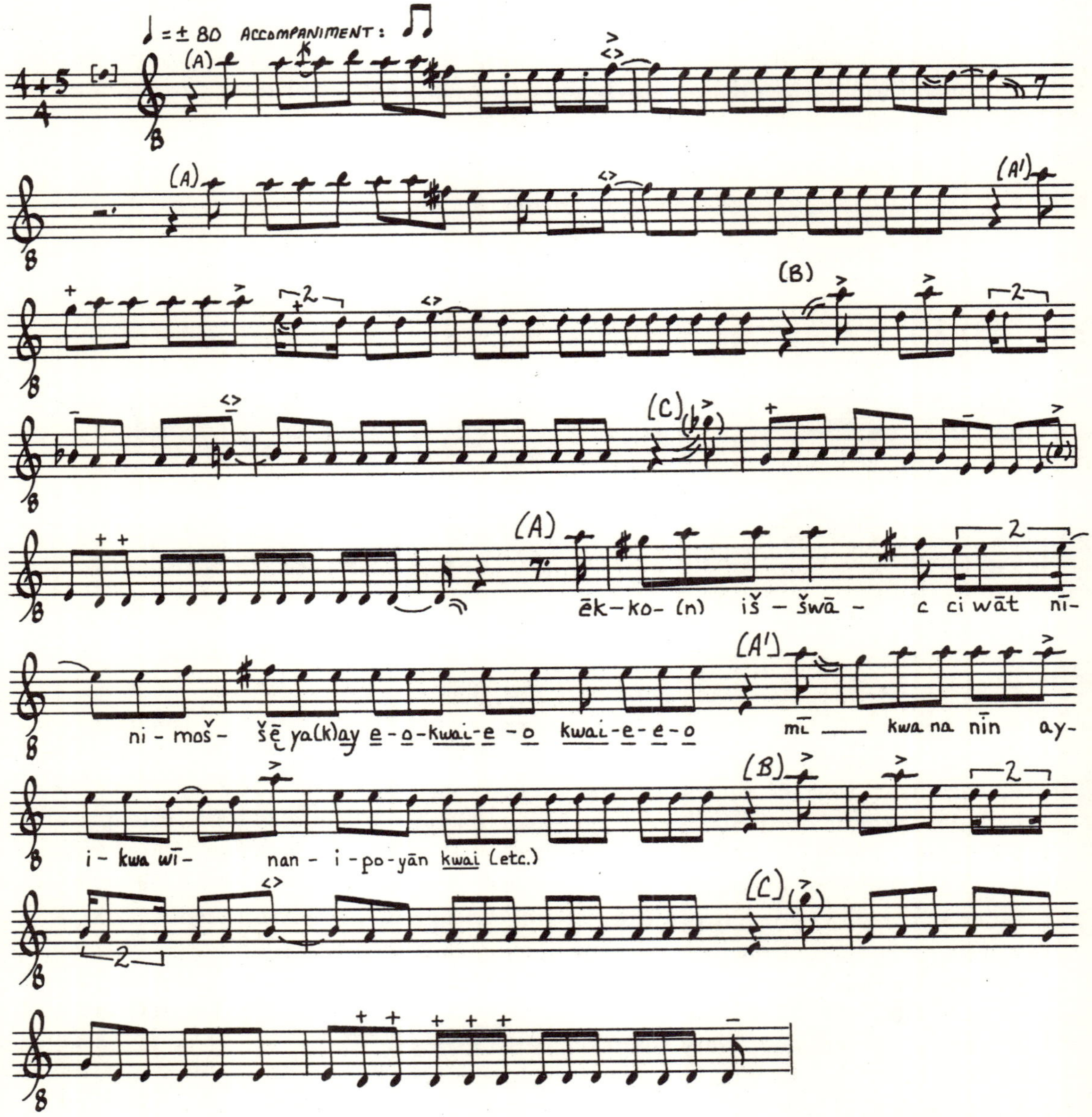

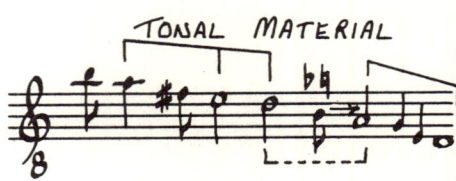

(translation: I have eight sweethearts; I will keep on dying.)

S1: transcribed
S2: as above

The second principal type of open form is represented by a melody which usually lacks the double introductory phrase, but whose distinctive feature is its conclusion; in place of the sustained final tone is a cadential formula based on repetitions of a brief phrase, which contains a melodic inflection — (ABCXXX), (ABCXX^{1}XX^1), etc.

Southern Dance Song (cat. 413) recorded by
Ĕ′niwûb′e at Lac du Flambeau, Wisconsin, October 1910.

This second type is composed exclusively of song genres identified by informants as old; the group of Wisconsin songs transmitted by animals in dreams,[31] the Pipe Dance songs, and the Southern Dance songs. Densmore's singers identified the Pipe Dance as "the principal 'good time dance' of the early Chippewa" (Densmore 1913: 293), and they believed it to have been created by a spirit (see cat. 281, 282, 408). The Southern Dance (šāwanōka), also said to be very old, was believed to have been transmitted by the Southern *manitō* to a people living south of the Ojibwa, most likely the Shawnee (see Hoffman 1896: 247).[32] First used for healing, its songs were later performed at peace gatherings (Densmore 1913: 129; see cat. 354, 355, 405, 414).

The repertoires of most of Densmore's singers contained examples of both open and closed form melodies. However, the age of her singers, though one might expect it to be a factor, does not seem to have determined whether or not their repertoires included songs whose melodies have open or closed forms.[33] All her older singers performed some songs with internal structural repetitions, and some younger singers sang songs with open form melodies. This heterogeneity of formal types in the singers' repertoires indicates that Densmore collected during a period of transition.

Special attention should be given to form in the songs of Densmore's oldest informant, Odjĭb′we,[34] and those songs recorded by Fletcher in 1899. The nearly complete absence from Odjĭb′we's songs of two of the three structural features found with regularity today (double introduction, incomplete repetition, and coda) may be significant. Because the size of his sample — the largest from any singer in her study — and the age of his songs, many of which date from before 1850, they may give us some insight into the older repertoire, assuming they were typical and accurately performed when Densmore recorded him, and not simply "staged behaviour."[35]

War Dance song (Dance of the Dog Feast).

Singer: Odjĭb'we
Place: White Earth, Minnesota
Date: August, 1909
Collector: Frances Densmore

Catalog No.: 361
Published: ii:93
Record No.: AFS10,544B2

S1: transcribed
S2: as above

War Dance song.

Singers: Canadian Indians (Ojibwa)
Place: Nett Lake, Minn. (Bois Fort)
Date: before January 7, 1915

Collector: Albert B. Reagan
Record No.: National Museum of Canada III G-58.

S1: as above
S2: as above
S3: transcribed
S4: as above
S5: as above + coda

More than half of the fifty melodies Odjĭb'we recorded have open forms. These open forms represent nearly every song type he recorded. Not one of his songs has a coda. In only three songs does the incomplete repetition appear.[36] Two of these are fully texted with a change of text occurring at the beginning of the incomplete repetition, a type of texting typical for *mite* songs and already archaic when Densmore collected.

Odjĭb'we's repertoire includes at least one song showing a closed form which belongs more to the style we know today (cat. 361). In addition to its incomplete repetition, which begins with material from the end of the (A) phrase, as do many songs today, other stylistic features of this textless War song appear to be modern and generally atypical of Odjĭb'we's other songs: the tonal range is wide, the melody is uncharacteristically long, and the phrase structure is closer to that of contemporary Ojibwa song.[37]

The six songs which Swift Flying Feather recorded for Fletcher reveal a similar distribution of formal structural types. (Feather's age at the time he recorded is not known; judging from a photograph of the Leech Lake delegation to Washington in 1899, he would appear to be about a generation younger than Odjĭb'we.) The singer's "Squaw Dance [Woman's Dance] song," War Dance song, and Moccasin Game song were each performed with open forms of the first type. The incomplete repetition appeared only once, in the third statement of a ceremonial song.

Excluding Odjĭb'we's War songs belonging to the older style, the War Dance songs from Densmore's and Reagan's samples show the highest incidence of the modern structural features. Next in order of song types to show a high percentage of closed forms are the Woman's Dance songs, three quarters of which contain the incomplete repetition and two of which have codas.

The newer structural features seem also to have begun to permeate the Moccasin Game repertoire. Although the older, open type accounts for half of the songs collected, a third of the Game songs contain the incomplete repetition. Densmore mentions divergent attitudes toward the Moccasin Game songs — older singers considering them to be sacred, younger singers using them simply for a pastime. This distinction may have been reflected in the style of performance as well, the melodies with open forms representing the older repertoire; those with internal structural repetitions, the newer.

There is evidence to suggest that the newer elements of song form emanated from the areas north and west of the Ojibwa; internal repetitions are characteristic of Sioux and Canadian Indian music of the period (see "The Influence of Sioux Music," Vennum 1975: 301-3).[38] The incomplete repetition, for example, occurs in eleven of the twelve songs which the Canadian Awûn'akûm'ĭgĭckûñ recorded for Densmore.[39] The incomplete repetition is also found in the three Nett Lake performances of Canadian songs, as is the double introduction. It occurs in Swift Flying Feather's "song sung when the Sioux and Ojibway meet ceremonially on a visit," which also contains a spoken text in Lakota. Baker recorded this last song in 1971 and identified it as a [Sioux] Drum ceremonial song.

Among the southwestern Ojibwa the newer structural style appears to have had its greatest diffusion in the northern sector, bordering the western Ontario Canadian Indians and the Sioux. The repertoires of the Red Lake and Ponemah singers show a high percentage of songs with the incomplete repetition. (All but one of A'jide'gijĭg's and Gi'wita'binĕs' songs contain it). Codas are frequent in the Nett Lake songs, and two songs from the Red Lake area conclude with them.

By contrast, Ojibwa music to the southeast, ca. 1910 — the repertoires of the two Wisconsin singers, E'niwûb'e and Mec'kawiga'bau — show that the newer structures occur much less fequently than in northern Minnesota. The incomplete repetition, for instance, is present in only about half of the Wisconsin songs, exclusive of the ceremonial Drum Dance songs.

The newer structures are reflected in Mec'kawiga'bau's twenty Drum Dance songs, *all* but one of which (cat. S.15) have the incomplete repetition, and all but three of which (cat. S.7, S.10, S.18) contain the double introduction. (Their omission of codas is a ritual requirement, as has been pointed out.) These are *Sioux* ceremonial songs, which were supposed to have accompanied the original drum presentation ca. 1870 in central Minnesota. The songs may even have been brought to Wisconsin by the Sioux themselves (see Armstrong 1892: 156-60).[40] In any case, these Drum Dance songs can be assumed to be close to their original state, for they are carefully transmitted whenever a drum is given away. Even if the recipients at a drum presentation already know the songs, it is customary for them to join the visiting donor delegation in a ritual rehearsal of the music (Densmore 1932: 155).

Other songs specifically identified as having a Siouan origin also contain the modern structural features. The Begging Dance was said to have originated with the Assiniboin Sioux; all but one of the songs of this type collected by Densmore contain the incomplete repetition.

While songs showing the newer forms appear to have been adopted relatively intact, there is some evidence that the new formal principles were also applied to the open form melodies of older Ojibwa songs.[41] There are at least two instances where this appears to have taken place. The first, Ki'miwûn's Dream song, "The Sky will Resound," recorded at Ponemah in 1910, conforms to the older, open type — (ABCC^{1}DE). This song is still performed in that village, where it is now known as the "Song of the Eagle," but in the contemporary version the newer structural elements are present: in their recording of this song (Canyon Records C-6082), the Ponemah singers have added an incomplete repetition, moved the text to the beginning of the repetition, and concluded the song with a coda. The differences can be summarized as follows:

Ki'miwûn (1910) $\|$:ABCC^{1}DE:$\|$

Ponemah Singers (1970) $\|$:ABCDE/B^{1}C^{1}DE:$\|$ B^{1}C^{1}DE

The second instance is Odjĭb'we's "At Gull Lake," a War song whose melody is in open form. This song has a concordant version in William Selkirk's "We Have Salt," though the concordance escaped Densmore (the texts are different). The complete form of Selkirk's song, however, is not immediately apparent from the cylinder recording. He sings the melody five times in succession, much in the way Odjĭb'we performs it. Then, after a brief pause, during which conversation can be heard on the recording, Selkirk starts his final rendition of the song. He begins, however, with a new textless phrase a third higher than before and sung twice. This is clearly a double introduction of the melody, showing that the portions he had sung previously were simply repetitions of the development section. (Densmore ignored the double introduction in her published transcription of the song.) Odjĭb'- we's performance of the song may be of the older version and Selkirk's the "modern" way (ca. 1910) of performing it.[42]

The existence, side by side, of songs showing open forms and those containing internal structural repetitions in most genres and in most singers' repertoires ca. 1910 shows this to have been a transitional period in Ojibwa music. Gradually, the songs with older open forms were either abandoned or reformed, and Ojibwa song form as we know it today was accepted as standard.

a. (opposite) Dream song: "The Sky Will Resound."

Singer: Kĭ'miwûn
Place: Ponemah, Minn. (Red Lake)
Date: July, 1910
Collector: Frances Densmore

Catalog No.: 296
Published: ii:270
Record No.: AFS10,537B2

♩ = 100 [84]   Accompaniment: ♫

b. Special Encore Song [Woman's Dance song].

Singers: Ponemah Chippewa Singers
Place: Ponemah, Minn. (Red Lake)
Date: 1971

Collector: Raymond Boley
Record No.: Canyon Record C-6082
            (side 2, no. 6)

♩ = 104   Accompaniment: ♫

a (translation: "The sky will resound finely, when I come making a noise.")

b (translation: "It's going to be a nice, peaceful day when I make my sound." [Brill 1974:80])

a S1: as above
S2: transcribed

b S1: transcribed
S2-3: AABCDE/B^{1}C^{1}DE + coda

TONAL MATERIAL

NOTES

1. The present paper is a revision of the writer's chapter on form in "Southwestern Ojibwa Music" (unpublished Ph.D. dissertation, Harvard University, 1975), pp. 140-67. Since the writing of the dissertation new data have emerged which substantially strenthen the arguments first presented therein. In particular, the number of historical recordings of Ojibwa music available for study has been enlarged through the discovery of cylinders from the Frances Densmore collection in the Library of Congress previously listed as missing, and the Library's transfer to preservation tapes of three cylinders recorded by Alice C. Fletcher and twelve cylinders from the Detroit Public Library.

In this paper Ojibwa texts, proper names, and English translations taken from Densmore's *Chippewa Music* (1910, 1913) are as she published them. All other Ojibwa words are transcribed according to the system of Leonard Bloomfield (1957), with the exception that the reduced vowels indicated in eastern Ojibwa with *e* (short) and *u* do not occur in the southwestern dialects used in the present discussion. Three substitutions have been made: *e* represents Bloomfield's long vowel *e·* ; (') represents the glottal stop; and vowel length is indicated by the macron (−) rather than the raised dot.

2. The recordings are deposited with the Archive of Traditional Music, Indiana University, and the Music Library, Harvard University.

3. A justification for excluding these genres from the present study is given in greater detail in Vennum 1975: 11-17.

Some of these song types have occupied a disproportionate share of the sample in past studies of Ojibwa music. *Mite* songs account for a third of Densmore's published collection and thus distorted Bruno Nettl's perception of song form in his "Chippewa and Menomini sub-area" (see Nettl 1954: 26). The writer also questions the attention given peyote songs by Paul Parthun in "Ojibwe Music in Minnesota" (unpublished Ph.D. dissertation, University of Minnesota, 1976), where they comprise more than six percent of his sample. Peyotism has made little headway with the Ojibwa (see Vennum 1975: 48-49), and the songs in Parthun's study were all collected from a single ceremony.

4. For music earlier in the century, see Curtis 1923: 73-74, 122-25, 169-70, 206-7; for contemporary music, see Powers 1970: 359-62.

5. An unusual reversal of the customary roles during the introduction was found in some Wisconsin performances. For several statements the group (or at least more than one singer) performed the first phase (A), while only one singer sang the second (A^1). In these performances the role of providing the second phrase passed from one singer to another with each statement.

In Reagan's Nett Lake recordings, both phrases of the double introduction in some statements are performed by the group (or at least more than one singer). Densmore may be referring to a similar practice among Ponemah singers when she notes that "in the beginning the leaders [sic] sang a few bars alone, after which the others took up the song" (Densmore 1913: 252).

Notational inconsistencies in Parthun's transcriptions (1976) make it difficult to tell what the roles of lead singer and group were in the performances. He uses

S[olo] and G[roup] above the music, but it is not clear what the performance distinctions are between "S   G" (Song No. 30), "SG" (Song No. 31), and "S:G" (Song No. 32). Nor do his song form schemata clarify matters, for they do not always correspond with his transcriptions, for instance Song No. 31, where he draws attention to a texted coda which is missing from the transcription (see also Song No. 42).

6. Using motifs as one means of unifying their melodies by the Ojibwa has been noted before. However, these motifs in the past have been inappropriately labelled "rhythmic units" by Densmore (1910: 10) — an oversimplified description of their make-up — or their use in a song identified as 'isorhythm' (see Nettl 1954: 25 and Parthun 1976: *passim*) — an exaggeration of their function. The choice of the term 'isorhythm' to describe such patterned repetition has already been appropriately questioned by Curt Sachs (1968: 122) in his assessment of Nettl's analysis of a Comanche song. Sachs makes the important distinction between repeated patterns which "have a strong and immediate motor appeal," such as are common in American Indian songs, and isorhythm, a 14th century structural device in European music whose complexities have little rhythmic attraction for the listener and usually must be studied from score to be perceived.

Parthun's use of the term to describe song form is equally questionable. The form of one song (Parthun 1976: 209) is actually that of the incomplete repetition, though it is labelled "isorhythmic." What Parthun means by "free isorhythm" (1976: 210) is not known.

7. In rare instances, all collected in Wisconsin, entirely new material supplanted the restatement of the development. Only one song collected for the study lacked the incomplete repetition; it was performed for a special "Stop and Go" Dance.

8. For example, the Four Winds, the four terrestrial cardinal points. Because the number four has a sacred meaning for most North American tribes, many of their songs have only four repetitions in performance, Northwest Coast potlatch songs, for instance (see Halpern 1968: 30). Cf., however, Yurok songs with only three repetitions.

9. For some ritual acts, however, the priest does not begin the song until he has estimated when the ritual act will conclude. Thus at Lac Vieux Desert, "when the funeral procession is part way to the ceremony, a chant is started so timed that it will be finished about the time they get to the grave" (Kinietz 1947: 145).

10. The Menominee singer also raises a finger to signal that he wishes the group to continue the song for another statement (Slotkin 1957: 88). Cf. the hand signals during the final four songs of the Menominee Drum Dance (Slotkin 1957: 96).

11. Densmore (1918: 471) describes bone whistles, called ši'yotaŋka, used in the Grass Dance of the Teton Sioux: "Three or four dancers might carry these whistles, but the signal was usually given by the recognized leader of the dancers. If the singers 'came near the end of the tune,' and he wished the dancing continued, he blew his whistle, whereupon they continued their repetitions of the melody."

The introduction of this custom on Minnesota reservations seems to have been through the urban Ojibwa dancers from Minneapolis and St. Paul. They undoubtedly adopted the practice through their contact with urban Sioux and their regular attendance at Sioux pow-wows in the Dakotas.

Although most younger singers recognize the purpose behind the use of the whistle, the practice is still a novelty on many Ojibwa reservations and may go unheeded by the singers. At the 1972 Ball Club (Leech Lake, Minnesota) pow-wow, for example, several dancers wore eagle-bone whistles of the Plains Sun Dance variety around their necks as part of their costumes. Near the end of a song, they would move near the drum, dance in place while facing it, and give several sharp "toots" on the whistles. It was obvious at the time that the singers attached no particular significance to the whistling, for they finished the song. Later, someone over the public address system had to inform them that the whistling was a request by the dancers for additional statements of the song and that the request must be granted.

12. The origin of the term 'tail' is obscure, though it may have originated with the Sioux and had some reference to a rear-guard action in warfare, later celebrated in a special dance. Cf. "dancing the tail" among the Teton Sioux (Densmore 1918: 472).

13. There is no evidence to support Densmore's contention that the Ojibwa used the "trail-off" (portamento) as one means by which to distinguish between song types, as did the Sioux, whose War songs ended with a portamento, but whose Grass Dance, Buffalo Dance, and Crow Owner Society songs "stopped short" (Densmore 1918: 11).

14. Apparently, regional practices vary in giving the signal. Powers (1970: 362) claims that the Minnesota Ojibwa often give *two* firm drum-strokes before the "tail," although I have never encountered this practice. Densmore reported it for the Teton Sioux (1918: 10). Parthun (1976: 37) mentions a signal to extend the song past the "tail" by following four accented beats at the "tail" followed by a fifth unstressed beat.

15. The coda may begin at a tempo slightly slower than that of the final statement, but very rapidly it returns to it. The pause, sharp tap, and crescendo are also features of the codas in Flathead War Dance songs (Merriam 1967: 252).

16. Except for occasional references to the incomplete repetition, there is no systematic analysis of contemporary song form in Parthun's recent study of Minnesota Ojibwa music.

17. In the recording *Chippewa* (Canyon Records C-6082), the lead singer, Johnson Kingbird of Ponemah, Minnesota, performs a *single* (A) phrase in the first statement (only) of each song. Because the other singers seem generally unfamiliar with the songs he has chosen, possibly Kingbird wished to cover their inability to "second" the (A) phrase alone upon first hearing him sing it.

18. A singer's age may also be reflected in his articulation of the coda or lack thereof: older singers pause between the final statement and the coda for one or two beats, whereas younger singers tend to abbreviate the pause to the point where there is almost none.

19. In a few songs in the contemporary sample, the codas seem to have been added by a singer as an afterthought, as though he suddenly remembered to attach the "tail." In these performances, more than the usual time elapsed after the final statement. One singer (usually *not* the lead) would start the coda alone at a tempo slightly slower than the one at which the final statement had been performed. The others, perhaps unprepared for this, would join him part way through the coda and complete the song.

20. For this reason, when Menominee Drum Society singers add the coda to a song, it is a signal to the Drum-heater to announce the special four final songs (Slotkin 1957: 95-96).

21. Performing only one coda seems more a reflection of age than of region. It is the usual practice of Baker (Wisconsin), Peter Seymour (Ontario), and Ray Robinson (central Minnesota), all older singers. Robinson, however, was once recorded adding a *third* coda to a song after the other singers added the first two.

In two of Densmore's recordings (cat. 171, 178), the coda did not conclude the song. Gi′nawigi′cĭg added a coda to the third statement of a Woman's Dance song but then proceeded directly to another statement, which was interrupted before its incomplete repetition. Possibly Densmore encouraged him to fill out the cylinder after the third statement.

22. Parthun (1976: 61) sees this as the distinction between the Grass Dance and the ordinary War Dance songs at a single tempo; in the former, the singers give an accented drumbeat to signal the tempo change.

23. On Canyon Records C-6106, the Kingbird Singers perform their songs in two tempos, with the coda at the end of the slower section and the coda omitted from the final, faster section. In effect, they have moved the coda from the end of the song to its mid-point.

24. Densmore discarded many cylinders which did not seem to present the song "once in a straightforward fashion"; thus she inadvertantly may have prevented our discovery of the true form of many songs she collected.

25. See Heider (1976), Chapter 3, "The Attributes of Ethnographic Film," p. 50 ff.

26. This was the first of only two songs Prentiss recorded for Densmore; the novelty of the recording experience and the interruptions may have induced nervousness, causing distortions in the form of the song.

Burton encountered the same difficulties. He described the recording of one song "sung by a woman who covered three quarters of the cylinder with false starts, giggling, exclamations expressive of extreme embarrassment. Encouraged by another woman who stood by, she at last mumbled the following melody and fled, her mind apparently in such disorder that she could not gather her wits sufficiently to dictate the words which are almost wholly inaudible on the cylinder" (Burton 1909: 272).

27. After one of Odjĭb′we's unaccompanied songs, the interpreter's instructions, asking him in Ojibwa to add the drum, are intelligible. In her text, Densmore confirms what she said (Densmore 1913: 90).

28. Heider (1976: 54). Heider gives as examples the battle and funeral scenes from the ethnographic film *Dead Birds*.

29. In attempting to verbalize about their music in the presence of ethnographers, Ojibwa frequently employ incorrect and often misleading terminology, possibly to appear erudite. Dudley's use of the term 'verse' is a case in point, for the songs to which he refers are textless. Until Baker demonstrated what he meant by 'bar,' for some time he had confounded me by stating that all Indian music was "made up of two bars." Baker and Dudley, in these instances, are using two different non-Indian musical terms to describe the same formal structure. 'Verse' and 'bar' are even synonymous musical terms for Baker.

30. Most of these songs are texted (another indication of their age), their texts coinciding with the (B) phrase — (ABCD) or (AABC) (see cat. 208, 423). Generally speaking, the Moccasin Game melodies performed by Densmore's older singers conform to the first open type. The one performed by A′jidegi′jĭg has an open form, as does that sung by Akĭ′waizi′. Gĭ′wita′bĭnĕs of Red Lake, whose age is given as ca. 50 and who sang "in the regular old way," performed six game songs, each with open form melodies, but only one with a double introduction. Both melodies of Ki′mi-wûn's Moccasin Game songs have open forms.

31. The five deer songs and two buffalo songs in the Wisconsin sample are closely enough related in origin, use, style, and provenance to constitute a separate genre, although Densmore included them among the Dream songs. The Ojibwa believed that each of these songs was taught by the animal mentioned in its text, and its performance included the sounds made by that animal, often incorporated into the cadential formula with which each brief statement closes.

32. The cadential formulae of the Southern Dance songs bear some resemblance to those of Plains Round Dance songs. This similarity might support the Ojibwa belief in a southern origin for these songs. Such formulae are also found in Cheyenne songs connected with gift giving (see Densmore 1936: 94ff.). Only one of the Southern Dance songs in Densmore's sample lacks the distinctive cadential formula.

33. The Moccasin Game songs may be exceptional. See above, note 30.

34. Though others may have been older, Odjĭb′we is the only singer whose exact age (89) at the time he recorded is given by Densmore.

35. Heider (1976: 56) cautions the viewer of ethnographic film to consider whether "... if the events were in some manner instigated or encouraged by the film maker, were they events in the current cultural repertory, or were they revived after more or less long abeyance?"

The assumption of this study, that Odjĭb′we's songs represent the oldest repertoire in Densmore's sample (exclusive of *mite* songs), is at odds with her own opinion, that the Waba′cĭñg and Wisconsin songs she collected represent "an older culture" than Odjĭb′we's War songs (Densmore 1913: 7-8). Densmore based her judgement on "the character of the songs and the singers."

36. Parthun (1976: 206) found that most Minnesota War Dance songs contained the incomplete repetition; the few exceptions were from his very oldest singers. However, the song which he selected from Densmore's transcriptions to illustrate the "older" War song is actually a *mite* song, which Densmore mistakenly assigned to the War song genre (Densmore 1913: 104).

37. Melodies with closed forms, such as Odjĭb′we's War song, have their greatest distribution among the social dance songs of the early part of the century. At that time, the War Dance and Woman's Dance — both vestiges of the war complex — were the two most frequently performed social dances, just as they are today (Densmore 1910: 168, 170, 172, 192; 1913: 284).

38. Deliberate imitation of the Fort Kipp (Sioux) style during the 1950's is acknowledged by one of Parthun's informants (Parthun 1976: 33-34; see also 36, 38). Presumably the singer is a Red Laker, as he mentions Dan Raincloud, a medicine man from that reservation, though none of Parthun's informants are identified and his interviews appear to be composites. There is a sigla provided in the appendix

of the dissertation to identify his thirty-six informants by age, sex, and reservation, but there is no reference to the sigla in the interviews. Parthun (1976: 38) attributes the Siouan influence to BIA suppression of traditional culture in the 1950's.

39. It was missing from one of his two Moccasin Game songs.

40. Did these songs with their double introductions reach the eastern Ojibwa early in the century? Burton (1909: 85-86) mentions "certain ceremonial songs where two singers alternate in stating the theme," the second beginning before the first has completed his phrase.

41. It is highly unlikely, however, that the new formal principles affected the *mite* repertoire, as is suggested by transcriptions of songs identified by Parthun as *mite* songs (1975: 106, 110), for it is doubtful that the orthodox *mitewiwin* would have tolerated a new style of performance for its traditional repertoire. Several aspects of Parthun's transcriptions suggest these to be Dream songs rather than *mite*, for example, the accompaniment patterns or, in song No. 3, the triplet vocal rhythm against the duple drum beat. *Mite* and Dream songs can also be distinguished through their manner of text performance, but since there are no text underlays in Parthun's transcriptions, it is not known whether the songs are texted or not, and if so, whether the text was performed continuously, as in *mite* songs, or was inserted once at the incomplete repetition, typical of Dream song performance. The "titles" to the songs given by Parthun's performer, such as "Where I am the earth stands still" and "Our god is coming," could be actual song texts belonging to either genre.

42. There is some evidence that older songs from the eastern Ojibwa repertoire were undergoing similar transformation at about the same time. A textless song published by Burton, which contains the double introduction, was said to have originally been a texted canoe song, "the singer telling of going to meet somebody, presumably a sweetheart." As collected by Burton, it was "sung to meaningless syllables throughout and often used in this form for dancing" (Burton 1909: 273).

REFERENCES CITED

Armstrong, Benjamin G.
    1892 *Early life among the Indians.* Ashland, Wisconsin: Press of A. W. Bowron.

Barrett, Samuel
    1911 "The dream dance of the Chippewa and Menominee Indians of northern Wisconsin." Bulletin of the Public Museum of the City of Milwaukee 1: 251-406.

Bloomfield, Leonard
    1957 *Eastern Ojibwa.* Ann Arbor: University of Michigan Press.

Burton, Frederick R.
    1909 *American primitive music; with especial attention to the songs of the Ojibways.* New York: Moffat, Yard and Company.

Curtis, Natalie
    1923 *The Indians' Book.* 2nd ed. New York: Harper and Brothers. Reprint eds., New York: Dover Publications, 1950; 1968.

Densmore, Frances
    1910 *Chippewa Music.* Bulletin 45. The Smithsonian Institution, Bureau of American Ethnology. Washington, D. C.: United States Government Printing Office.
    1913 *Chippewa Music – II.* Bulletin 53. Bureau of American Ethnology.
    1918 *Teton Sioux Music.* Bulletin 61. Bureau of American Ethnology.
    1932 *Menominee Music.* Bulletin 102. Bureau of American Ethnology.
    1936 *Cheyenne and Arapaho Music.* Southwest Museum Papers, No. 10. Pasadena, California.

Halpern, Ida
    1968 "Music of the British Columbia Northwest Coast Indians." In *Proceedings of the Centennial Workshop in Ethnomusicology, Vancouver, 1967,* pp. 23-41. Edited by Peter Crossley-Holland. Victoria, Canada: The Government of the Province of British Columbia.

Heider, Karl G.
    1976 *Ethnographic Film.* Austin: University of Texas Press.

Hoffman, Walter J.
    1891 "The Mitewiwin; or, 'Grand Medicine Society' of the Ojibwa." In *Bureau of American Ethnology 7th Annual Report,* pp. 143-300. The Smithsonian Institution. Washington, D. C.: United States Government Printing Office.
    1896 "The Menominee Indians." In *Bureau of American Ethnology 14th Annual Report,* pp. 11-328. The Smithsonian Institution.

Keating, William H.
    1825 *Narrative of an Expedition to the Source of St. Peter's River . . . ,* Vol. 1. Philadelphia: H. C. Carey and I. Lea.

Kinietz, Vernon
    1947 *Chippewa village: the story of Katikitegon.* Bulletin 25. Cranbrook Institute of Science. Bloomfield Hills, Michigan.

Nettl, Bruno
    1954 *North American Indian musical styles.* Memoirs of the American Folklore Society, vol. 45. Philadelphia: American Folklore Society.

Parthun, Paul
    1976 "Ojibwe music in Minnesota." Unpublished Ph.D. dissertation, University of Minnesota.

Powers, William K.
    1970 Review of American Indian Soundchief Library recordings. *Ethnomusicology* 14: 358-69.

Rynkiewich, Michael A.
    1968 "Chippewa pow-wows." Unpublished Master's thesis, University of Minnesota.

Sachs, Curt
    1965 *The Wellsprings of Music.* Edited by Jaap Kunst, et al. New York: McGraw Hill Book Company.

Schoolcraft, Henry R.
    1855 *Information Respecting the Historical Condition and Prospects of the Indian Tribes of the United States.* Vol. V. Philadelphia: J. B. Lippencott.

Slotkin, James S.
    1957 *The Menominee pow-wow: a study in cultural decay.* Milwaukee Public Museum Publications in Anthropology, No. 4.

Vennum, Thomas
    1973 "Introduction" to Frances Densmore, *Chippewa Music* (1910, 1913). Minneapolis: Ross and Haines.
    1975 "Southwestern Ojibwa music." Unpublished Ph.D. dissertation, Harvard University.

OKUSHARE,

MUSIC FOR A WINTER CEREMONY:

THE TURTLE DANCE SONGS OF SAN JUAN PUEBLO

Maria La Vigna

Sacred musical repertoires of American Indian societies tend to operate as closed systems. There is less influx of new songs and/or texts into the repertoire; rather, existing songs are transmitted orally to succeeding generations. Although substantial portions of these repertoires are preserved because of their special powers over man and his environment, some Indian communities recognize also the creative input of new combinations of sounds for these same effects. From the San Juan Pueblo in New Mexico, a Tewa-speaking village along the banks of the Rio Grande, certain sacred ceremonies call for music and song texts to be composed anew each year. Although these ceremonies are briefly discussed in the literature devoted to Pueblo music, no comprehensive statement has been published concerning the techniques or rules used in composing this music.

Scholars in the past have recommended studies to identify the intricacies of the formal structures in all Pueblo music. Edward Dozier states that in the Rio Grande Pueblos, new sets of songs and words are composed for particular ceremonies, fitting a prescribed "rhythmic mold." Although many of these songs have now been recorded, no one has investigated their technical characteristics (Dozier 1958: 269-70). Don L. Roberts questions whether a composer always fits his songs into a set mold, and if such is the case, whether specialized formulas and signals hinder the compositional process (Roberts 1972: 254). Charlotte Frisbie suggests that composers may follow certain models, mnemonic devices, formulas, and/or patterns. If composers are bound to such traditional restrictions, she questions how much freedom exists for individual artists (Frisbie 1977: 46).

Only one work has appeared to date that describes both the music and dance of Tewa Pueblo ceremonialism. In spite of its being generously supplied with musical transcriptions and song texts, the thrust of Gertrude Kurath's *Music and Dance of the Tewa Pueblos* details the choreography, dance-plaza circuits, and accompanying music for various ceremonies publicly performed in Tewa-speaking villages. In this volume, Antonio Garcia, a native of San Juan Pueblo, settled the question of the employment of a set mold by stating that the composers do obey traditional restrictions (Garcia *in* Kurath 1970: 39), but a study detailing these characteristics was not included. While not exhaustive, this article identifies some of the unique characteristics of the music composed for one of these ceremonies.[1]

The Repertoire. The San Juan *Okushare*, Turtle Dance, is part of a large ceremonial repertoire, which has been classified into five major areas ranging from sacred to secular (see Dozier 1957, 1958, 1970). In order to understand the relationship of this ceremony to the entire repertoire, it will be helpful to summarize these categories briefly. This classification system is artificially imposed; the singers appear not to recognize categories in their ceremonial repertoire except for those borrowed from neighboring tribes and foreign cultures.

On a continuum from sacred to secular, the most sacred ceremonies are those associated with the masked *kachina* cult[2] and the secret societies. These rituals are carefully guarded and are restricted to members and novitiates only. No recordings have been made of this music because of traditional bans; thus, little is known by anyone outside of the participants about either the music or the ritual practices associated with these ceremonies.

A second set of performances involves communal ceremonies. The public portion of these ceremonies is a dance given in the courtyard plazas. These dances may be viewed by visitors, but all outsiders are excluded from viewing the activities which precede and follow the dances.

The third group includes the activities of special ceremonial associations, particularly those of the warriors and hunters. The public performances sponsored by these associations consist primarily of war dances and/or the imitation of game animals. These three categories together represent the sacred core of Rio Grande Pueblo ceremonialism and appear to be almost totally free from Spanish or Euro-American influences.

A fourth set of ceremonies, essentially secular in nature, is performed for amusement or entertainment. Many Pueblo villages have borrowed songs and dances from neighboring tribes. Yet, despite the origins of these public ceremonies, the dance and song patterns reveal basically Pueblo or pan-Indian characteristics rather than Spanish or Euro-American elements.

The final category comprises ceremonies, introduced in the sixteenth and seventeenth centuries, that are associated with the Spanish or Spanish-Mexican Indians. These dances and ceremonies closely follow the calendar of the Catholic Church, and are definitely of European or Mexican Indian provenance.

The Okushare belongs to the second category of communal ceremonies and is considered the most sacred from this category. It has been referred to as a 'maskless kachina dance' (Parsons 1939: 913) since the choreography and music closely resemble the kachina ceremonies performed in the *kiva*.[3] According to Don L. Roberts, informants state that they dress as *kachinas* except that they "don't put the head on" (Roberts 1972: 251). Masks were probably worn originally but were removed to appease Spanish civil and church authorities who were offended by certain rites contained in these ceremonies (Dozier 1958: 270).

The Okushare is one of three ceremonies whose music and song texts are composed anew each year. The ceremony probably functioned originally as an acknowledgement of the winter solstice and followed a period known as the "Days of the Sun" (Ortiz 1969: 104). Hence, new songs may have been prescribed to celebrate the birth of the winter season. Sometime after the Spanish arrival at the Southwest, the Okushare was attached to the date of December 26th, most likely in response to the most important calendrical date of the Catholic Church the day before. Today, the Okushare is viewed both as an observance of the new year and as a rite of thanksgiving for the year just completed. The other two ceremonies, *Tunshare* (Basket Dance) and *Pogonshare* (Cloud Dance), alternate each year just before the Summer moiety takes over the leadership of the village from the Winter moiety.[4] Songs for all other ceremonies are unchanging (Ortiz 1969: 105).

The Composer and The Process of Composition. In the creation of the music for the Okushare, the composers from San Juan employ a unique system of compositional process. To engage in the activity of composing, the individual must possess certain attributes. According to one composer from San Juan,[5] there are four attributes necessary to compose a song (besides the obvious one of tribal membership): interest, tune, words, and memory.

Concerning interest, he states:

> A person has to have interest in what they want to become. Without interest in singing, I won't go through this. I've got to be interested in singing or otherwise I won't make the grade (Cipriano Garcia, 26 April 1976).

The attitude of a man who wishes to become a composer is vital, for one is selected on the basis of his interest in singing to join a small group of men who are recognized as the community's corps of composers.

Antonio Garcia stated that the selection of composers to create songs for a specific ceremony presented no difficulty because only a handful of gifted men possess the genius for such craft. Although the *xamayo*, chorus masters, train younger men, the talent is often inherited (Garcia *in* Kurath 1970: 38-39).

Concerning tune and words, the composer continues:

> And then comes the tune. I think up a tune. I sing it to myself or sometimes I hum it to myself. After I've got it finished, I think of the words. Words that would make sense to a particular dance, for instance, like the Turtle. Sometimes we mention the directions and the colors; or sometimes we mention the clouds, the sun, the rain, the rain gods, better known as the *Kachinas*. You have to think of all these words, but then you have got to use the words in the right places at the right time (Cipriano Garcia, *op. cit.*).

Before a composer presents a song to his contemporaries, he may spend two months fitting words to melody, making sure that song texts and musical idioms are appropriate for the ceremony in question. On one occasion, however, another song master was officially requested to create a composition within a twenty-four-hour period. On a one-day trip to Albuquerque he thought of the melodies; on his return, he fitted the appropriate words to the music; and one hour after reaching the pueblo, he presented the song to his fellow composers.

The last attribute is memory. The composer refers to himself as a "computer bank," whereby he recalls a specific song from a certain dance in a particular year. The following sequence of events demonstrates this remarkable process of recollection. (None of the songs from this large repertoire are written down in any form.)

The songs created for the Okushare in 1974 were performed in San Juan on December 26th. In September of 1975 these same songs were recorded and transcribed in their entirety. Just after this recording session, a new set of songs was composed and performed for the Okushare on December 26, 1975. In April, 1976, two of the composers from San Juan participated in a one-day seminar at UCLA, where they performed many songs from their repertoire. Included in this session was one of the compositions from the Okushare created in 1974. This song was also recorded and transcribed, and later compared with the recording made in September of 1975. Although new songs had been composed in the interim, the rendition of the 1974 composition recorded in April of 1976 was exactly the same as that recorded in 1975.

This process of recollection is extremely important to the junior as well as the senior composer for they both draw upon past experiences and knowledge of their musical repertoire to create new compositions. Memory, of course, serves another purpose: it helps to preserve the set or fixed repertoire. From the incident described above, it appears that once the songs have been composed, they pass into the repertoire, whose method of retention is oral — not notational.

The four prerequisites — interest, tune, words, and memory — according to the composer, can be summarized in one word: talent. The men responsible for creating new compositions, as well as for maintaining songs which have been handed down for generations, are clearly recognized by the community as talented individuals. Without these chorus masters, the preparation and performance of the ceremonial repertoire simply could not be carried out.

About ten days before the Okushare, the composers gather at the home of the War Chief, the pueblo official responsible for this ceremony. When these sessions commence, one of the song masters asks if anyone had composed a song or songs for the Okushare, thereby deferring first to his colleagues. The composers then make modifications as a group, suggesting changes, additions or deletions to each other's songs until a consensus on their acceptability is reached. In the event that no compositions are offered, the senior members will have composed, as a back-up measure, the required number of songs for the Okushare. This communal system, perhaps wasteful by our standards, insures both continuity of the repertoire and solidarity among the group. Often, however, a composition which is not performed in one year will be offered the next.

Don Roberts suggested that modifications are usually made by one or two of the officially designated song leaders and that these adjustments must fit a preconceived mold.[6] One song leader stated that the most important changes made are in the text. Certain word-sets have a fixed sequence and must be used in their correct order, for instance, male before female, corn before wheat. The composer recalled one occasion in which he had changed the word order of another composer's song because of the incorrect sequence of several word-sets.   When asked if he had changed any of the melodic material, he stated that he "would not change the tune," for the composition would no longer belong to his colleague; he "did not want to make him feel bad" (Cipriano Garcia, 26 September 1977).

This process of alteration is not unique to San Juan, but obtains in other pueblos. A music educator described the process among the Hopi Indians of Arizona as follows:

> Once the composer has the song firmly in mind, he will sing it to others in the kiva, where they will learn and contribute to it. This group participation is not thought of as a correction of the composer, but is rather thought of as the natural process any song must go through. It would be extremely rare for a composer to bring in a song which would not be altered in some way before it was deemed ready for performance.[7]

These accounts give some insight into how songs are selected and how composers, with their individual ideas, gather together to shape each other's compositions.

Concepts Behind "Newly Composed." An understanding of what is meant by "newly composed" is crucial to the description of the Okushare. The following list of incidents makes clear that the concept of newness is not what we might expect.

Transcribing the songs composed for the 1974 Okushare proved to be an intriguing project. While transcribing these songs, it became apparent that different compositions shared common melodic material. After transcriptions of the songs composed for 1971 were completed, it was found that melodic material contained in these songs had actually been borrowed for 1974. Finally, after securing a recording of the 1976 Okushare, it was noted that wholesale melodic borrowing had occurred.

On December 26, 1976, I observed the Okushare in San Juan. On the day before, the *Ange'in*, Evening Dance, had been performed. I was informed that the music and text of this dance are newly composed not only for the Okushare, but also for the Tunshare and Pogonshare. Later, a recording and transcription of the Ange'in accompanying the Okushare were completed. In April of 1977, the composers again traveled to UCLA to participate in a one-day seminar, performing some of their songs and dances. During this session, the Ange'in accompanying the Pogonshare (performed in San Juan on January 30, 1977) was demonstrated. This Ange'in bore such remarkable resemblance to the one performed for the Okushare in December, 1976, that I assumed no new material had been composed. With these discoveries in mind, I asked the composers what was actually meant by the phrase "newly composed."

A song composed five or even twenty years ago is considered new when performed in another year. A particular song might achieve widespread popularity among composers as well as among members of the community. From time to time, a song may be performed in its original state, but it is perceived as new because it had been rendered in another year (see Kurath 1970: 132).

The composers informed me that, in the case of the Ange'in, certain words in the text had been altered to accommodate the ceremony which this dance accompanies. In spite of the fact that music and a major portion of the text are the same in the Ange'in for both the Okushare and Pogonshare, both renderings are considered newly composed. Hence, even a slight change in the text is classified as new.

In two of the songs created for 1974, the text had been composed by the father of one of the song masters. The song master had remembered the words, but fabricated new melodies for his father's song texts. This situation can reverse itself, whereby melodies from an old song will remain intact while the text is newly composed.

On one occasion, I exhibited to a composer the process of borrowing material from one song to another. Various articles, each representing a section from a song of a certain year, were placed on a table. After I had arranged the items to represent a new composition, the composer admitted that part of the compositional process is to arrange materials taken from other songs. He noted, however, that when borrowing occurs, the placement of the phrase unit borrowed from an old song will be the same in the new composition as in the old song. In other words, phrase "a" from one song will not appear in the section designated for phrase "e" in another — it will appear after the opening of the new song, just as in its original context. In the analysis of the songs from the Okushare discussed below, the musical transcriptions include a splendid example of the borrowing of a complete phrase unit from 1971 to 1976, The substitution of text and/or melody lent from other compositions may also account for the homogeneity inherent in these songs.

One might suspect that borrowing is more frequent than the introduction of new ideas. This is not entirely the case, however, because at a particular point in the song structure, new ideas are presented and these may not resemble any material from previous years.

Performance of The Okushare. About six days before the performance of the Okushare, the composers, along with thirty to fifty male dancers, gather in the practice kiva where composers transmit the songs orally with accompanying choreography. Central to these kiva practice sessions is the *sawipinge*, the group of lead singers who occupy the center of the dance line (Garcia *in* Kurath 1970: 38). The sawipinge usually includes the composers as well as a few other men selected for this core of lead singers.

For the next six nights, the dancer-singers learn the songs and choreography in order to insure precision on the actual day of performance. Older male members who have been participating in this ceremony for years attend on the night before the performance. Because of their experience, many of them know what to expect in the practice sessions and some can learn the songs and choreography after one rendering. Some male members who have married and moved away make a special effort to return to their native pueblo just to participate in this ceremony.

The composers are responsible for four songs to the Okushare as well as to the Ange'in. The Ange'in is performed late in the afternoon on December 25th and is also sung immediately after the performance of the Turtle Dance songs. Early on the morning of December 26th, the dancer-singers gather at the practice kiva for a final rehearsal. Certain rites are performed here, but visitors are not permitted to observe them. Costumes are checked to insure that everyone has the proper paraphernalia; when all are ready, the Turtle dancers file out of the practice kiva, proceeding to

Fig. 1. Plaza Circuit for Turtle Dance.
December 26, 1976
San Juan Pueblo

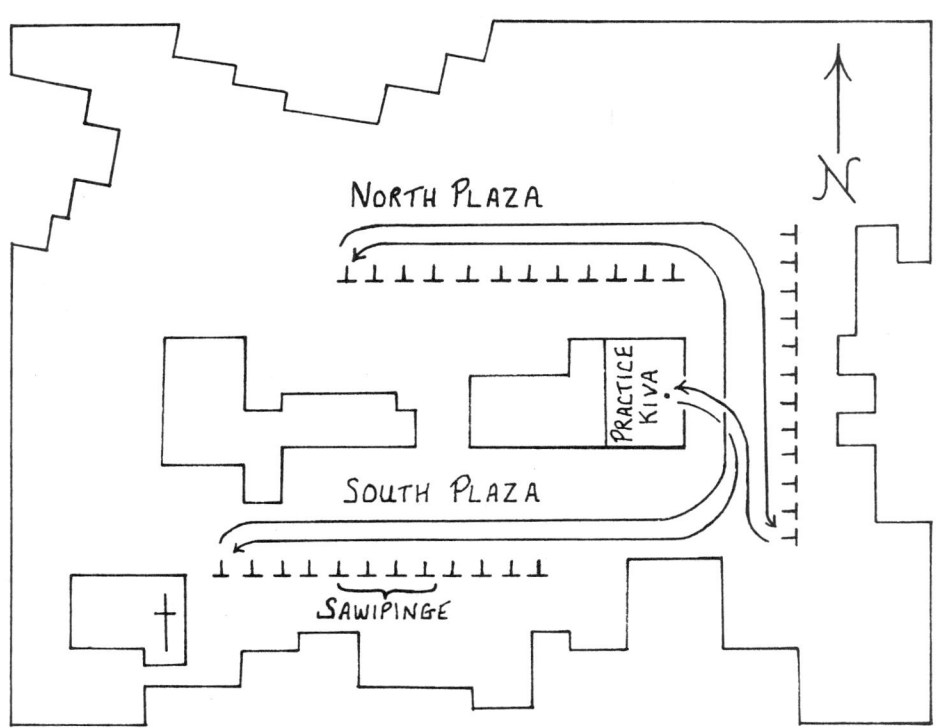

the south plaza. After reaching this area, the dancers line up shoulder to shoulder, facing north, and begin the first song. When the first rendering of the initial song has been completed, the men file out to the north plaza. While still facing north they sing the first song again. This procedure is repeated in the east plaza, except that the dancers are now facing west. After the third rendition, the dancers file back into the practice kiva to give the fourth and final rendering of the first song. Only one verse, however, is sung while in the kiva. The second, third, and fourth songs are presented in the same manner, and by late afternoon the songs for the Okushare are concluded. The final song to be performed is the Ange'in and it employs the same plaza circuit pattern just described in connection with the Okushare. Figure 1 shows the plaza circuit for the Okushare performed on December 26, 1976, with the practice kiva indicated in relation to the dance plazas.[8]

84   SELECTED REPORTS

Costuming for all dancers is identical: headdress, dance kilt, body painting, and musical instruments, which are both worn and carried. A gourd rattle is carried in the dancer's right hand along with a spray of evergreen branches. Attached to the end of the handle is a rawhide string, through which the dancer slips his hand to prevent him from accidentally dropping the rattle. He carries only a spray of evergreen branches in his left hand.

The dancer may wear a leather belt with jingle bells around his waist. Bells may also be worn as leg rattles; these are tied on just below the knees. Occasionally an individual may not have the leg bell rattles, but every dancer must wear a turtle shell rattle.

The turtle shell rattle is always worn just below the right knee. The turtle is hollowed out and deer hoof tinklers or pig knuckles are attached to the outside of the shell, with leather thongs drawn through holes drilled in the upper shell. Leather thongs drawn through holes in the lower shell serve to tie the turtle rattle onto the dancer's knee.

Fig. 2. Turtle Shell Rattle (*oeku*),
Gourd Rattle (*poewíyé*), and Leg Bell Rattle (*puŋ*).

Since spectators are prohibited from photographing the Okushare, photographs of the instruments used in their normal setting are not available. Instruments were photographed outside their context, however, and are shown in Fig. 2. Except for the headdress, all items such as costuming, body paint, and instruments used in the Okushare closely resemble those in the Pogonshare (see Nora Yeh's article in this issue for photographs of the Pogonshare).

The choreography for the Okushare is the simplest of the newly composed category. The basic step is called the *antege*, meaning 'foot lifting' (Kurath 1970: 82). Emphasis is always placed on the right foot. The upbeat corresponds to the raising of the right knee while the weight is supported by the left foot. The down beat, corresponding to the accented lowering of the right foot, sets in motion the deer hoof tinklers rapping against the turtle shell rattle. This also sounds the bell leg rattles, if worn.

Dancers remain stationary when executing the antege. Transitions from one section of a song to another — consisting of specified musical pauses — are the only changes in choreographic movement. Initially facing north, the dancers turn toward the west, toward the east, and finally back to the north again, where they proceed to the next section of the song. Many of these choreographic details will become evident in the musical transcriptions below.

Songs of the Okushare. The sample used here for analysis includes fifteen songs: three isolated examples from 1954, 1961[9] and 1969[10]; and three complete sets of four songs composed for the years 1971,[11] 1974,[12] and 1976.[13] In the sets, the songs are ordered around criteria not known at this time, but for the sake of continuity, comparison and space, only excerpts from the first songs of 1971, 1974, and 1976 are presented in the musical transcriptions. The selection of these songs rather than the second, third, or fourth, is based upon the treatment of the material. Two of the songs, those of 1971 and 1976, are similar in treatment but the example from 1974 is unique. The 1971 example was composed by one of the elder song masters, who has been musically active for the last thirty years. The 1976 song was composed by his elder brother, who has also been composing for many years. The 1974 song belongs to a younger man, whose first attempt at composing for the Okushare is recorded here.

The excerpts include only the material newly composed for each of the three songs. Phrase units taken from corresponding sections are arranged in chronological sequence. For example, each phrase "a" from the three years is presented simultaneously for purposes of comparison. As a preface to these excerpts, Fig. 3 summarizes the special symbols used in the transcriptions. The International Phonetic Alphabet was used for the orthography of the song texts.

Upon hearing the songs of the Okushare for the first time, the compositions seem very complex by virtue of their length and what appears to be the employment of a large amount of new melodic material. Closer examination of the songs reveals that duration is partly due to the formal structure, and that the melodic material composed in a ten-minute song is actually of about two and one half minutes.

Songs for the Okushare are all cast into a five-part form: $A^1 A^2 B^1 B^2 A^1$. The composers refer to this basic structure as "five verses." Within each of the five verses, a further ordering of material is in operation. Based on the use of the melodic material, which is interdependent with the song text, each of the five verses can be subdivided into four parts.

After the dancers have filed into the plaza, one of the song leaders from the sawipinge shakes his gourd rattle, thereby signaling the dancers to face north and begin the antege. The dancers set the tempo in unison, and after some eleven beats, the text begins. The tempo for the Okushare is generally ♩ = 72 and remains constant throughout the duration of the songs.

Next the men begin a phrase that belongs to the Okushare. It has been termed the *puchano* by one composer, but has no translatable meaning. I have designated it as a standard phrase unit (S.P.U.); it occurs in every song composed for the Okushare. The puchano is always sung in the lower register of the men's voice range, and the text consists only of vocables (non-lexical syllables). The phrase itself is a repeated four-beat sub-unit, but the entire phrase should be conceived as an eight-beat unit. This phrase is "the stamp" for the Okushare; there are other such units belonging to the other two ceremonies whose music and song texts are composed anew. These phrases are exclusive property of their respective ceremonies and are not interchangeable. Together, the introduction and standard phrase unit (puchano), illustrated in Figure 4, represent Part 1 in Section A of the song structure and must occur in every composition.

Part 2 of Section A was identified by the composers as the "beginning of the song" because it always introduces meaningful text. I have divided this subsection into two phrase units, which are designated as phrases "a" and "b". This division rests upon the employment of phrase "b" later in the development of the song. Phrase "a" is generally located in the middle register of the voice range. Melodic contour is variable, as is the length.

In Figure 5, phrase "a" for 1971 begins in the middle register, descending to the lower register. For 1974, the first six beats of phrase "a" initiate from the middle register, but are then restated a fifth higher. In 1976, however, phrase "a" begins in a higher register and eventually descends. Different melodic treatment of the same text occurs in the first seven beats of phrase "a" for 1971 and the first six beats of 1976. Here the text has been borrowed as well as the descending contour, yet both phrases remain distinct from one another.

Phrase "b" must end in the lower register. With regard to Figure 5, phrase "b" for 1971 and 1976 is located in the lower register. For 1974, however, the lower register is approached from the octave above. All three phrases use similar material, as found in the final eight beats for 1971 and 1974; and the entire phrase for 1976 (also eight beats). This eight-beat phrase structure occurs in many other Turtle Dance songs and contains vocable syllables only. I have designated it as a common phrase unit. Although this phrase is often employed, it is not standardized in the song structure as is the case with the standard phrase unit found in Part 1. At least one other common phrase unit has been found in other Turtle Dance songs. The frequent occurrence of these particular phrases suggests that they are part of the composers' musical vocabulary. One composer regards their function as an aesthetic placement in order to "finish that part of the tune." In other words, meaningful text should be completed with a vocable phrase unit.

Fig. 3. Signs Used In Transcriptions.

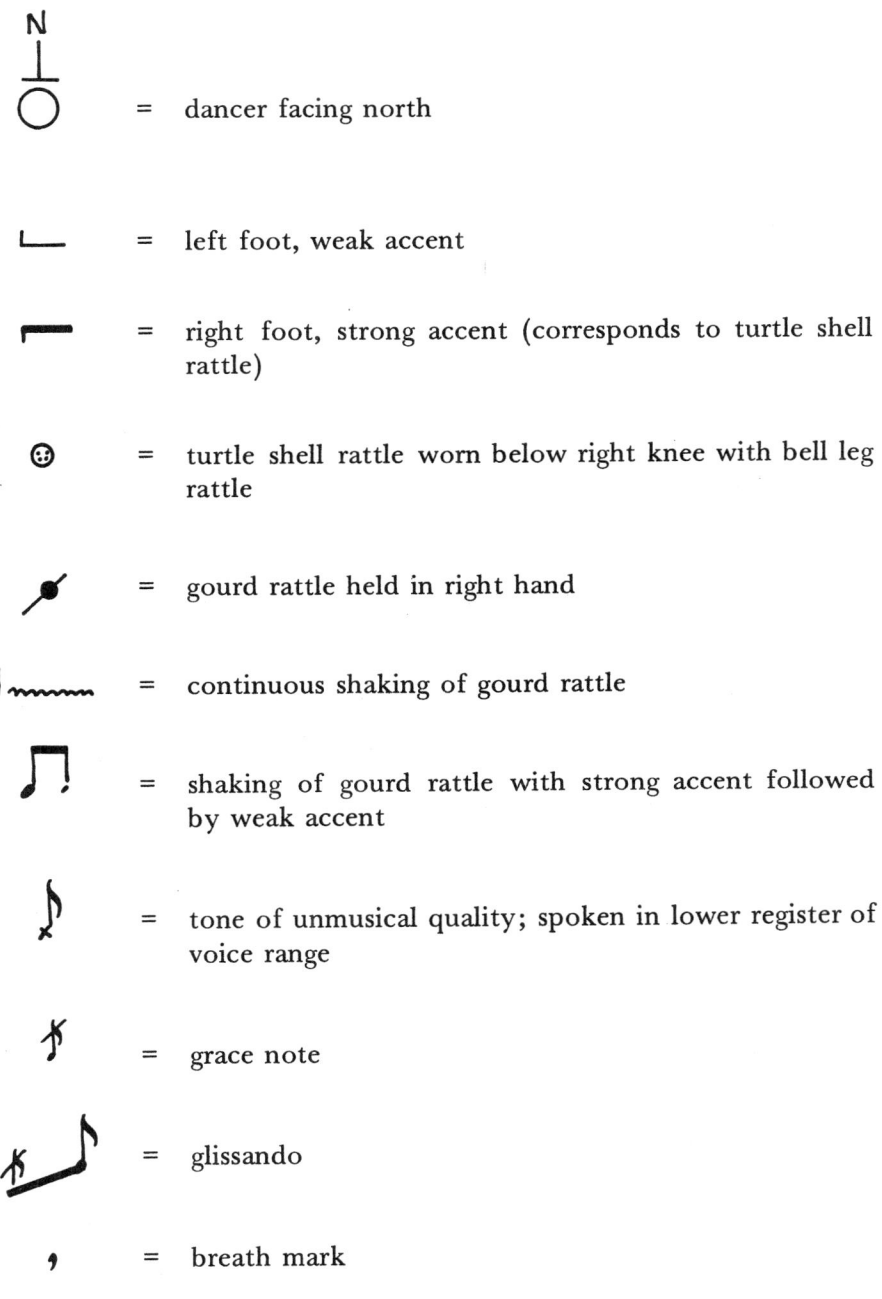

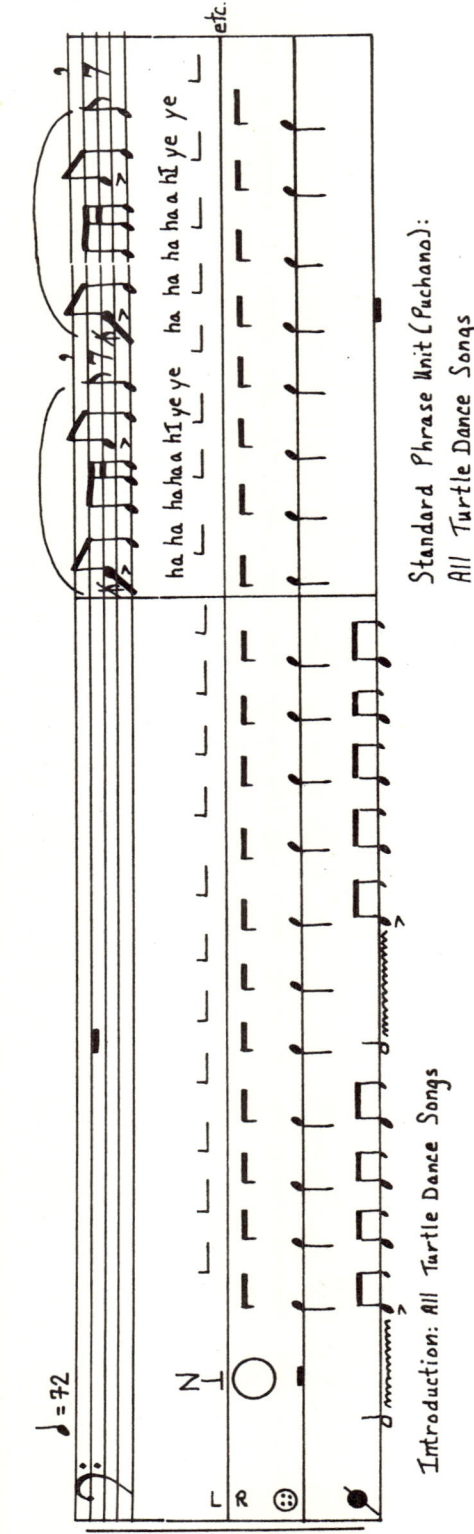

Fig. 4. Section A: Part 1.

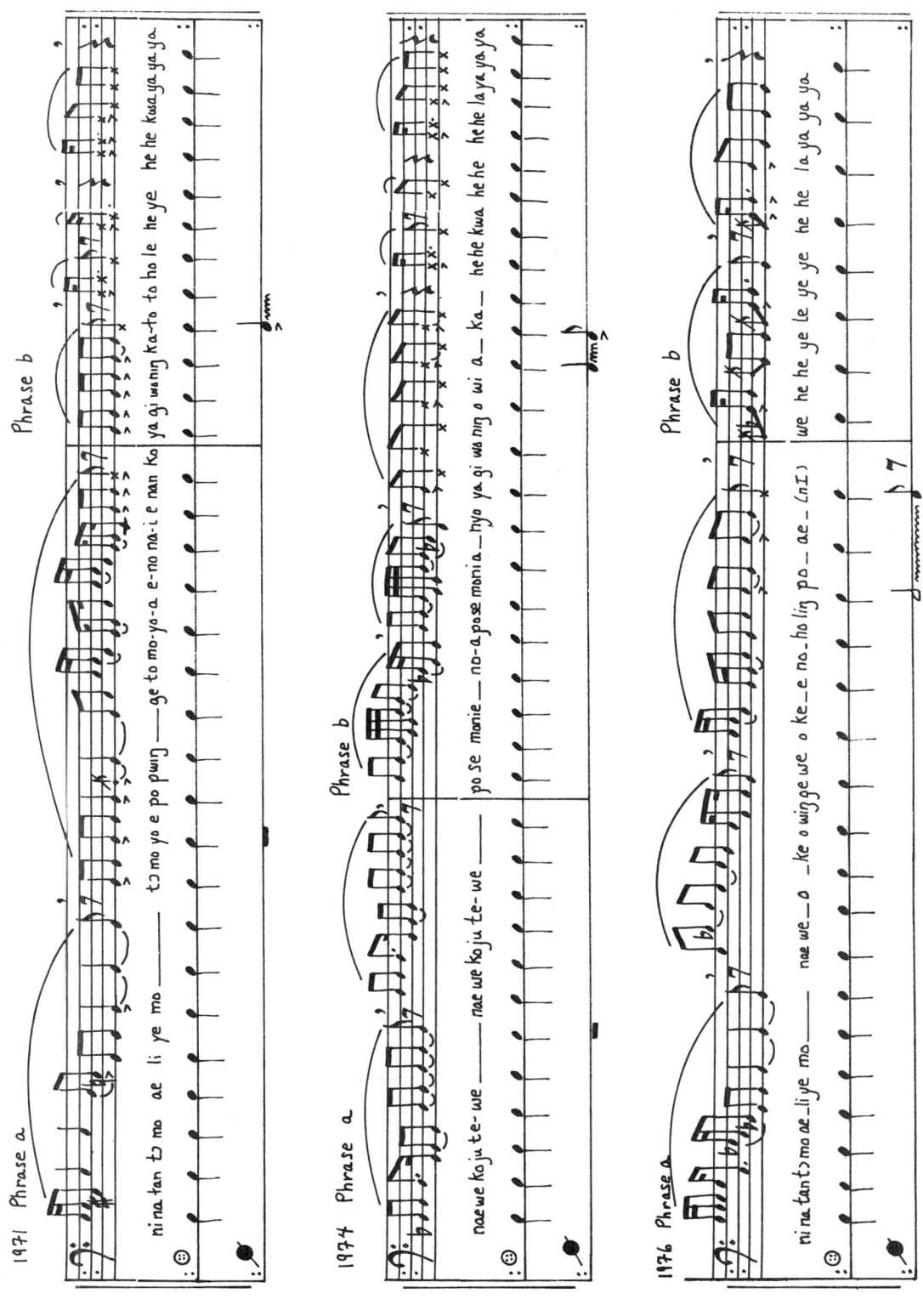

Fig. 5. Section A: Part 2.

90 SELECTED REPORTS

Fig. 6. Section A: Part 3.

After the statement of phrase "a" immediately followed by phrase "b," both phrases are restated, completing Part 2 of Section A. In the repetition, however, a change in text may take place. Usually only one word is changed, but this does not affect the melodic material to any great degree.

The repetition can be viewed in two ways. Phrases "a" and "b" together may be conceived as an entire unit that is repeated to form a large paired phrase unit. The composers, however, do not recognize it as a repetition of material, but rather as a method of restatement or recurrence; the purpose is to mention the counterpart of the particular word changed. The clue is in the meaning of the text. If, for example, the text alludes to kachina boys singing, the repeat will account for the kachina girls. When this type of substitution occurs, the word-sets have an ordered sequence. In the above example, male must be mentioned before female; if the cardinal directions are included, they must appear in the sequence of north-west-south-east.[14]

The composers identify Part 3 of Section A (indicated as phrase "c" in Fig. 6) as the chorus, for it reappears in Section B of the song structure. Usually set in the higher register, the text may contain non-lexical syllables, or the entire unit may have meaningful text. When meaningful text occurs, it is followed by vocable syllables.

Phrase "c" for 1971 contains vocables only, whereas "c" for 1976 employs meaningful text (illustrated in Fig. 6). The last four beats of 1976 contain vocable syllables, and it is this short common phrase unit that has been found in other Turtle Dance songs. The phrases for both 1971 and 1976 are placed in the higher register and are repeated to complete Part 3. No text change occurs for 1971 since the entire phrase employs vocables. 1976 does have a text change in the repeat, but only one word is changed, leaving the melodic material unaffected.

Phrase "c" for 1974 is a special case. It is found in the middle register and is repeated after the first seven beats. The phrase contains meaningful text, and in addition, these words are familiar — the opening phrase "a" for 1974 (in Fig. 5) contains the same words. Here the composer has supplied the text with new material within the same song. Although the composer retained the text and paired phrase concept, phrase "c" is nevertheless very distinct from phrase "a". The two phrases together are repeated, forming Part 3 of Section A. In all of the Turtle Dance songs examined, only this example borrows a complete phrase unit from Part 2, inserting it in Part 3. Consequently, this procedure lessens the amount of melodic material composed.

One other device makes its appearance in Part 3. It is characteristic not only of the Okushare, but appears in many other dances from the ceremonial repertoire as well. The basic temporal unit so far has been duple. That is, the kinetic (antege), percussion (turtle shell rattle), and melodic patterns have been executed in the basic pulsation of accent-release-accent-release. The accent corresponds to the right foot; the release represents the weight on the left foot. The device for shifting this pattern is the *t'a*, which literally means 'pause' (Kurath 1970: 89). After a series of apparently duple bars, a change to a triple pattern is accomplished by the dancers extending the antege through the third beat:

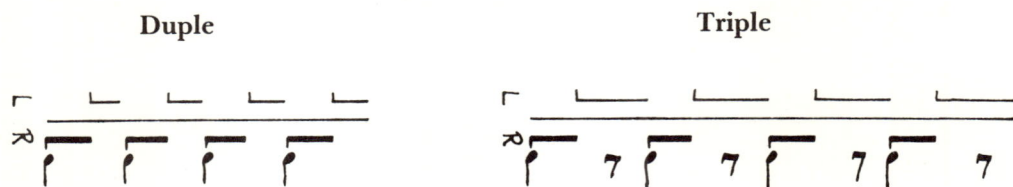

After the eleventh beat of phrase "c" for 1971, the music marks the third count while the antege pauses. Often, however, the antege as well as the music pause for the third count, as they do after the sixth full beat of phrase "c" for 1974.

The placement of the *t'a* is variable. In the song for 1976 it does not occur until Part 4. In other examples it is placed in Part 2, just after the standard phrase unit, the puchano. The only place where the t'a is not used is in Part 1. The introductory phrase and standard phrase unit are never altered; they remain consistent and unchanged in every Turtle Dance song.

The final Part 4 of Section A is referred to as the "ending part" of the verse. It is characterized by a gradual descent to the lower register, and may contain two phrase units. Phrase "d" is optional; with one exception, it is separated from phrase "e" because it is not repeated. When used, it is followed by phrase "e," which is repeated, forming Part 4 of Section A. Part 4 contains the least borrowing between songs. In the fifteen songs surveyed, Part 4 of each example remained distinct from its counterparts.

Both songs for 1971 and 1976 contain phrase "d," but this phrase is absent from 1974. It may contain either vocables or meaningful text, and uses the higher register. Phrase "d" for 1971 (illustrated in Fig. 7) employs vocables, whereas 1976 contains meaningful text. It is not until phrase "d" that the t'a occurs in the song composed for 1976.

The t'a, even if it has made an appearance in a previous part, will always be found in Part 4. Two types of t'a have been used in the excerpts presented. A third type, however, is exhibited at the beginning of phrase "e" for 1974. At this point, emphasis is placed on each foot equally. The basic pulse of the song quickens briefly but returns to the fundamental antege step in the last seven beats of the phrase.

The gourd rattles have been employed up to this point chiefly in three ways: 1) as a signal for the dancer-singers to begin; 2) as a device for emphasizing particularly important words appearing in the text; and 3) as a signal to repeat an entire verse. The rattle is sounded at structural points of the song — just before the end of a section to be repeated.

The composers do not view the brief shaking as a signal for a repetition; to them, the rattle calls attention to important words in the text. In Part 4, especially phrase "e," the rhythmic shaking of the rattle signals the end of a verse, which is then repeated. It also adds textural and rhythmic emphasis to the melodic material and to the underlying basic pulse, the latter of which is outlined by the turtle shell rattles.

The four parts just discussed (puchano, beginning, chorus, and ending) represent Section A^1, or the first verse of the five-part song structure. A^2, the second verse, contains the same melodic and rhythmic substance but certain words in the text may be changed. If, for example, the directions north and west appear in the first verse, south and east will occur in the second. A choreographic movement is added at the beginning of the second verse; it is described with the third verse below, for it is employed in the second through fifth verses.

The third verse, Section B^1, is also divided into four parts. Part 1 contains both an introduction and a standard phrase unit. The introductory phrase, illustrated in Figure 8, is similar to that in Figure 4, but here the gourd rattle signals the dancers to turn in place. The first continuous shaking of the rattle initiates a turn to the west; the second shake then instigates a turn to the east; and the final shake indicates a turn to the north. Facing north, the dancer-singers begin the standard phrase unit for Section B.

This unit, unlike the one in Section A, is meaningful. It is called *hapimbe*, meaning 'middle section' or 'middle verse' (in other Tewa-speaking villages it has different connotations). This particular phrase unit, like the one in Section A, is in the lower register and must be used at this point in all Turtle Dance songs. The introductory phrase and standard phrase unit, or hapimbe, together represent Part 1 for Section B and are not repeated.

Part 2 of Section B contains one or more phrases. In all cases, the songs must contain new material, designated here as phrase "f," but this may be followed by a phrase or portion of one previously introduced in Section A. Phrase "f" for 1971 (Fig. 9) issues forth phrase "b" from Section A, while phrase "f" for 1974 adjoins a portion of phrase "b." For 1976, the phrase is succeeded by a short phrase "g" and recaptures phrase "b" from Section A. In each case, the phrases conclude with vocable syllables. Phrases "f," "g," and/or "b" are repeated, forming Part 2 of Section B.

If Part 4 of Section A is earmarked for composers' ingenuity, then Part 2 of Section B is the locus where ideas coincide. Nowhere else does borrowing occur to the extent that it does in this portion of the song structure. Part 2 for 1976 is an exact restatement of the same phrase for 1971. The composer has borrowed this entire phrase unit from 1971 and placed it in his song for 1976. In the 1974 example, the composer may have been influenced by this phrase, for his rendering is very similar. The remarkable similarity of these three phrases, transcribed in Figure 9, leaves no doubt that the borrowing of phrase units from one song to another (regardless of the original composer) is a significant part of the compositional process.

In Part 2 of Section B, meaningful text must be present in the first portion of the phrase unit. The text should deal with a personality from the kachina pantheon, as is the case with the excerpts presented in Figure 9. One composer's treatment may be continually borrowed by others, but this is not viewed as an infringement upon the original composition. The composer of the 1971 song stated that he was delighted to see a portion of his song work well for another composer's creation.

After Part 2 of Section B, no new material is introduced except for minor text changes. Parts 3 and 4 of Section B are restated from Section A, completing the third section or verse of the song form. Section B^2, the fourth verse, may have text changes, but they do not conspicuously modify the melodic material. The fifth and final verse is an exact rendering of the first verse and completes the five-part song form.

Fig. 7. Section A: Part 4.

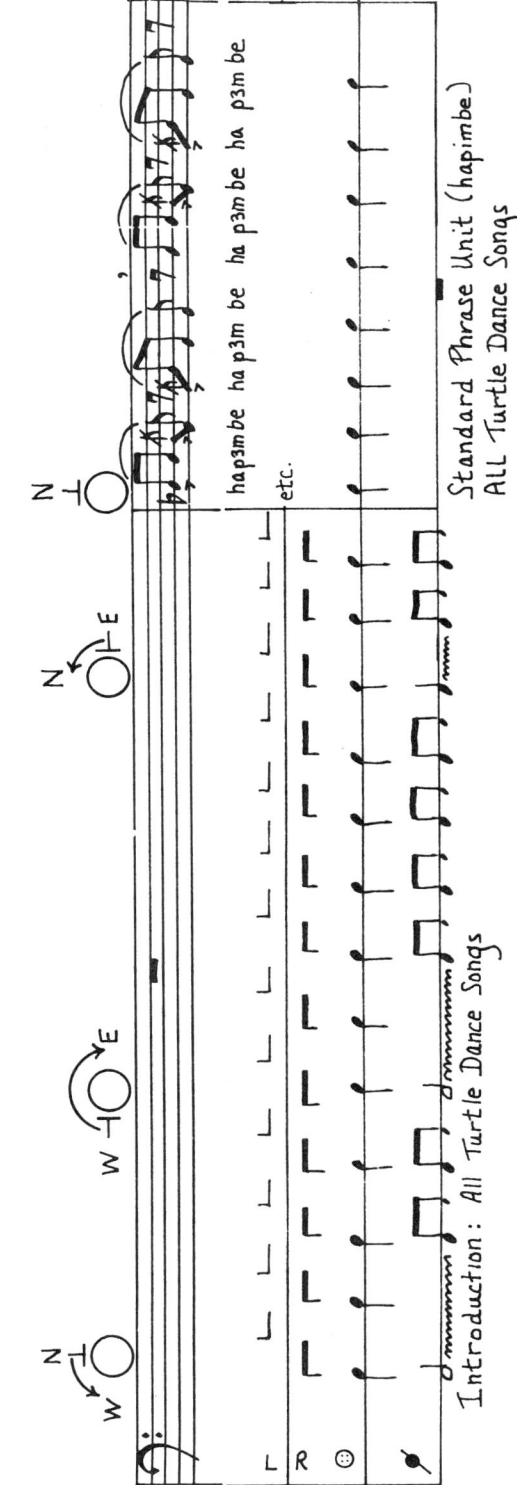

Fig. 8. Section B: Part 1.

Fig. 9. Section B: Part 2.

The music which is newly composed in the five-part structure is contained in the entire first verse and the initial two parts of the third verse. The remainder is a recurrence of music with text changes. The most difficult part of the compositional process, said one composer, "is the fitting in of words after the tune has been composed" (Cipriano Garcia, *op. cit.*). Melodies cannot be altered significantly to accomodate severe text changes. Because the song form demands the repetition of melodies, the composer must consider carefully what portion of his text can be changed without marring his original musical ideas for a given composition.

Conclusions. From the foregoing discussion and analysis, what has been coined as a "preconceived mold" is indeed an operative element in this genre of the ceremonial repertoire from the San Juan Pueblo. The composers, however, are not consciously aware of this preconceived mold. When asked why the songs must fall into the patterns just described, no answer was given other than "this is the way the ancestors gave it to us — it is up to us to carry it on." There is a sense of respect for and adherence to the song structure along with the recognition that it simultaneously permits the input of fresh ideas into an old and traditional form.

An archetypal song form was derived from the fifteen songs examined in order to indicate the basic outline of the structure, including elements characteristic to each of the various parts. Illustrated in Figure 10, this scheme may be viewed as one "preconceived mold" which scholars have referred to in the past.

The analytic breakdown of the songs presented in this article is only one method by which the songs may be perceived. Although I applied some technical terms to identify the basic components of the song structure which are not employed by the composers, two members concurred that my identification was correct. An awareness of some of the details discovered in these songs did not occur to the composers until they were questioned about the formal aspects inherent in their compositions. The mode of perception experienced by the composers and singers will require further investigation.

Although this study, unfortunately, did not investigate the song texts accompanying the music composed for the Okushare, certain themes generally occur in the texts of the Okushare that are not found in the newly composed texts of the Tunshare and Pogonshare. Subjects expressed in the texts, too, remain exclusive property of their respective ceremonies.

The sacred musical repertoire of the San Juan Pueblo has been preserved much in the same manner as some of the earliest sacred music in the West. Westerners, however, developed a system of notation to accommodate the increasing wealth and complexity of compositions being supplied constantly to its sacred repertoire. The Tewa have adhered to the traditional method of preservation through oral means, as have many other cultures. In San Juan, a portion of the sacred repertoire continues to expand, still rejecting written devices for the purposes of recollection. The mind of one composer alone may be considered as a reference manual to the entire musical life of this small thriving village in the southwestern part of the United States. The composer is a poet, musician, performer, and mental scribe. Imbued with the responsibility of preserving music given to him, he is charged also with creating music prescribed by his cultural traditions.

NOTES

1. Portions of this article were initially presented at the Annual Meeting of the Society for Ethnomusicology held in Philadelphia, November, 1976.

2. A *kachina* cult is an association that usually comprises male members of a pueblo, and in some villages female members as well. The cult is concerned with supernatural beings vaguely connected with ancestral spirits and believed to have the power to bring rain.

3. A *kiva* is a pueblo ceremonial structure. In some Pueblos it is wholly or partly underground; it is either circular or rectangular in shape.

4. These two ceremonies no longer alternate every year. See Nora Yeh's article in this issue for a discussion of the Pogonshare.

5. Cipriano Garcia, in a videotaped interview recorded April 26, 1976. Peter and Cipriano Garcia, two composers from San Juan, were the guest lecturers for two sessions at UCLA, 26 April 1976 and 25 April 1977. A subsequent interview with Cipriano Garcia was held in San Juan Pueblo, 26 September 1977. The project was made possible by grants received from the University of California program in Innovative Undergraduate Instruction and the National Endowment for the Arts.

6. Personal letter, 16 March 1976.

7. Robert Rhodes, letter to Charlotte Heth, 12 May 1976.

8. The ground plan for the circuit pattern was taken from Gertrude Kurath 1970: 54.

9. Tape recording given to the author by Don L. Roberts. This tape was originally recorded by Antonio Garcia. The two songs composed for 1954 and 1961 have been transcribed in Kurath 1970: 136-37.

10. This example has been released commercially on Canyon Records ARP 6065.

11. This complete set of songs has been released commercially on Indian House Records 1101.

12. This complete set of songs was recorded by Charlotte Heth for New World Records, 8 September, 1975, and subsequently was published in *Okushareh: Turtle Dance Songs of San Juan Pueblo* by Charlotte Heth and Alfonso Ortiz, 1979 (New World Records NW 301).

13. This complete set of songs was recorded by the author in San Juan Pueblo, 5 January 1977.

14. For further examples of this type of text change, see the complete translations of the Turtle Dance Songs for 1971 on the record jacket cover of Indian House Records 1101.

Figure 10. ARCHETYPAL SONG FORM FOR OKUSHARE.

	Part 1		Part 2 (Beginning)		Part 3 (Chorus)	Part 4 (Ending)	
	Introduction	SPU* (Puchano)	‖: Phrase "a"	Phrase "b" :‖	‖: Phrase "c" :‖	‖: Phrase "d" (optional)	Phrase "e" :‖
SECTION A¹ (1st Verse)	Gourd Signal	Lower Register Vocables Only No T'a No Gourd Signal	Middle Register Meaningful Text followed by Vocables T'a may occur Gourd Signal		Higher Register Meaningful Text followed by Vocables or Vocables Only T'a may occur Gourd Signal	Higher Register Meaningful Text or Vocables Only T'a may occur No Gourd Signal	Descent to Lower Register Vocables Only T'a must occur Gourd Signal

SECTION A² (2nd Verse) Same as A¹ but with text changes

	Part 1		Part 2 (Beginning)		Part 3 (Chorus)	Part 4 (Ending)	
	Introduction	SPU* (Hapimbe)	‖: Phrase "f"	Phrase "g" and/or "b" :‖	‖: Phrase "c" :‖	‖: Phrase "d" (optional)	Phrase "e" :‖
SECTION B¹ (3rd Verse)	Gourd Signal	Lower Register Meaningful Text No T'a No Gourd Signal	Descent to Lower Register Meaningful Text followed by Vocables T'a may occur Gourd Signal in Phrase "g" or "b"		See Phrase "c" from Part 3 of Section A¹ above; may have possible text changes	See Phrase "d" from Part 4 of Section A¹ above; may have possible text changes	See Phrase "e" from Part 4 of Section A¹ above; no text changes

SECTION B² (4th Verse) Same as B¹ but with text changes

SECTION A¹ (5th Verse) Same as A¹ above (no changes)

*SPU = Standard Phrase Unit

REFERENCES CITED

Dozier, Edward P.
    1957   "Rio Grande Pueblo Ceremonial Patterns." *New Mexico Quarterly Review,* Summer Issue.
    1958   "Cultural Matrix of Singing and Chanting in Tewa Pueblos." *International Journal of American Linguistics* 24.
    1970   *The Pueblo Indians of North America.* New York: Holt, Rinehart & Winston, Inc.

Frisbie, Charlotte J.
    1977   *Music and Dance Research of Southwestern United States Indians.* Detroit Studies in Music Bibliography, No. 36. Information Coordinators, Inc.

Kurath, Gertrude P. and Antonio Garcia
    1970   *Music and Dance of the Tewa Pueblos.* Santa Fe: Museum of New Mexico Press.

Ortiz, Alfonso
    1969   *The Tewa World.* Chicago: University of Chicago Press.

Parsons, Elsie Clews
    1939   *Pueblo Indian Religion,* Vol. 2. Chicago: University of Chicago Press.

Roberts, Don L.
    1972   "The Ethnomusicology of The Eastern Pueblos." In *New Perspectives on The Pueblos.* Edited by Alfonso Ortiz. Albuquerque: University of New Mexico Press.

Fig. 1. Antege portion of Pogonshare.

Fig. 2. The symmetrical antege formation is defined by the two females. Each male holds a gourd rattle in his right hand and some evergreen branches in his left hand.

THE POGONSHARE CEREMONY OF THE TEWA

SAN JUAN, NEW MEXICO[1]

Nora Yeh

Pogonshare, one of a series of ceremonial fertility dances among the Eastern Pueblo Indians in San Juan, New Mexico, is one of the most significant ritual activities in the Tewa calendar year. Together with other ceremonies, Pogonshare determines and influences the economic, spiritual, and socio-political well-being of the entire village.

Little information can be found about the Pogonshare in the literature on the Tewa Pueblo of San Juan. When described, it is discussed in the context of a full year's ceremonial cycle, by Elsie C. Parsons (1929: 189-90) and Gertrude Kurath (1970: 150-51, 164-65), for instance; mentioned as a fragment of the Tewa world in an anthropological, philosophical study (Alfonso Ortiz 1969: 104; 169, nos. 13 and 14); or it is included together with other dances (Antonio and Carlos Garcia 1968: 239-44). The Pogonshare has never been studied as an independent entity through systematic, musicological investigation.

The title of this particular ceremony, unlike those of other ceremonies at San Juan, is ambiguous in both the Tewa language and in its translations. In Tewa, it is either called "Pogonshare," from *po* 'gourd' and *share*, 'dance,' or *Powinshare*, a seemingly old term which also means "Gourd Dance." It has been translated into English as "Three Times Dance" by Parsons; "Corn Maiden Dance" by Kurath, A. and C. Garcia, and Vera P. Laski; "Squash Dance" by Ortiz; "Cloud Dance" by Cipriano Garcia; and "Pumpkin Dance" or "Gourd Dance" by Tony Isaacs (1972). "Gourd Dance" is probably the most appropriate and direct translation, although "Cloud Dance is the translation most commonly known. According to Cipriano Garcia, the latter name derives from the similarity between the female dancer's headdress and the shape and color of clouds (see Figs. 1, 2, 10, and 11).

---

[1] This article would not be complete without the encouragement of Charlotte Heth; the information provided by Cipriano Garcia; the advice and criticism from Maria La Vigna, Abraham Schwadron, and Philip Sonnichsen. The writer wishes hereby to acknowledge and thank them for their assistance.

Although most ceremonial dances among the Tewa are traditionally oriented, the *Pogonshare, Tunshare* ("Basket Dance"), and *Okushare*[2] ("Turtle Dance") are the only three dances for which new music is composed annually. The purposes of this paper will be to study the importance of the Pogonshare to San Juan Pueblo and to present a detailed analysis of the Pogonshare music.

According to the calendar of the agricultural cycle at San Juan, the end of January or the beginning of February is the time when the earth has been ploughed, the seeds have been planted, and the crops are waiting to be nurtured into budding new life. The most important purpose of the Pogonshare ceremony is to pray for another year of fine, abundant crops and to ask for moisture in the form of snow, rain, or dew. The natural environment of the Tewa in the Southwest is arid land, but through irrigation and the cooperation of natural and supernatural forces, an intricate jigsaw puzzle is created, in which the Pogonshare is an essential element. The Tewa perform the Pogonshare at the time of year when fresh, as well as stored, food is least available (Ford 1972: 11), and thus it is a ritual intended to seek new life.

The actual performance of Pogonshare usually lasts one full day, but the preparation and preceding activities begin much earlier. The spruce branches held by the dancers are acquired in the previous December, before the Okushare is held. Twelve days before the Pogonshare ceremony, tribal officials, including the War Chief and his five assistants, meet to decide which one of the two dances (Tunshare or Pogonshare) should be performed. If Pogonshare is chosen, certain decisions must be made: which eight female dancers should be selected to participate; when the four-day rehearsal should take place at War Chief's house (to be followed by final rehearsals inside the *kiva*, or ceremonial chamber); and which songs should be chosen (for a description of some of these processes see A. and C. Garcia 1968: 239-44). Traditionally, the appointment of the War Chief, who is responsible for all seasonal ceremonies, alternates between the Summer and Winter moieties. Either Tunshare or Pogonshare is the first ceremonial duty of the newly elected official. When the Summer Chief is in office, Pogonshare is normally performed; when the Winter Chief is in office, Tunshare is scheduled (see Ortiz 1969: 103, regarding dual organization).

Of the two, Pogonshare is more frequently performed because of the uneven proportion of the population between Summer and Winter moieties and the far greater expense and labor involved in the Tunshare ceremony. Moreover, Tunshare requires an equal number of male and female participants, who are not always available. Pogonshare, on the other hand, simply requires all of the able-bodied males in the village plus eight females.

The composers of the music for Pogonshare are appointed by the tribal officials. According to Antonio and Carlos Garcia, "The selection of composers presents no problems because only three gifted men have a genius for new song creation, and they are invariably appointed for new songs . . . " (A. and C. Garcia 1968: 239). These musicians must create appropriate ceremonial music in a matter of a few days. With a preconceived mold of text and melodic formulae passed down from their forefathers, the composers, through joint effort, create new pieces for the upcoming event.

---

[2] For a discussion of *Okushare*, see Maria La Vigna's article, pp. 77-99.

Fig. 3. The wasa formation.
The drummer and his assistant stand next to sawipinge.

Fig. 4. Male dancer with turtle shell rattle, gourd rattle, and bells.

When the new musical material is completed, the four-day rehearsal is undertaken at the home of the War Chief. Cipriano Garcia (1977) outlines the rehearsal schedule as follows: on the first night the participants begin to learn the new songs by listening to the composer-singers; on the second night the participants become involved by humming the new material; on the third night the actual singing is undertaken, and on the fourth night the *t'an*, dance steps, are incorporated with the singing.

On the evening before the actual Pogonshare ceremony, two events take place. The first is the *Ange'in*, in the nature of a "ritualistic prelude," designed to insure good weather and a successful ceremony the next day. Only males participate, and their dress is the same as that worn for the Pogonshare. In addition, however, these men wear a dark blue or black blanket at knee length over the dance costume. Following the Ange'in, a final rehearsal of the Pogonshare is held inside the small kiva.

In recent years the Pogonshare ceremony has been scheduled for an appropriate Sunday at the end of January or the beginning of February. The ceremony is a sequence of events, the public portion of which takes the better part of a Sunday afternoon and involves four circuits of three plazas and the kiva. A specific ceremony attended by this writer on January 30, 1977, will be outlined subsequently.

All the participants in Pogonshare are elaborately and brightly dressed; they do not change their costumes during the ceremony. Each item of paraphernalia and every color used in the costumes holds symbolic meanings. The shape of the female dancers' headresses represents clouds, for example; the white tassels hanging down the back from each male dancer's waist imitate rain (Figs. 1 and 2). Further details regarding symbolism will be discussed in the progress of this article.

Every male dancer wears a headdress of two eagle feathers, one macaw feather, and ribbons. His face is marked with rouge or black stripes, and he wears scarves and necklaces around his neck. The upper torso is bare and is smeared with gray clay on the upper half and white on the lower half. Each upper arm is wrapped with a leather or beaded arm band three to four inches wide; evergreen branches are inserted inside each arm band. A leather belt with jingle bells encircles the dancer's waist. The left hand holds evergreen branches while the right hand holds a gourd rattle.

A white dance kilt embroidered with designs at the edge reaches to just above the dancer's knee. White tassels hang down his back from a handwoven sash. White and gray clay is applied to upper and lower legs respectively. Bells are tied around both knees, and one turtle shell rattle is attached to the side of the right knee. Red, white, or yellow yarns are also tied around the knees and knotted in the front. Moccasins, either plain white or beaded, are covered by fur pieces at the ankles (Figs. 3 and 4).

A pair of identical headdresses which are worn by two female dancers attract the most attention. Fan-shaped, made from eagle tail feathers and bright orange yucca fiber, the two headdresses are handed over from the first pair of dancers to the second, the second to the third, and the third to the fourth during the performance of the four circuits. Sixteen ears of corn in four different colors, each wrapped in evergreen, are held by the female dancers, one ear in each hand.

The female dancers wear no paint or decoration on their faces. But they exhibit many necklaces made of silver and turquoise, and numerous rings adorn the fingers.

105

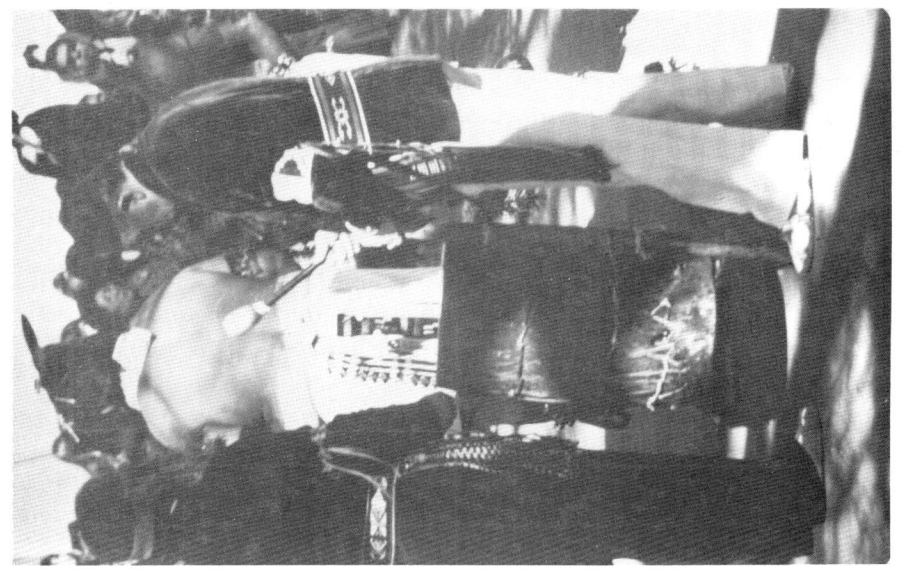

Fig. 6. Manner of playing the drum.

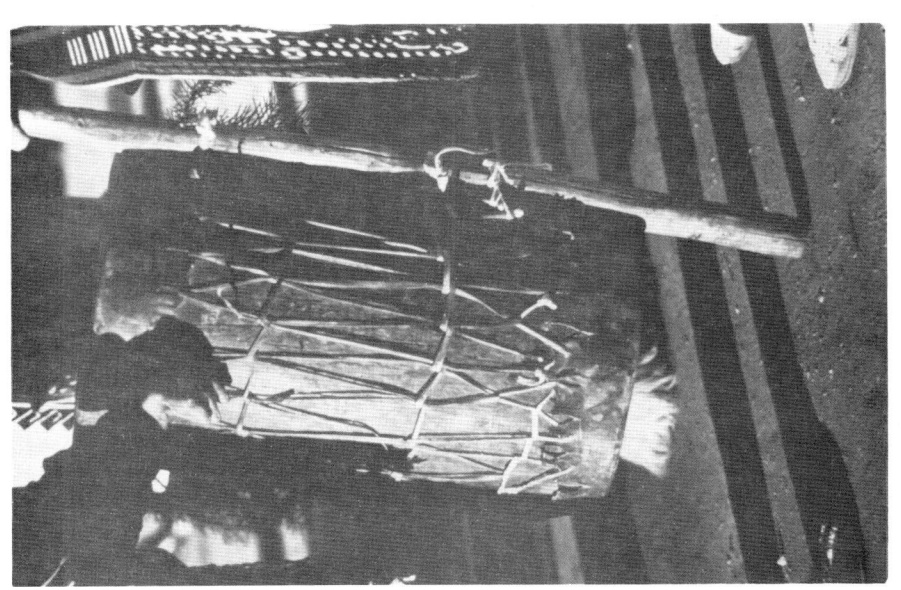

Fig. 5. The drum fastened to a pole in its characteristic playing position.

Each woman wears a thick black dress reaching to mid-calf in length, with long sleeves colorfully embroidered at the cuff and with a sash tied around the waist. Another garment — a bright, thin, lacy piece of cloth tied at the right shoulder (exposing the left shoulder) and reaching approximately to the knee — is worn as an overdress. Arm bands worn by the women are similar to those of the men. The only difference is that, instead of evergreen branches, bright orange fibers are tied to the arms. White buckskin leggings and moccasins complete the womens' dancing outfit. Such costumes are unique to Pogonshare.

The drummers wear a so-called "Apache outfit": head band, bright colored velvet shirt, multi-colored woven sash with tassel on the side, beaded arm bands (one on each arm), long pants, and moccasins (Fig. 6).

A group of officials known as *Towa é*, the middle level of a tripartite political organization within the Tewa (see Ortiz 1969: 61-77) and whose role encompasses a number of duties and obligations during Pogonshare, wear ordinary street clothes except for a blanket worn over the shoulder.

Four types of instruments are used in Pogonshare: a drum attached to a stick supported by the drummer and his assistant (although only the drummer plays); gourd rattles held in the right hand and played by each male dancer; turtle shell rattles worn below the right knee by each male dancer; waist and knee bells, also worn by each of the male dancers.

The drum (*tambe* in the Tewa language) is made of a cottonwood log slightly modified into a cylindrical barrel shape and covered with rawhide at each end. A pole about ten inches longer than the drum's height is fastened to the side lengthwise, with five inches protruding at each end. During the performance this pole serves as a single-legged stand at the lower end to prevent the drum from touching the ground and as a handle to be steadied at the upper end by the drummer or his assistant (Figs. 5 and 6). The particular drum used at San Juan Pueblo is said to be very old and its maker unknown. Like the drums used by many other North American Indian tribes, this instrument is much respected among the Tewa. An example of their reverence is given by Cipriano Garcia (1977), who noted that when repairs were done to the drum in 1964, a "Butterfly Dance" (*Ti'ishare*) was held in its honor. This old drum has never been painted; if it were to be painted for any reason, a general meeting would have to be called to approve such action. To the Tewa, drums have supernatural powers.

The stick beater (*tambefe*) used on the drum is sometimes made from the branch of a willow tree. The stick is padded with buckskin sewn together at the tip. The drummer holds the stick in his right hand as he plays during the dance.

Throughout the Pogonshare the drummer and his assistant traditionally stand to play and they must stay close to the lead singers-dancers-composers, known as *sawipinge* in Tewa (literally "center of dance line") at both *wasa* ("entrance") and the ensuing *antege* ("footlifting"). The drummer is expected to be extremely familiar with the music, possess a good rhythmic sense, have tremendous physical endurance, and be able to sustain long hours of persistent concentration.

The basic drum pattern (1.) consists of alternating strong and weak beats, but occasionally other patterns are also included:

Drum Patterns: 1. ♩♪ 2. ♩♪♪♪ 3. ♩♪♪ (2)

The gourd rattle (*po'pwiye*) is an unpainted gourd pierced through the stem by a stick which forms the handle. Beads, gravel, and/or kernels of corn are placed within. A thong is tied to the handle for carrying on the wrist. Anyone in the Tewa society may construct it. When shaken, its sound is supposed to imitate the pattering of rain (Billard 1974: 53) and, indeed, the instrument is said to have rain power.

Two basic patterns of shaking technique are found in the Pogonshare:

Gourd Rattle Patterns:

1. ♩♪ or ♩♪♪♪ or ♩♪♪ (2)   A sharp stroke is made on every accent, as shown on the drum patterns 1, 2, and 3.

2. ♩ ~~~~~~   a "tremolo" effect:

a. at the beginning of the wasa and the antege as a part of introductory phrase — a cue meaning "everybody is ready";
b. during a particular section of the ceremony as a marker to emphasize and underline the important words within a song text. For example, "coming" and "singing" of *kachina* (a spirit) are sung with the tremolo rattle accompaniment;
c. to communicate when the dancers should turn (during wasa) and when they should step out of line (in the case of the female dancers during antege).

Because the music used in this article was recorded outside of a performance context, the singer, Cipriano Garcia, was recorded alone, accompanying himself with a drum. As such, the transcription does not include the rattle part.

The turtle shell rattle (*oeku*) is made from a water turtle. Holes are drilled on the curved surfaces of the carapace near the head and tail. Long deerskin thongs are passed through these holes, attaching below the dancer's right knee; the ventral plastron comes into direct contact with the leg. Four to five deer hooves, functioning as leg rattles, are attached to the deerskin thongs (Fig. 4). The deer hooves create a rhythmic effect through the dancers' foot stamping movements, which coincide with the various accents illustrated under the drum patterns:

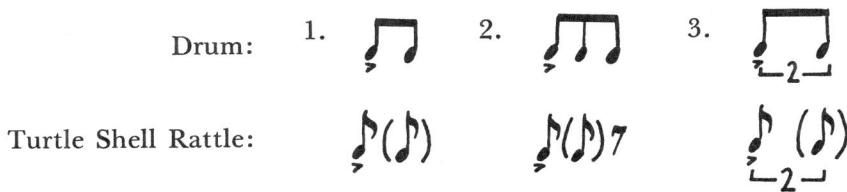

Several metal slit and tongued bells (known as *pun*) are worn by every male dancer around the waist and knees. The size of the bells varies; some are as large as a golf ball. Since both the bells and the turtle shell/deer hoof rattles are worn by all male dancers, the rhythmic patterns of the bells are identical to those of the turtle shell/deer hoof rattle (Figs. 4 and 11).

The Tewa Cosmology.

In Tewa cosmology, the four cardinal points have particular significance and meaning. According to Tewa mythology, the Tewa have their origins in a mythical lake known as *Sipofene*, literally "Sandy Lake," located far to the north of San Juan (Ortiz 1969: 13). The north is related to the Winter moiety and its colors are blue and green, which symbolize the growing crops.

East is also associated with and sponsored by the Winter moiety. The east is identified with the sun, which is believed to be the source of all life as the primary fertilizing agent in nature. During a portion of the first of the six rites of passage, the "naming ritual," the infant is presented to the rising sun in order to gather blessings for the child (Ortiz 1969: 31). Of the twelve kivas used by the Tewa, ten have their doors built facing east or southeast. The white color of this direction represents winter moisture or snow.

West is shared by both Winter and Summer moieties and is, therefore, a neutral direction. The color of this direction is yellow, symbolizing sunshine. The holiest and most important mountain, *Tsikomo*, lies to the west of San Juan.

South belongs exclusively to the Summer moiety; it is the direction from which the "warm gods" come. Its color is red, represented by the rouge used by men in warfare and hunting. Black is also associated with the summer colors but is not associated with any direction. It does, however, symbolize the rain-laden cumulus clouds of spring and winter.

As indicated in Fig. 7, the sixteen ears of corn held by the four pairs of women dancers, one ear of corn in each hand, are blue, yellow, red, and white. The corn represents the Corn Mother (Ortiz 1969: 89) while the four colors represent the cardinal directions, the seasons, and the "natural substances" which enlarge growth. The cardinal directions, the Winter as well as the Summer moieties, the spiritual beings, ancestors, and mythological personalities, i.e., the whole universe of time and space, is represented and symbolically encompassed in this one-day festivity.

Because moisture is critical to Rio Grande pueblos, including San Juan, one of the duties of high town officials is to sponsor rain retreats during the seasons when rain is needed (Parsons 1929: 178-79; Ortiz 1969: 107-8). One of the functions of the men belonging to the medicine society is to "control clouds." Clouds are particularly sacred; as Ortiz has noted, "In the Tewa's — as all Pueblo Indians' — unceasing quest for rainfall, that which seems to bring them closer to the source of this precious moisture, is endowed with unusual sacredness" (Ortiz 1969: 25).

With regard to symbolism, we may summarize by saying that in the greater world in which we live, all things, supernatural and natural, subconscious and conscious, spiritual and physical, play an influential role. The Tewa feel that either excess or insufficiency in nature causes an imbalance. Disaster results, thus affecting the lives of men and women. In order to temper such extremes and to make peace with other worlds as well as our own, the performance of rituals for various purposes, from sacred to secular levels — kachina dances, maskless kachina dances, animal dances, corn dances, borrowed dances, and social dances — is indispensable.

The Pogonshare Festival.

The following diagrams are based on the author's observations in the pueblo of San Juan on January 30, 1977. The Tewa, like other Pueblo groups, traditionally maintain a consistency in the basic format of Pogonshare, including dance sections, the rotational system used between the three plazas and the kiva, the time allocated to each event, the use of colors in each circuit, and the musical organization.

As mentioned previously, the Pogonshare ceremony involves two basic dance patterns: wasa ("entrance") and antege ("footlifting"), both organized in a specific rotational pattern, as noted below. Wasa involves mixed men and women in a side-stepping pattern with the lines of dancers alternating right and left directions. In antege, a single line of male dancers does an in-place, duple rhythm step while the female dancers execute a crossing pattern, or zig-zag, in front of the men.

Fig. 7. Schedule and Sequence of Pogonshare Dance Circuits.

Circuits	Dance Sections	Stations	Males Facing	Corn Color	Musical Organization
One:	Wasa I	Entrance to South Plaza	⊣ and ⊢ [3]	blue	(Wasa–Antege) X 3 [4] + 1 shortened Antege
	Antege I		⊥		
11:45 am	Wasa II	Entrance to North Plaza	⊣ and ⊢		
to	Antege II		⊥		
	Wasa III	Entrance to East Plaza	⊤ and ⊥		
1:00 pm	Antege III		⊣		
	Antege IV	Kiva	not known		
Two:	Antege V	South Plaza	⊥	yellow	Antege X 3 + 1 shortened Antege
1:15 pm	Antege VI	North Plaza	⊥		
to	Antege VII	East Plaza	⊣		
2:05 pm	Antege VIII	Kiva	not known		
Three:	Antege IX	South Plaza	⊥	red	Antege X 3 + 1 shortened Antege
2:25 pm	Antege X	North Plaza	⊥		
to	Antege XI	East Plaza	⊣		
3:15 pm	Antege XII	Kiva	not known		

[3] Please see Key to Figure 9.

[4] See the detailed musical analysis of Wasa I and Antege I in Tables 1 and 2.

Circuits	Dance Sections	Stations	Males Facing	Corn Color	Musical Organization
Four:	Wasa IV	Entrance to South Plaza	⊣ and ⊢	white	(Wasa—Antege) X 3 + 1 shortened Antege
4:15 pm	Antege XIII		⊥		
	Wasa V	Entrance to North Plaza	⊣ and ⊢		
to	Antege XIV		⊥		
	Wasa VI	Entrance to East Plaza	⊤ and ⊥		
5:30 pm	Antege XV		⊣		
	Antege XVI	Kiva	not known		

Fig. 8a. Circuits One and Four.

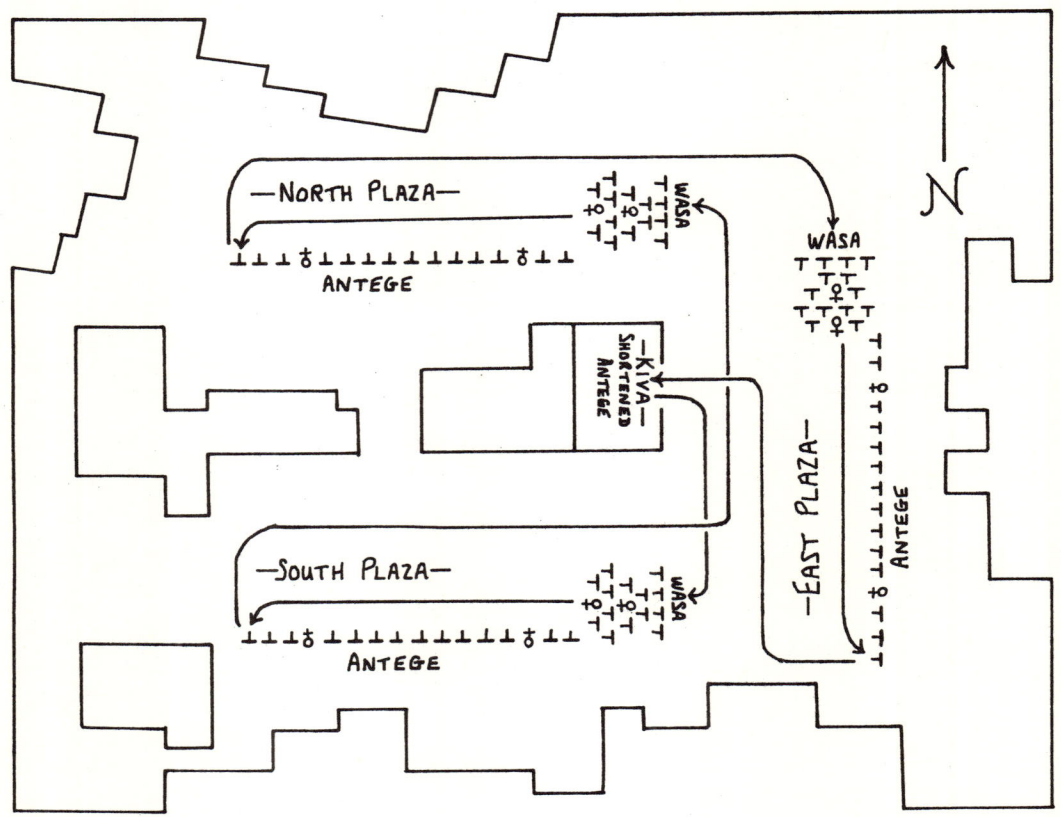

Fig. 8b. Circuits Two and Three.

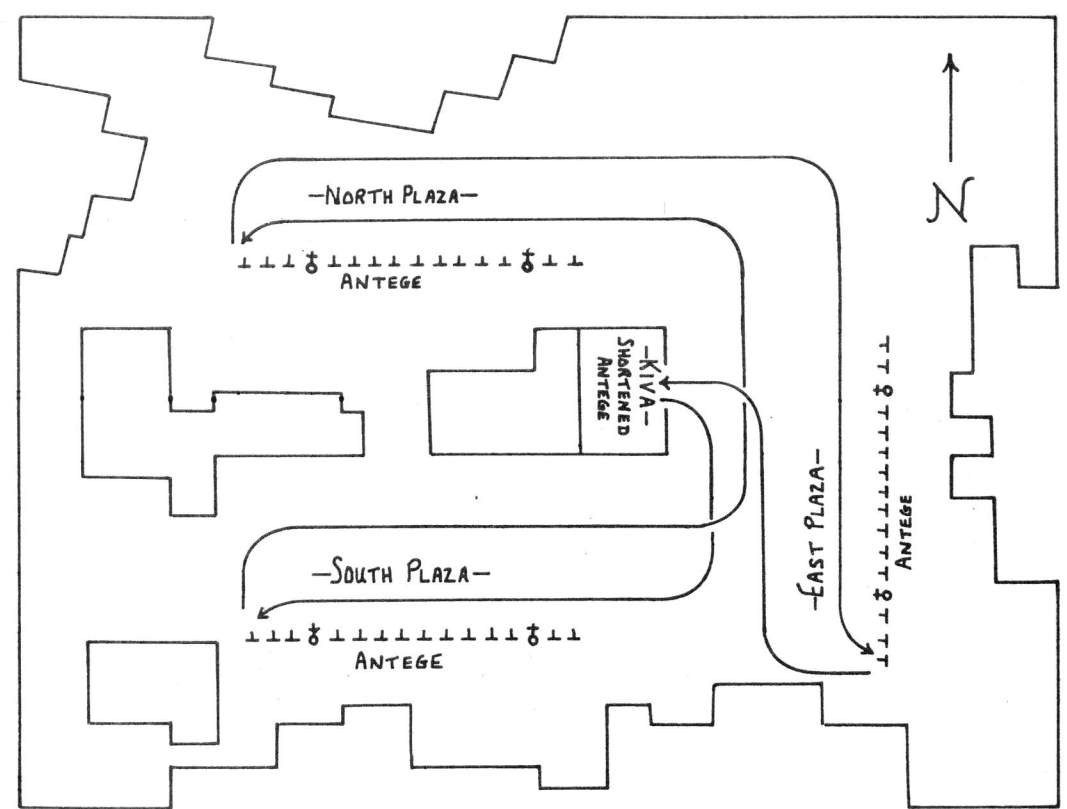

Dance Circuits:

1) From kiva to entrance of south plaza — wasa I, IV[5]
2) Line formation at south plaza — antege I, V, IX, XIII
3) To entrance of north plaza passing in front of kiva — wasa II, V
4) Line formation at north plaza — antege II, VI, X, XIV
5) To entrance of east plaza — wasa III, VI
6) Line formation at east plaza — antege III, VII, XI, XV
7) Inside kiva for final rendition — antege IV, VIII, XII, XVI (shortened).

---

[5] Please note that wasa are danced only in the first and last circuits; wasa and antege formations are magnified in Figures 9 and 12.

There are five parts in the music within each wasa and each antege. These five parts are organized in an A A B B A pattern; the second and third A's and the second B are exact repetitions, in both music and text, of the first A and B respectively. Further discussion will confirm that such particular structure is fundamental and necessary for the Tewa ritual performance.

Wasa, meaning "entrance," is the first dance and alternates with the antege in a prescribed manner during the first and last circuits, but does not appear in the second and third circuits. The following is a description of Wasa I, i.e., the first wasa performed at the entrance to the south plaza.

The male dancers and the first pair of female dancers are led by a Towa é out of the kiva to the eastern side of the south plaza in single file. Then, in groups of two, three, or four, the dancers line up facing west in shoulder-to-shoulder position and start dancing by stamping the right foot on the accented beats (with very little exception), the left foot following on unaccented beats (see Fig. 3; also the transcription of footlifting patterns, p. 135 ff.). The parallel lines of dancers move sideways and alternate lines move in opposite directions, i.e., lines one, three, five, etc., step sideways towards the right or north while lines two, four, six, etc., step sideways towards the left or south (see Fig. 9, Diagram A). The process is reversed when the dancers face a different direction.

At the "tremolo" signal on the gourd rattles, which are shaken by the lead singers-dancers and are immediately imitated by the rest of the dancers, the lines change to face the opposite direction, i.e., the east (Diagram B). At another signal the dancers turn to face west again and move in the same manner. During this portion the entire group moves gradually, almost imperceptibly, towards the center of the south plaza — westward. The two drummers situate themselves on the southern side of the dancers and closely follow the lead singers. At the closing of the wasa, the dancers are led in single file by the Towa é to the middle of the south plaza. The antege then follows.

Fig. 9 (opposite). Choreography of Wasa.

Key to the transcriptions:

⊣ = male facing west

⊢ = male facing east

⊢O = female facing west

O⊢ = female facing east

↑ = sideways movement of dancers toward the north

↓ = sideways movement toward the south

☉ = drum and drummers.

WASA DIAGRAM A.

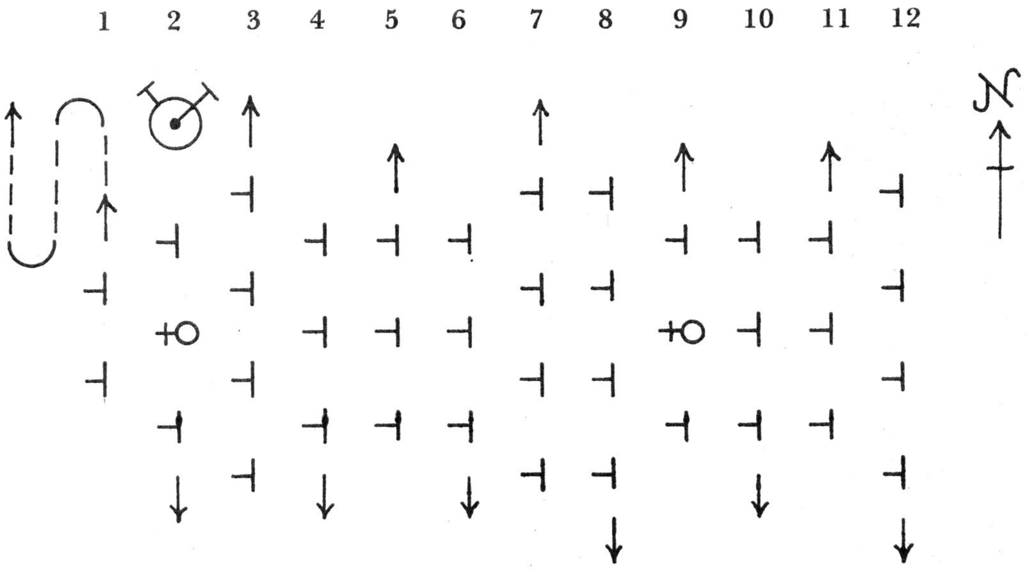

WASA DIAGRAM B.

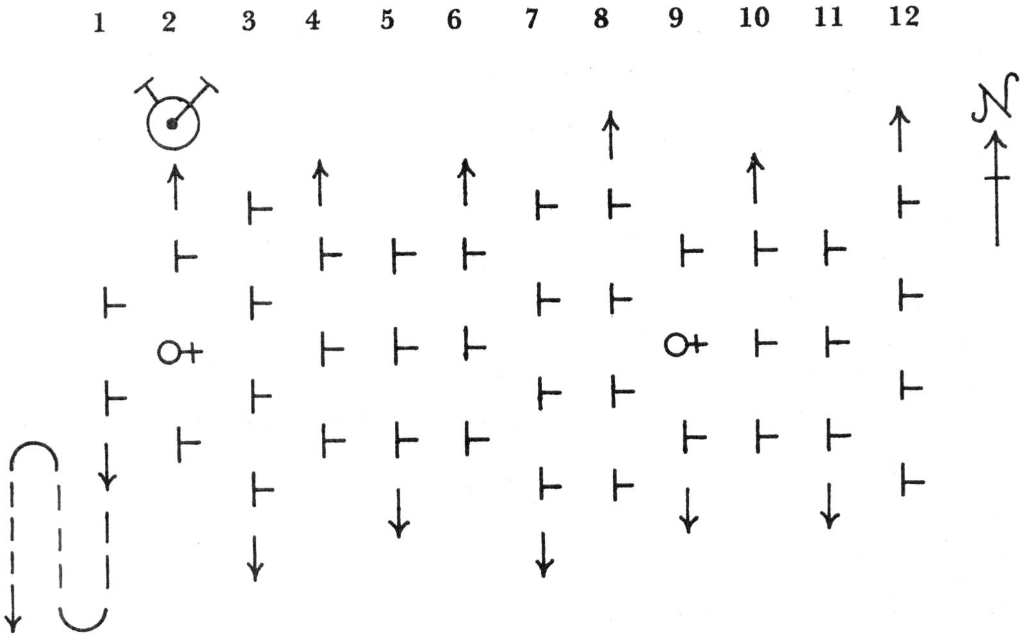

Antege, literally "footlifting step," is performed in conjunction with a wasa, or separately, depending on the particular circuit. The dancers line up shoulder-to-shoulder facing north. By this time each of the two female dancers can be spotted as the fourth dancer from either end of the line. The singers-dancers are in the middle portion of the line while the drummers are immediately behind them, i.e., south of the line (Fig. 6). While all males dance in place throughout the antege, the females dance in different patterns.

After section A is sung and danced in line (Fig. 10 a.), the female dancers gradually step out to the front of the line and dance toward the center of the line; then they dance past each other toward opposite ends of the line, forming a zigzag pattern by stepping forward diagonally with their right feet touching the ground on accented beats (Figs. 2 and 10 b.). Usually the women change directions (90-degree angle) every three to four steps on the right foot while the left foot advances to close the step.

When each female dancer reaches an end of the line, she turns around counter-clockwise and checks to see if her counterpart has made an identical progression to the opposite end (Figs. 10 b-d and 12). Then they begin to zigzag toward the center of the line and past each other again. The zigzag pattern is repeated several times at the center of the line (Fig. 10 b-e). The number of repetitions depends on the length of the line of male dancers and the speed of the pair of female dancers while adjusting to the music. Towards the end of the antege the female dancers move back to their original positions to be in line with the males. At the closing of the antege section, each of the male dancers holds his spruce branch and gourd rattle together against his mouth, whispering the word *Twanini*, meaning "Long Life."

Antege I lasts approximately fourteen minutes. In the diagram of the choreography of antege (Fig. 10), a. shows the initial arrangement of the dancers, the drummer, and his assistant in the south plaza, after the first wasa. In parts b, c, d, and e, the two women dancers step out from the line and dance in zigzag pattern toward each other, passing each other, as described above. The empty spaces left in line by the women are filled by the male dancers on each end of the line as they move gradually toward the center. The reverse process takes place when the female dancers return to their places in line at the end of the antege. It should be noted that the steps of only one female dancer are shown here. The other dancer would be doing the exact opposite; thus, the two female dancers make symmetrical patterns in the choreography.

There is no rule as to how many times back and forth a pair of female dancers must make their zigzag patterns because the length of the male dancers' line may vary according to the number of eligible males participating each year, whereas the length of the music remains relatively unchanged. In this particular instance, the pattern of one female dancer corresponds to the musical sections in the manner indicated in Fig. 10.

As a gesture of thanksgiving, the families of the dancers throw gifts to the spectators during the antege each time the female dancers step out to perform zigzag patterns. The gifts include a variety of candies; household items such as aluminum foil, clothes pins, sponges, spoons, towels, paper towels, soap, scoops, paper plates; fruits, including bananas and oranges. Gift throwing is also customary during the Harvest Dance (*Tembishare*) and the Butterfly Dance (*Ti'ishare*) ceremonies.

Fig. 10. Choreography of Antege.

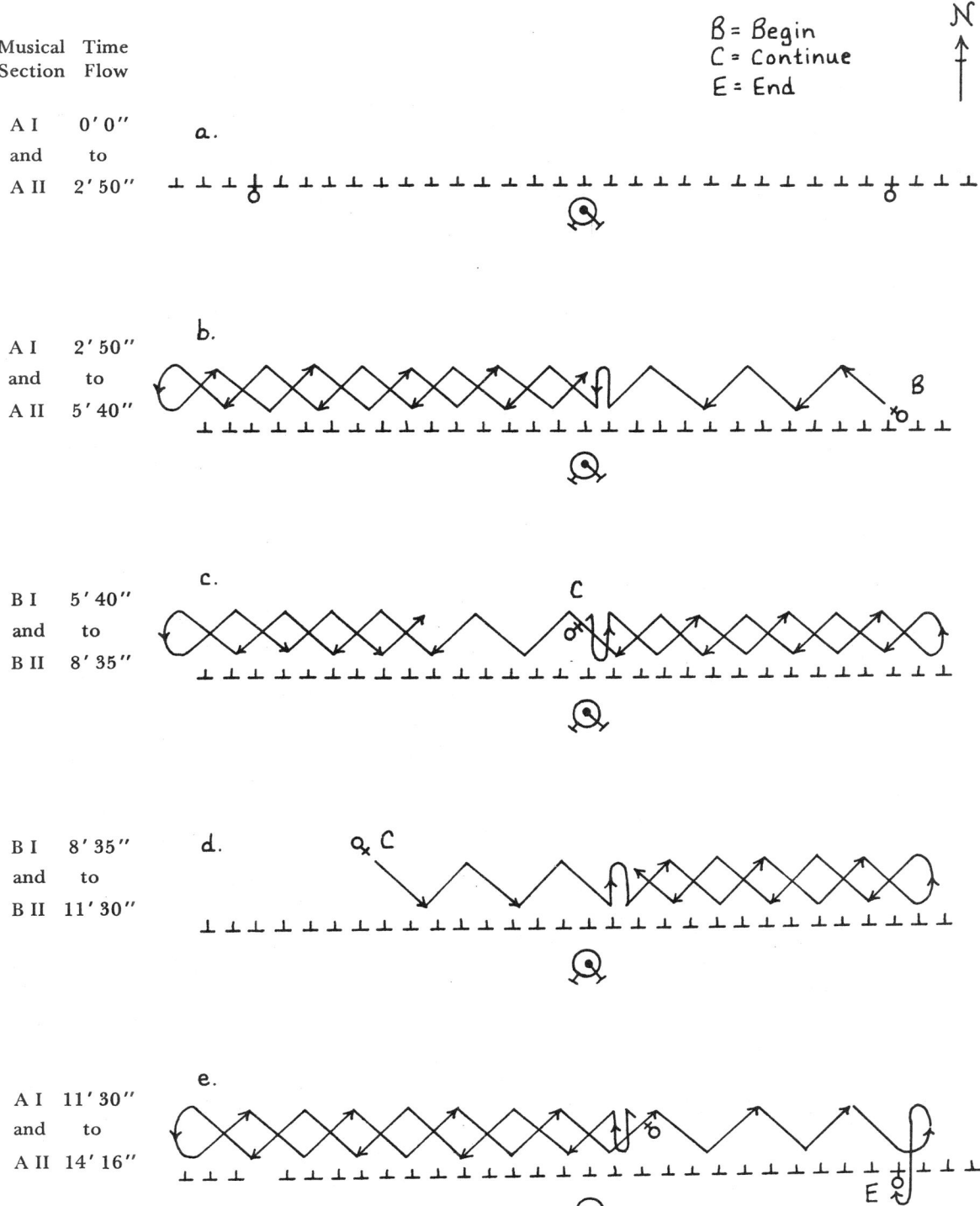

Fig. 12. One female dancer turns counter-clockwise at end of formation in antege.

Fig. 11. Dancers in Circuit Two.

The presentation is in recognition of the gifts Earth Mother has given to the community. At one time, the gifts actually thrown were agricultural products such as ears of corn, squashes, bread, and fruits.

Gifts are bestowed upon the female dancers when they dance back into line in all plazas during the antege. Money, blankets, and many gift-wrapped boxes are presented and piled in front of these female dancers, mostly by women. The gifts are removed while the dancing in that plaza concludes. Such gift distribution occurs throughout the ceremony. The spectators have twelve chances to catch gifts thrown among them while each female dancer has three opportunities to receive gifts at south, north, and east plazas consecutively.

Because it is a serious occasion, the dancers show respectful and sincere expression. While men look toward the distant directions to which they sing and pray, the women dance with downcast eyes and total concentration (Fig. 11). When the dance in one plaza is finished, the participants are led by an official and walk in single file to the next plaza. During these brief intermissions the dancers seem relaxed and enjoy small jokes, mitigating the solemn atmosphere. Vera Laski has commented on their inner feelings during such occasions:

> Most white people, most Christians, will find it difficult to understand the happy laughter in a religious ceremony, and even more, the great inner happiness in solemnity; both are easily misinterpreted. Once, while witnessing a Corn Dance in the Rio Grande Valley, I overheard a well-meaning white woman, who knew little about Indians, make the respectful remark: 'How serious these dancers look. None of them has a smile.' Later, a more sensitive observer with a much deeper feeling for the Pueblo Indian commented on the very same event, the same dancers, by saying: 'It was wonderful. Never have I seen the dancers so happy' (Laski 1958: 80).

According to Elsie Parsons (1929: 190), *pu't'ani* (a type of kachina or spirit) appeared and interfered with the women dancers during the Pogonshare ceremony of 1923. The present writer witnessed no such "interference" in 1977; it is probable that this practice is no longer carried out. In this respect, Pogonshare seems to fit into the second group of ceremonies which Laski describes: "Among the religious ceremonies of San Juan, we can distinguish between those in which the Kachina always appear, and others in which, at least nowadays, no Cloudbeings [*oxua povi*] participate. There is also a third group of ceremony in which the Kachina may or may not be present" (Laski 1958: 19). She adds that in the Deer Dance, "the Kachina used to appear, but they no longer come. It is evident that, in former times, the Kachina appeared more often than they do now, and at a much greater variety of ceremonies" (*ibid.*: 20).

Don Roberts points out that "... the Pueblo people do not divide their dances into categories other than sacred/secular or ours/not ours. By noting similar characteristics, Rio Grande dances can be grouped into six basic classifications: kachina dances, maskless kachina dances, animal dances, corn dances, borrowed dances, and social dances" (Roberts 1972: 251). The Pogonshare belongs to the category of maskless kachina dances. Roberts explains, furthermore:

Maskless kachina dances are so designated since, except for the absence of masks, their choreography and music closely resemble kachina ceremonies. Dances of this type usually feature a self-accompanying line of male dancers and are among the most beautiful of all eastern Pueblo dances. It is likely that these dramas were originally masked and that the Catholic priests forced the removal of the masks through charges of idolatry. Some informants state they dress as kachinas for these ceremonies except they 'don't put the head on' (*ibid.*).

With regard to the text as a determining factor in the musical structure of the Tewa, it is evident that the texts employ considerable use of symmetry and paraphrasing, for example, south and east versus north and west; men versus women; blue, yellow versus red, white, etc. As a result, paired melodic structure has been created to accommodate such couplets. There is a certain preconceived order and accompanying host of words in the song text. For instance, in a paired phrase or period, "male" or "man" must be mentioned in the antecedent; "female" or "woman" in the consequent phrase. Other qualifications on textual contents are: 1. The fundamental vocabulary of the text repertoire in every Pogonshare composition must include directions; colors; forms of water; men and women or boys and girls; movements, such as singing, dancing; and crops, plants, animals, and spirits.   2. There should be a distinction between the Tewa in song and conversational Tewa. "Cloud" in daily Tewa is *oxua*, for example, but in ritual context it is *oxua povi*, literally "cloud flower." 3. "Hummingbird" may appear only in the text of the *hapembe* ("middle section") of the Pogonshare — as "yellow birds" is treated in the Basket Dance and "parrots" in the Turtle Dance.

The Music of Pogonshare.

Music to the Tewa is a means of communication intended to regulate and harmonize cosmological relationships. Singing, largely in unison on ceremonial occasions, is similar in function to that of other American Indian tribes: it expresses power. In the description of another ritual context, Laski writes, "Although all these songs are different, one from another, they sing them at the same time and swing their rattles, and these many different songs make it become very powerful" (Laski 1958: 101-2).

To my knowledge, the only written information on the music of Pogonshare consists of a brief summary by Antonio and Carlos Garcia (1968: 240) and one page of transcription in staff notation by Gertrude Kurath (1970: 164). In "A Comparison of Pueblo and Pima Musical Styles" (1936: 283-417) George Herzog discusses Pueblo music with regard to manner of singing (vocal technique), melody (tonality), rhythm and accompaniment, structure (form), and types, but without specific reference to Pogonshare.

The present analysis is based on a recording made by Cipriano Garcia at San Juan, New Mexico, on January 23, 1977 — a performance which I observed. Prior to undertaking the analysis I compared the Garcia recording with two commercially available recordings, and found these virtually identical with Garcia's in terms of format. The two recordings are *Pueblo Indian Songs from San Juan* (Canyon Records 6065) and *Cloud Dance Songs of the San Juan Pueblo* (Indian House Records 1102).

In the following paragraphs I will treat the entire musical format in the setting of the ceremony: the sections, subsections, and their smallest units, with a detailed examination of the horizontal as well as the vertical segments of the musical texture of the vocal style and the relationship between these segments.

In the sectional structure of music and dance noted in Fig. 13, one can observe that the musical structure of each formation at a given time (one entire wasa or one entire antege portion at one of the plazas) consists of five portions or parts in which each part is repeated once: A A B B A. These five parts are similar to the numerical symbolism of the Tewa four (see Ortiz 1969: 139, no. 2) because five is *four plus one*, and the last *one* is intended to round out or complete the processes of a ritual section or step. The author was informed by Cipriano Garcia that in every performance, whether presented in context or outside of the environment (i.e., in a strange city, a foreign country, at a studio, etc.), the final A section must be finished inside the kiva upon returning to the village. Furthermore, it is held that when necessary, the second A and the second B may be eliminated — as is the case on both commercial recordings cited above, as well as in demonstration sessions — but never the third and final A. Such particularized sectionalization is a tradition which is also followed in other ceremonial performances among the Tewa, including the Butterfly and Turtle Dances.

As indicated in Fig. 13, each portion (A, B, and A) is subdivided into two sections (A I, A II, B I, B II), of which the second sections are identical (B II = A II). Tables 1 and 2 show the organization of phrases within an A B A section format in the 1977 Pogonshare.

Generally the music begins with low pitches in a melodic introduction. A middle and higher range of pitches follows. After these are expressed, the undulating contours descend to one of the low notes heard at the beginning of the melodic introduction. The most important pitch of the scale is the tonic, defined as an F sharp below low C in this particular example.

From Tables 1 and 2 it is evident that usually there are fewer notes in the scale of wasa than in that of antege. In the present transcription there are nine notes in the former and eleven in the latter. The ranges of both wasa and antege are the same: an octave plus a minor sixth. The most frequently used notes are within one octave, f sharp to F sharp. The interval of a minor third occurs most frequently. It is followed by major third, major second, perfect fourth, perfect fifth, minor second, diminished fourth, and major sixth. Since half steps as well as diminished fourths are found, the scale is not as anhemitonic as many people believe it to be in North American Indian music. On a deeper level, each scale is extremely individualistic, depending on the particular piece and specific section.

More than sixty percent of the melodic progression is downward. Phrases begin on one of the high notes and descend to one of the two lowest notes. If and when an upward step or skip is sung, it is apt to return to the note sung previously. Because the singing is to be heard by all participants of the ceremony, as well as the

Fig. 13. Musical Organization of Pogonshare.[6]

WASA:

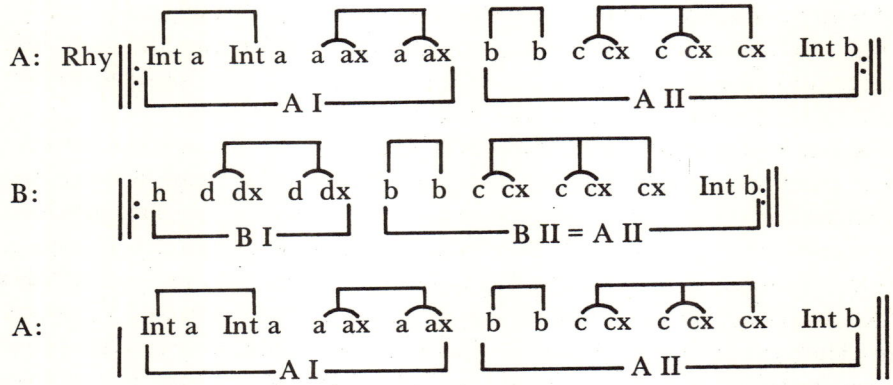

ANTEGE:

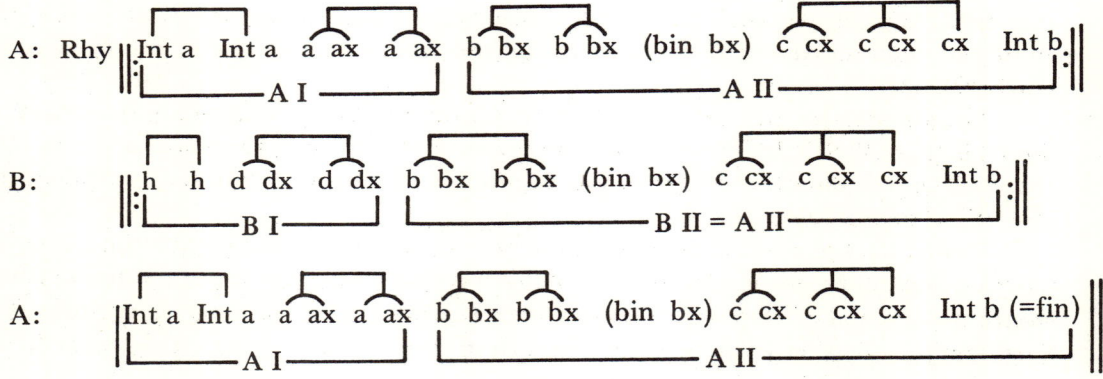

Musical Sections in Ritual Order:

Circuit One: (I wasa → I antege) X 3 + 1 shortened antege.

Circuit Two: II antege X 3 + 1 shortened antege.

Circuit Three: III antege X 3 + 1 shortened antege.

Circuit Four: (II wasa — IV antege) X 3 + shortened antege.

[6] Please see Key to Tables 1 and 2 (p. 124), "Units," for an explanation of the following letters.

spectators and the spirits in distant places, the dynamic level is quite loud. The higher the pitches, the louder they seem; consequently, the lower notes, being so soft, often seem inaudible.

Under "Materials" in Tables 1 and 2, one will note that the new materials are Rhy, Int a, a, ax, b, c, cs, Int b, h, d, and dx in wasa; Rhy, Int a, a, ax, b, bs, bin, c, cx, Int b, h, d, and dx in antege. With regard to "Duration," these new materials last altogether 84 seconds in wasa and 144 seconds in antege, including accelerando phrases in the case of paired phrase structure. The compact sources are expanded and stretched through the techniques of repeating, returning, reiterating, and reorganizing into a tightly constructed musical body. These techniques may be observed in many other Tewa ceremonies; they are utilized not only for a particular year by an individual composer-singer but also for many years to come by generation after generation of musicians among the Tewa.

The text is rhythmic without being mechanically regulated into a certain metric mode. The significance of the text is underscored by the fact that a phrase is partially repeated for a third time in order to accommodate text (phrase 15 of antege). Textual treatment is generally syllabic, but the portions with vocables tend to be melismatic. For instance, unit c of wasa is mainly syllabic while cx is melismatic and ends with a terminal note which lasts four beats. There are two outstanding characteristics in the Tewa vocal style: first, heavy pulsations in the lower tessitura; second, notable accents at the beginning of phrases, especially in the initiation of the non-lexical portions.

The rhythmic structure is basically simple, consisting of alternate strong and weak beats. But due to some metric changes, it is more complex than one might assume. It is heterometric, with three types of meter. These types are identical to those of the drum patterns discussed earlier.

The length of a phrase which is repeated to achieve paired phrase structure is extremely irregular. For example, with reference to "Counts" and "Duration" in Table 1, it should be noted that while phrases 4 and 5 each contain 24 beats (22 duple and 2 triple), phrases 6 and 7 each contain only 15 beats (9 duple and 6 triple). In other words, while the paired phrases are symmetric by comparison, the lengths of two or more pairs are asymmetric.

The tempo in wasa is steady throughout the entire section (74 mm), except for the concluding phrases of each section (phrases 11, 20, 29, and 30). In antege, the tempo varies more frequently:
1. 30 mm in the rhythmic and melodic introduction of A;
2. accelerando from 30 mm to 88 mm and its establishment in the second half of A;
3. maintenance of 88 mm in A section;
4. a sudden drop to 35 mm in the melodic interlude (int b);
5. accelerando from 35 mm to 88 mm and its establishment in the second half of B, similar to 2 above;
6. maintenance of 88 mm in B section, like that of 3 above;
7. exact recurrence of steps 1, 2, and 3 of the above;
8. conclusion in 35 mm, another int b.

Thus, the building up of tension through tempo happens five times in a full version of A A B B A structure in one antege.

Climax is achieved by reaching the highest note in the course of one period. Sometimes this highest pitch is touched upon only slightly, as in wasa phrases 6 and 7; or it can be repeated or held for a few beats, as in antege phrases 6 and 7. These occur in the beginning of A II sections. In addition to pitch level, the rhythmic density, i.e., the shortening of duration in the A II sections of antege helps to build up the intensity. Triple meter occurs most frequently in A II and B II sections but not exclusively so, as in the case of wasa phrases 4 and 5.

Shift of pitch level takes place in the antege: F sharp in A I section; F natural in phrases 6, 7, 8 in A II; and back to F sharp in 9, 10, and the rest of the section. This practice seems to be common. Frances Densmore noted a similar occurrence among the Santo Domingo Pueblos (Densmore 1938: 182-83).

In every wasa or antege a rhythmic introduction initiates the performance. This is followed by a pair of melodic, introductory phrases which serve as identification markers. These precede the main body of paired phrase materials, whose numbers correspond with the paired textual structure.

Sections	No. of Pairs	Phrase
A I	2:	[2, 3]
		[4, 5]
A II	2:	[6, 7]
		[8, 9]
B I	1:	[13, 14]
B II	2:	[15, 16]
		[17, 18]

A number of phrase tails (indicated by bin, bx, cx, for example, under "Units" in Tables 1 and 2) and interludes (int b) also serve as coda towards the end. The texts of these tails, interludes, and codas are vocables (see "Motifs").

Most melodic phrases begin with accented beats. When the voice enters on an off-beat, however, the accent shifts from strong beat to weak beat so that a "syncopation" effect is felt. When paired melodic phrases occur, their equivalent in the double structure of the text also occurs. But if part of a paired phrase melody is sung again, the text no longer recurs; rather, an entirely different set of textual material is sung (e.g., bin of antege). Each phrase of the pair can be further divided into motifs; a phrase may consist of one to five motifs. Every motif is separated by a breath or a short rest (𝄾), indicated by a solid barline in the transcription. Every motif has a different number of beats and syllables. At these variable junctures, the composers have freedom in their work. Any unit which is larger than these motifs is essentially prescribed and inherited from an established musical model.

It is doubtful whether musical terms such as major and minor mode might be applied to this musical style because, on examination, we find that different sections have different pitch selections, and the number of tones selected in these sections varies drastically (see Tables 1 and 2, "Scale"). Moreover, while the ranges of these sections may be the same, the tones sung may not necessarily be identical (*cf.* "Scale" and "Contour").

To summarize, the writer has endeavored to examine the meaning and purpose of Pogonshare to the Tewa, its musical structure within a larger cultural framework, and its significance as a musical entity. The following characteristics have been determined:

1. The Pogonshare ceremony begins and ends with circuits consisting of wasa and antege.
2. Every wasa and antege opens with an introductory phrase which can only belong to Pogonshare, i.e., a Tewa musical expert can immediately identify this particular dance by listening to the initial phrase. He can further identify which year's version it is and to which of the four circuits of that version an excerpt belongs by listening to the first melodic period.
3. As the music of the antege proceeds, the tempo begins to accelerate noticeably until the end of the section. Then it suddenly drops back almost to the original tempo before picking up again (see Tables 1 and 2, "Tempo"). Compared with other San Juan dances, Pogonshare is medium in tempo; it is slower than the Butterfly Dance but faster than the Turtle Dance.
4. The textual context of Pogonshare is distinct in meaning from other Tewa ceremonies.
5. The Tewa musician composes according to a set of predetermined rules. This hereditary, basic pattern consists of introductory beats; tempo setter and identifying code, paired phrases with parallel text being found throughout the main body of the composition. Interludes or bridge phrases and ending coda in specific vocables complete the composition.
6. Different from the Okushare and the Tunshare, several conscious and intentional "accelerandi" as well as predictable changes of "tessitura" may be perceived with each antege of the Pogonshare.

Key to Tables 1 and 2:

Counts:	22+2	22 duple counts, 2 triplets
Units:	Rhy	rhythmic introduction
	Int a, Int b	melodic introduction or interlude
	ax, bx, cs, dx	unchanging portions with vocables
	h	hapimbe
	bin	portion of b material
	fin	end
Motifs:	v	vocables, non-lexical syllables
	s	meaningful text
Intervals:	<u>4</u> 4th	4 intervals of perfect fourths
	<u>11</u> m3	11 intervals of minor thirds
	<u>6</u> M3	6 intervals of major thirds
	<u>2</u> 1/2	2 half steps
	<u>4</u> D4	4 intervals of diminished fourths
Up:	3	The melody ascends three times.
Down:	14	The melody descends fourteen times.
Duration:	2	The phrase lasts for two seconds.
Scale and Contour:		only the notes and the contour of the <u>new</u> material are provided.

Table 1: Analysis of Wasa I.

Section	Phrases	Counts	Units	Motifs	Range	Intervals	Up	Down	Meter	Duration	Dynamics	Materials	Scale	Contour
A I	1	2	Rhy	no singing	—	—	—	—	74 mm	2	mf	new		
	⌈2	13	Int a	2v	m6	4 4th	3	3		11		new		
	⌊3	13	Int a	2v	m6	4 4th	3	3		11		old		
	⌈4	22+2	a ax	11s+4s+10s+4v	8va	11 m3, 6 M3, 4 4th, 2 5th, 2 1/2	6	14		20		new		
	⌊5	22+2	a ax	11s+4s+10s+4v	8va	11 m3, 6 M3, 4 4th, 2 5th, 2 1/2	6	14		20		old		
II	⌈6	9+6	b	13s+14s	8va	8 M2, 3 4th, 1 m3	6	6		14		new		
	⌊7	9+6	b	13s+14s	8va	8 M2, 3 4th, 1 m3	6	6		14		old		
	⌈8	17+2	c cx	12s+3v	8va	5 M3, 3 M2, 2 m3	3	9		15		new		
	⌊9	16+2	c cx	12s+3v	8va	5 M3, 3 M2, 2 m3	3	10		15		old		
	10	6	c cx	4v	m3	3 m3	0	3		7		old		
	11	7	Int b	3v	m3	3 m3	1	2	40 mm	4		new		
B I	12	2	h	3s	m3	1 m3	0	1	74 mm	2		new		
	⌈13	23	d dx	7s+7s+9s+1v	m10	10 m3, 9 M2, 2 4th	8	14		18		new		
	⌊14	23	d dx	7s+7s+9s+1v	m10	10 m3, 9 M2, 2 4th	7	13		18		old		
II	⌈15=6	9+6	b	13s+14s	8va	8 M2, 3 4th, 1 m3	5	5		14		old		
	⌊16=7	9+6	b	13s+14s	8va	8 M2, 3 4th, 1 m3	5	5		14		old		
	⌈17=8	17+2	c cx	12s+3v	8va	5 M3, 3 M2, 2 m3, 1 4th, 1 5th	3	9		15		old		
	⌊18=9	17+2	c cx	12s+3v	8va	5 M3, 3 M2, 2 m3, 1 4th, 1 5th	3	9		15		old		
	19=10	6	c cx	4v	m3	3 m3	0	4		7		old		
	20=11	7	Int b	3v	m3	3 m3	1	2	40 mm	4		old		
A I	⌈21=2	13	Int a	2v	m6	4 4th	3	3	74 mm	11		old		
	⌊22=3	13	Int a	2v	m6	4 4th	3	3		11		old		
	⌈23=4	22+2	a ax	11s+4s+10s+4v	8va	11 m3, 6 M3, 4 4th, 2 5th, 2 1/2	6	14		20		old		
	⌊24=5	22+2	a ax	11s+5s+10s+4v	8va	11 m3, 6 M3, 4 4th, 2 5th, 2 1/2	6	14		20		old		
II	⌈25=6	9+6	b	13s+14s	8va	8 M2, 3 4th, 1 m3	6	6		14		old		
	⌊26=7	9+6	b	13s+14s	8va	8 M2, 3 4th, 1 m3	6	6		14		old		
	⌈27=8	17+2	c cx	12s+3v	8va	5 M3, 3 M2, 2 m3, 1 4th, 1 5th	3	9		15		old		
	⌊28=9	17+2	c cx	12s+3v	8va	5 M3, 3 M2, 2 m3, 1 4th, 1 5th	3	9		15		old		
	29=10	6	c cx	4v	m3	1 m3	0	3	40 mm	7		old		
	30	3	fin	1v	m3	1 m3	0	1		3		old		

Table 2: Analysis of Antege I.

Section	Phrases	Counts	Units	Motifs	Range	Intervals	Up	Down	Meter	Duration	Dynamics	Materials	Scale	Contour
A I	1	3	Rhy	no singing	—	—	—	—	30 mm	2	mf	new		
	⌈2	4	Int a	2v	m3	3 m3	1	2	30	9		new		
	⌊3	4	Int a	2v	m3	3 m3	1	2	30	9		old		
	⌈4	32	a ax	11s+6s+9s+5v	8va	22 m3, 6 M3, 2 4th, 2 8va	12	20	30–84	34	f	new		
	⌊5	32	a ax	11s+6s+9s+5v	8va	22 m3, 6 M3, 2 4th, 2 8va	10	18	84	23		old		
II	⌈6	31	b bx	7s+10s+6s+4s+6v	8va	8 1/2, 7 M3, 6 m3, 5 M2, 2 M6, 1 4th	9	19	84–88	19		new		
	⌊7	31	b bx	7s+10s+6s+4s+6v	8va	8 1/2, 7 M3, 6 m3, 5 M2, 2 M6, 1 4th	9	19	88	21		old		
	8	15	bin bx	17s+6v	8va	4 1/2, 4 m3, 3 M3, 2 M2, 1 4th	5	9	88	10		old		
	⌈9	13+6	c	14v+2v	m10	7 m3, 4 M3, 4 D4, 4 1/2, 3 5th, 2 4th, 1 M2	11	13	88	16		new		
	⌊10	13+6	c	14v+2v	m10	7 m3, 4 M3, 4 D4, 4 1/2, 3 5th, 2 4th, 1 M2	11	13	88	14		old		
	11	11	cx	5v	5th	2 D4, 2 1/2, 1 m3, 1 M3	6	6	88	7		old		
	12	4	Int b	3v	m3	1 m3	0	1	35	6	mf	new		
B I	⌈13	4	h	6s	m3	3 m3	1	2	35	9		new		
	⌊14	4	h	6s	m3	3 m3	1	2	35	7		old		
	⌈15	38	d dx	10s+12s+9s+5v	8va	29 m3, 6 M3, 2 M2, 1 4th, 1 5th	14	23	35–84	38	f	new		
	⌊16	38	d dx	10s+12s+9s+5v	8va	29 m3, 6 M3, 2 M2, 1 4th, 1 5th	14	23	84	28		old		
II	⌈17=6	31	b bx	7s+10s+6s+4s+6v	8va	8 1/2, 7 M3, 6 m3, 5 M2, 2 M6, 1 4th	9	19	84–88	19		old		
	⌊18=7	31	b bx	7s+10s+6s+4s+6v	8va	8 1/2, 7 M3, 6 m3, 5 M2, 2 M6, 1 4th	9	19	88	21		old		
	19=8	15	bin bx	17s+6v	8va	4 1/2, 4 m3, 3 M3, 2 M2, 1 4th	5	9	88	21		old		
	⌈20=9	13+6	c	14v+2v	m10	7 m3, 4 M3, 4 D4, 4 1/2, 3 5th, 2 4th, 1 M2	11	13	88	16		old		
	⌊21=10	13+6	c	14v+2v	m10	7 m3, 4 M3, 4 D4, 4 1/2, 3 5th, 2 4th, 1 M2	11	13	88	14		old		
	⌈22=11	11	cx	5v	5th	2 D4, 2 1/2, 1 m3, 1 M3	6	6	88	7		old		
	⌊23=12	4	Int b	3v	m3	1 m3	0	1	35	6	mf	old		
A I	⌈24=2	4	Int a	2v	m3	3 m3	1	2	35	9		old		
	⌊25=3	4	Int a	2v	m3	3 m3	1	2	35	7		old		
	⌈26=4	32	a ax	11s+6s+9s+5v	8va	29 m3, 6 M3, 2 M2, 1 4th, 1 5th	12	20	35–84	34	f	old		
	⌊27=5	32	a ax	11s+6s+9s+5v	8va	29 m3, 6 M3, 2 M2, 1 4th, 1 5th	10	18	84	23		old		
II	⌈28=6	31	b bx	7s+10s+6s+4s+6v	8va	8 1/2, 7 M3, 6 m3, 5 M2, 2 M6, 1 4th	9	19	84–88	19		old		
	⌊29=7	31	b bx	7s+10s+6s+4s+6v	8va	8 1/2, 7 M3, 6 m3, 5 M2, 2 M6, 1 4th	9	19	88	21		old		
	30=8	15	bin bx	17s+6v	8va	4 1/2, 4 m3, 3 M3, 2 M2, 1 4th	5	9	88	10		old		
	⌈31=9	13+6	c	14v+2v	m10	7 m3, 4 M3, 4 D4, 4 1/2, 3 5th, 2 4th, 1 M2	11	13	88	16		old		
	⌊32=10	13+6	c	14v+2v	m10	7 m3, 4 M3, 4 D4, 4 1/2, 3 5th, 2 4th, 1 M2	11	13	88	14		old		
	33=11	11	cx	5v	5v	2 D4, 2 1/2, 1 m3, 1 M3	6	6	88	7		old		
	34=12	4	Int b	3v	m3	1 3m	0	1	35	6		old		

REFERENCES CITED

Billard, Jules B.
    1974   Editor. *The World of the American Indian*. Washington, D.C.: National Geographic Society.

Densmore, Frances
    1938   *Music of Santo Domingo Pueblo, New Mexico*. Southwest Museum Papers, No. 12. Pasadena, California.

Dozier, Edward P.
    1970   *The Pueblo Indians of North America*. New York: Holt, Rinehart & Winston, Inc.

Ford, Richard I.
    1972   "An Ecological Perspective on the Eastern Pueblos." In *New Perspectives on the Pueblos*. Edited by Alfonso Ortiz. Albuquerque: University of New Mexico Press.

Garcia, Antonio and Carlos Garcia
    1968   "Ritual Preludes to Tewa Indian Dances." *Ethnomusicology* 12, No. 2.

Garcia, Cipriano
    1977   Interview with Maria La Vigna. Recorded at San Juan Pueblo, 26 September 1977.

Herzog, George
    1936   "A Comparison of Pueblo and Pima Musical Styles." *The Journal of American Folklore*, Vol. 49, No. 194. Edited by Ruth Benedict. New York: American Folklore Society.

Heth, Charlotte
    1976   *Songs of Earth, Water, Fire and Sky: Music of the American Indian*. New World Records 246.

Isaacs, Tony
    1972   *Cloud Dance Songs of San Juan Pueblo*. Indian House Records 1102.

Kurath, Gertrude P.
    1970   *Music and Dance of the Tewa Pueblos*. Santa Fe: Museum of New Mexico Press.

Laski, Vera P.
    1958   *Seeking Life*. American Folklore Society Memoirs, Vol. 50.

La Vigna, Maria
    1976   "The Turtle Dance Songs of the San Juan Pueblo Indians." Manuscript read at the Annual Meeting, Society for Ethnomusicology. Philadelphia, 11 November.

Ortiz, Alfonso
    1969   *The Tewa World*. Chicago: University of Chicago Press.

Parsons, Elsie Clews
    1929   *The Social Organization of the Tewa of New Mexico*. American Anthropological Association Memoirs, No. 36.

Roberts, Don L.
    1972   "The Ethnomusicology of the Eastern Pueblo." In *New Perspectives on the Pueblos*. Edited by Alfonso Ortiz. Albuquerque: University of New Mexico Press.

126

WASA I

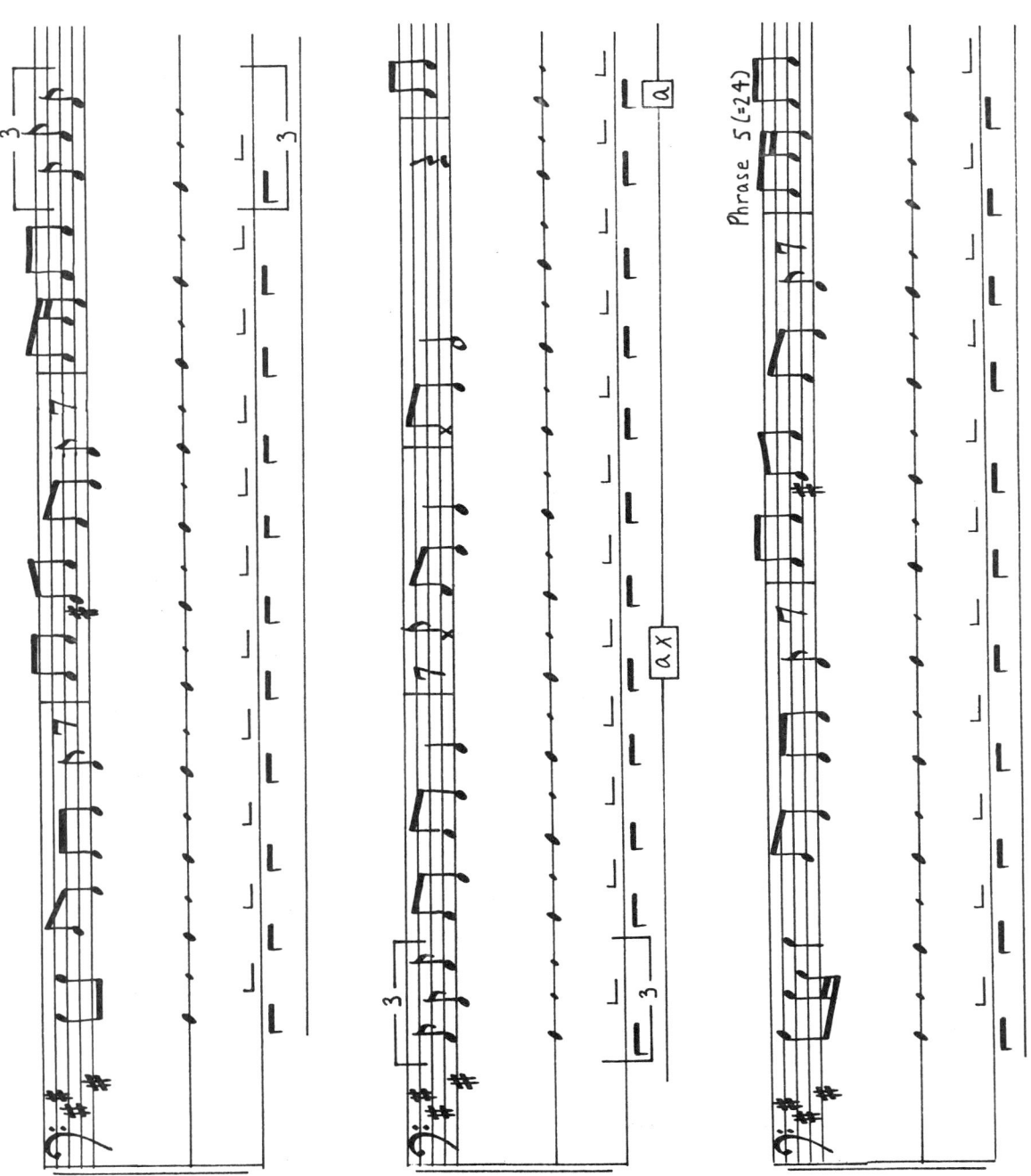

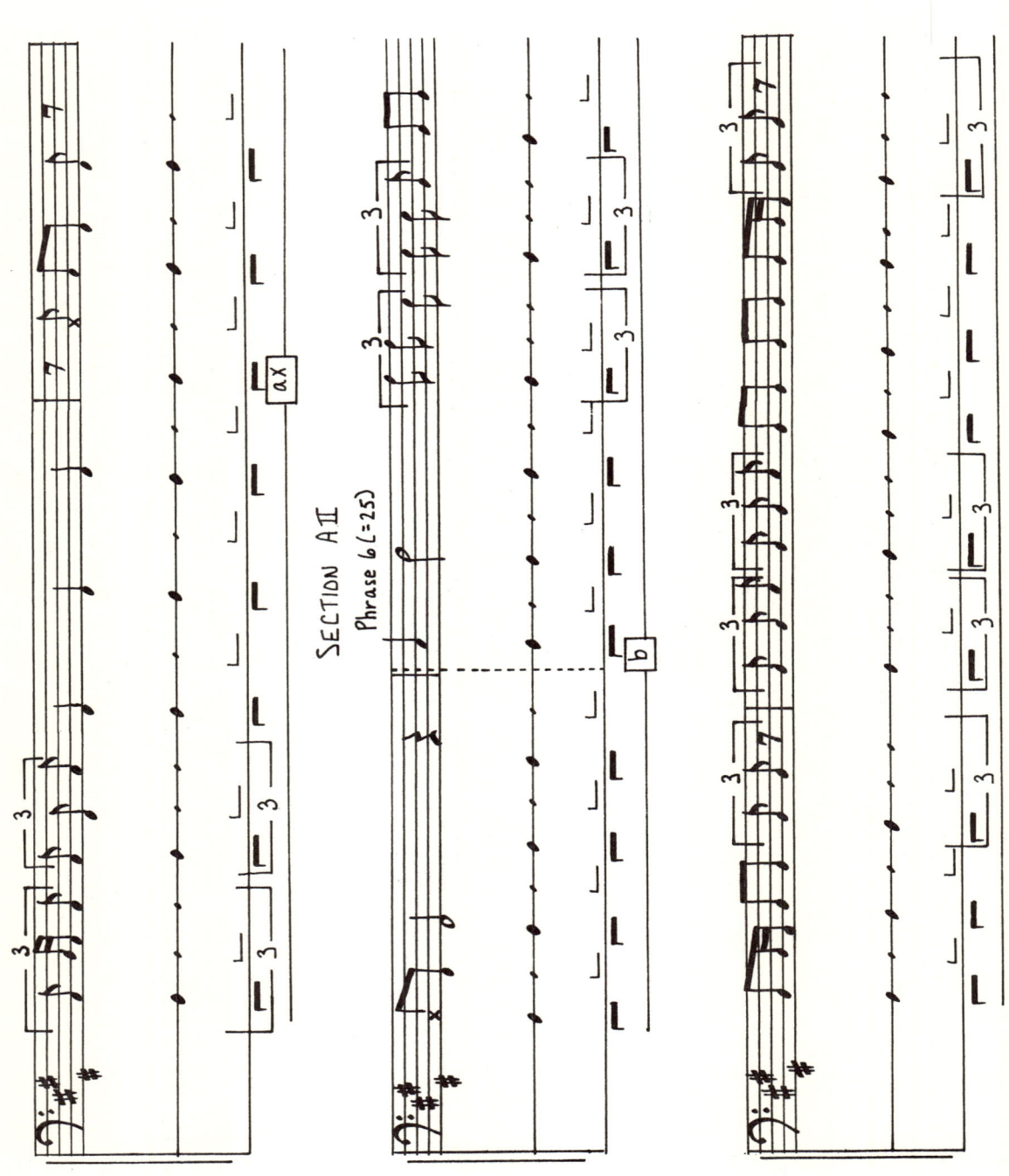

129

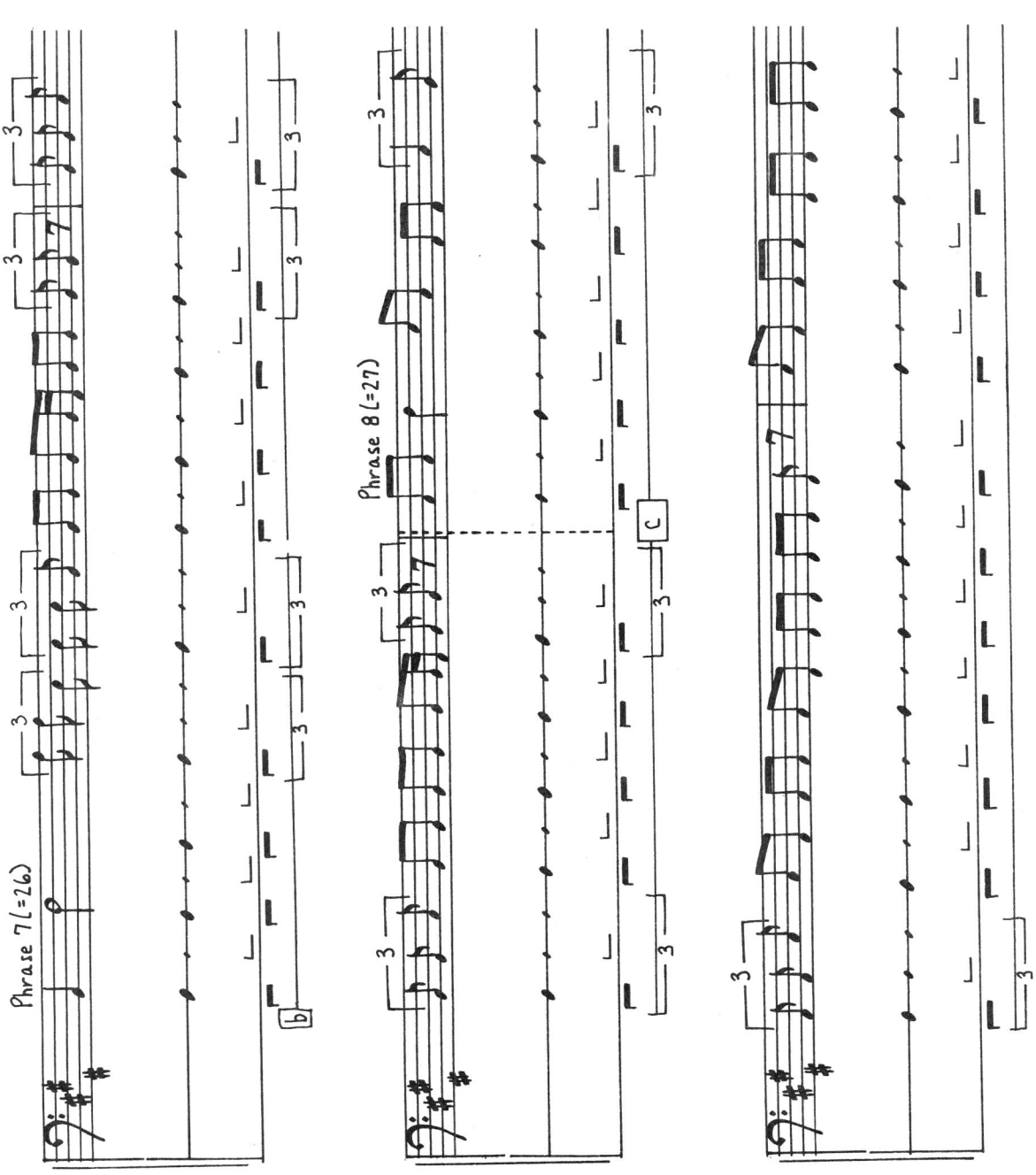

130

132

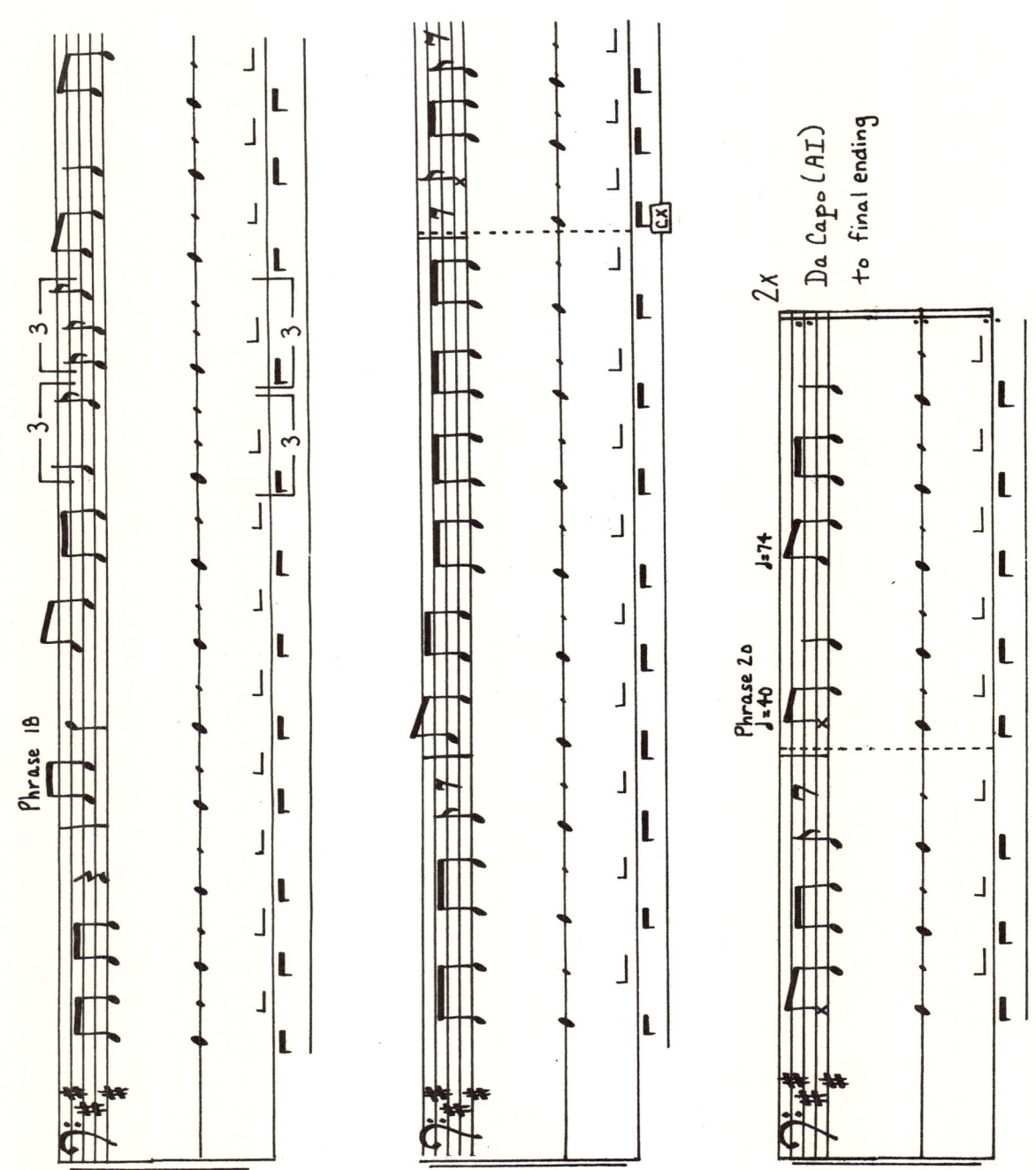

ANTEGE I

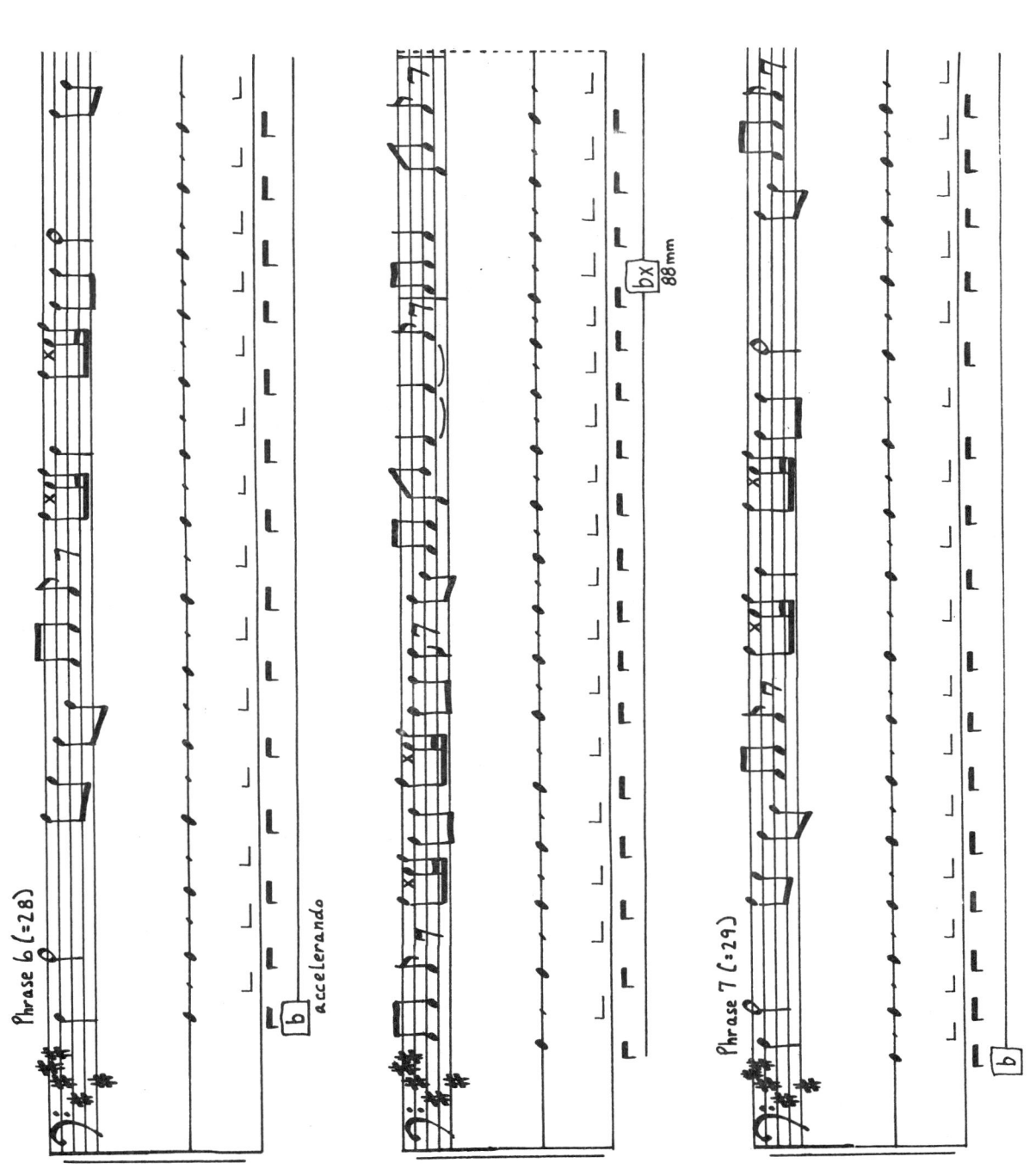

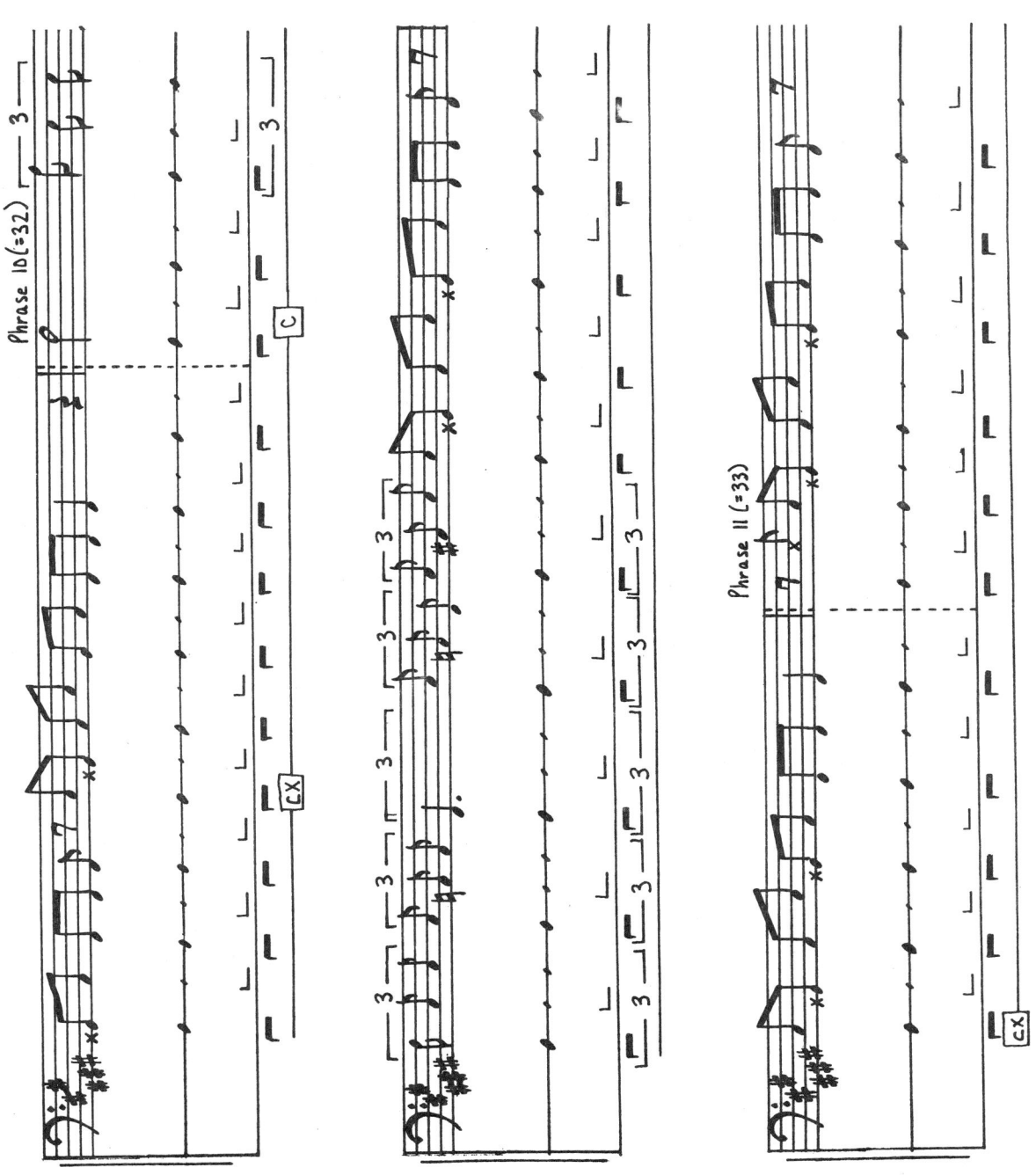

140

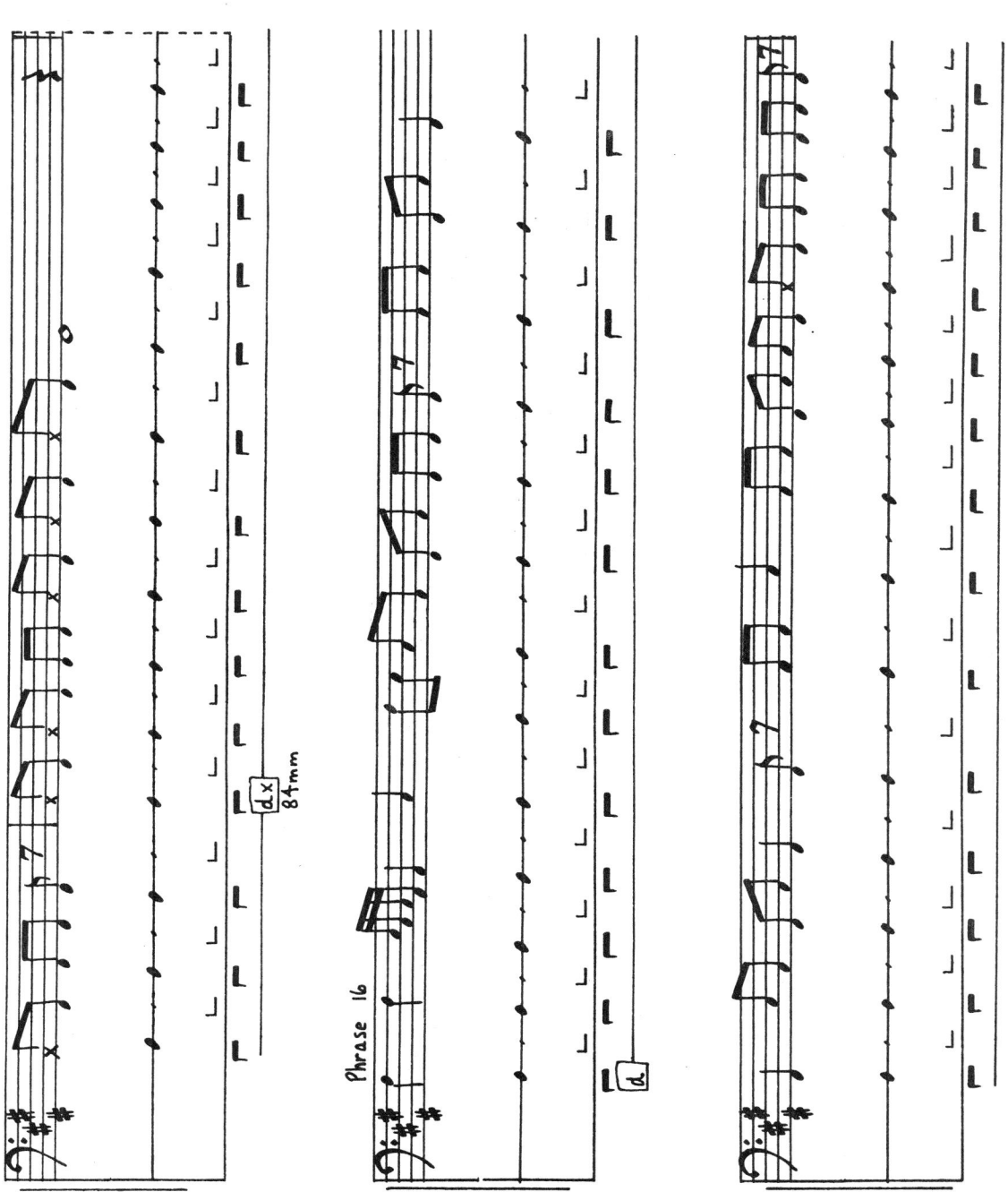

142

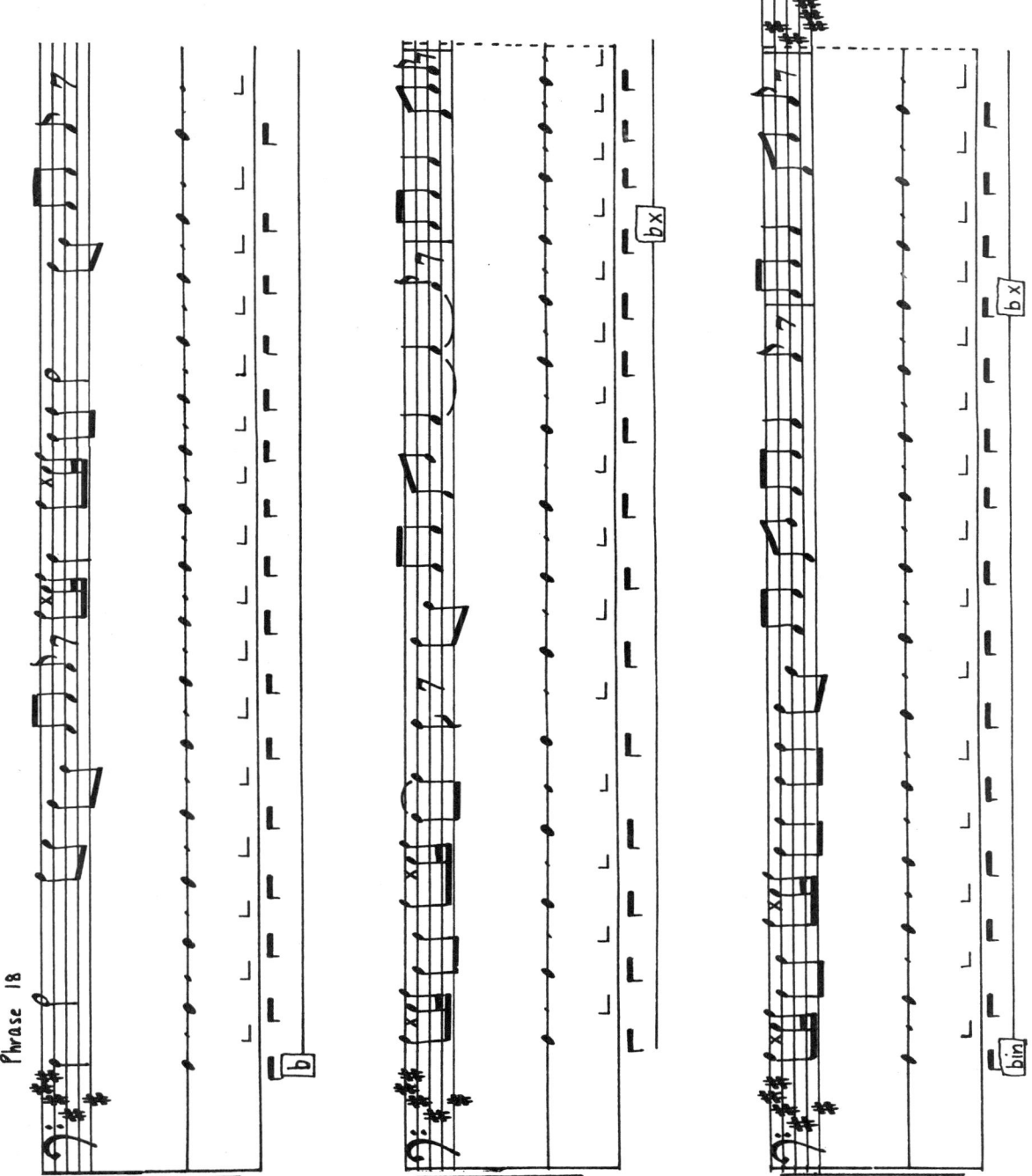

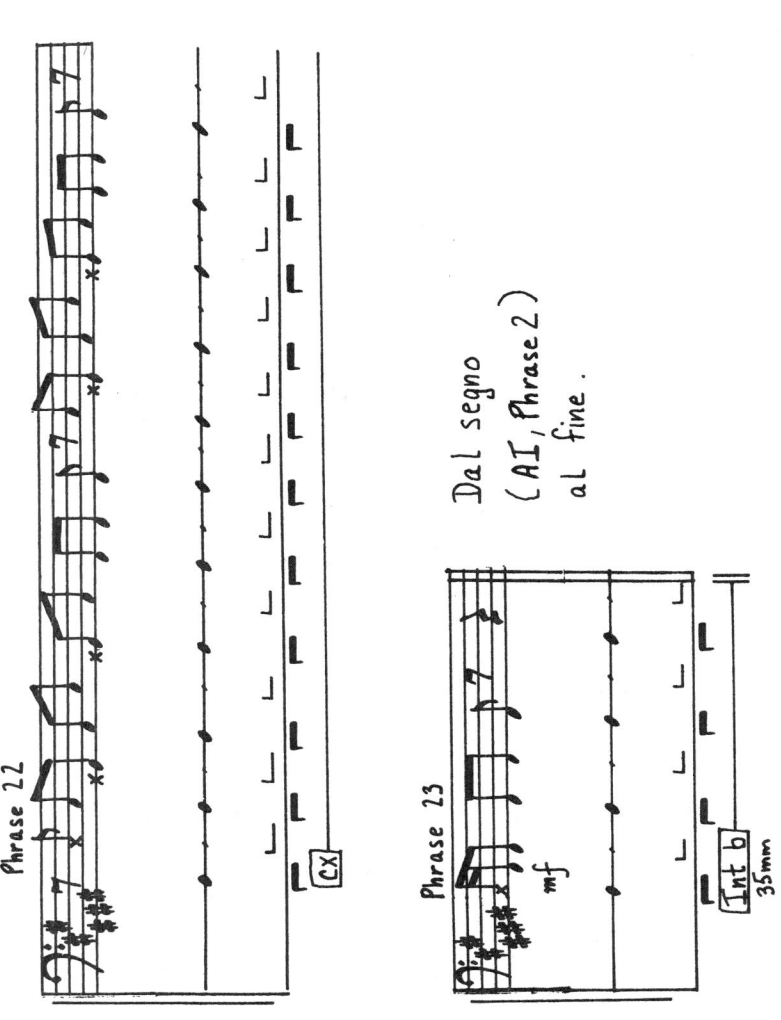

OCCASIONS FOR THE PERFORMANCE
OF
NATIVE CHOCTAW MUSIC[1]

David E. Draper

The recent revival of interest in American Indian music will undoubtedly expand our current knowledge concerning expressive behavior of Native Americans. Since music is still a viable part of the culture in many tribes, we may soon expect to learn a great deal more than is presently available about esthetics, ideology, and symbolic behavior, among other possibilities. With this expansion of existing knowledge, we may also expect a re-examination of research completed previously. Thus, we may indeed have an opportunity to improve the quality of the material currently available. This article will aid the latter category since the music of the Mississippi Choctaw has been studied, albeit superficially, in the past.

Approximately four thousand Choctaw still reside in Mississippi. About one thousand individuals remained in the original territory at the time of the 'Trail of Tears,' and it is from this group that the present population is descended. Choctaw speakers currently reside in seven communities in the vicinity of Philadelphia, Mississippi. Some individuals live on reservation land; others do not.

The changing economic pattern in Mississippi (and the South in general) over the last few decades has effected changes for the Choctaw. Particularly on an economic level, these people exhibit a high level of acculturation. Yet, in other spheres of their lives, they retain a distinctive Choctaw identity. Prominent in this retention of identity is the maintenance of native ideological, symbolic systems. Choctaw is still the first language of this population. Males are forced to learn English in order to compete economically. Older females, especially in conservative communities, refuse to speak English. Second, the institution of the native shaman still exists as a viable part of this culture. It is the shaman's role to verbalize aspects of the ideology for native speakers. The third factor is the retention of their presumably aboriginal musical system. As will be examined below, this repertory is highly symbolic and intimately linked with the ideological system of the Choctaw.

The degree of acculturation and/or assimilation for the Mississippi Choctaw remains a complex issue, and its discussion is beyond the scope of the present work. The seven communities form a continuum from the conservative or traditional to the acculturated. Christian missionaries entered Choctaw country in 1819, and the continuing presence of such individuals has been a critical factor in the degree of acculturation exhibited. For traditional, ethnographic descriptions, the reader is referred to the publications of Swanton (1911, 1931) and Bushnell (1909). A contemporary perspective may be found in Peterson (1970).

The Musical System.

At present the musical system of the Mississippi Choctaw includes both indigenous and acculturated musical forms. Although this article will focus on specific elements of the musical repertory from the pre-contact period, it seems advisable to provide an overview of all existing categories of musical performance. The reader can then place the subsequent discussion in a more accurate perspective for contemporary Choctaw society.

Native Choctaw Music.

The ethnographic literature on the Choctaw from the early post-contact years is not as complete as that available for some tribes. Thus, our knowledge of the ritual and ceremonial life is extremely limited. We do not know, for example, if the Choctaw had attained a "state religion," as reported for the neighboring Natchez tribe. If such a level of cultural complexity were achieved, complete with priests and associated characteristics, we have no understanding of how the institution of the native shaman would have interlocked with such communal ritual structures in aboriginal Choctaw life.

The only ritual of which we have retained some knowledge is the stick-ball game. The ideological, political, and economic functions of this occasion are, in large part, described in the ethnographic literature mentioned above. This paper will be concerned only with the associated musical repertory. The author was fortunate in obtaining a recording of one ball game song from a native shaman in 1969, shortly before the latter's death. Another piece, the "Hogalillie, ho!," reportedly sung by the players before the game, was recorded by an elderly song leader. Densmore (1943) includes two transcriptions of flute songs performed by the shaman that are no longer remembered. These examples comprise the extant knowledge of ball game music, which presumably was a rich repertory. As is illustrated by comparable examples cross-culturally, when the occasion for performance of music ceases to exist, the related musical repertory also disappears.

A repertory of native music referred to as *hitla tuluwa*,[2] "dance-songs," has survived to the present day. This music is performed outdoors, exclusively by groups of Choctaw speakers, and represents what does remain of the aboriginal ceremonial complex of the Mississippi Choctaw. Since these dance songs form the basis of the present paper, the occasions for their performance will be discussed in detail below.

Apart from the *hitla tuluwa* category, very few examples of native music have survived. The present writer has been fortunate in collecting several miscellaneous songs. The latter include a "lazy song," a lullaby, and a drinking song (based on the indigenous corn beer). A personal song sung by the ball game players before going to the ball field was recorded, although it is unclear whether or not this example should be considered as part of the 'ritual' category of native music.

Abba isht tuluwa.

Christian missionaries are reported to have entered Choctaw territory shortly after the turn of the nineteenth century. A repertory of Christian hymns, the *abba isht tuluwa* ("God songs"), emerged soon thereafter. Hymnbooks, containing only the texts of these hymns, were published as early as 1827, and continue to be printed and used in the Protestant Choctaw churches. The texts of one hundred sixty different hymns appear in the current edition of this hymnal. Thirty tunes, used interchangeably with the various texts, have been collected and transcribed. Two of these examples have identifiable models: "In the Sweet Bye and Bye" and "Amazing Grace." A recent, unpublished dissertation (Stevenson 1977) suggests that other examples may have pre-existent melodic models.

These hymns are similar in many respects to the *hitla tuluwa* repertory. Performances of the hymns traditionally have been led by a male song leader, following the practice exhibited in the aboriginal music. Melodic outlines are based on the whole-tone scale and are primarily pentatonic. There is no influence of harmony in the monophonic melodic outline that is sung unaccompanied. Females double the male vocal part an octave higher, as in the *hitla tuluwa* repertory. Texts are set exclusively in the Choctaw language, and those that have been translated suggest that the texts, at least, were original contributions of the Choctaw and the missionaries. These pieces continue to be performed in the Baptist and Methodist churches in the seven communities. Their popularity appears to be waning, but this may be a reflection of the non-Indian missionaries who currently reside there.

Oboha hitla.

The *oboha hitla*, "inside dances," currently represent the most popular of the acculturated musical forms. Since this repertory is classified in the *hitla*, or 'dance,' category, it is distinguished from the aboriginal dances by being designated as 'inside' songs, i.e., to be performed indoors, in contrast to the *hitla tuluwa*. They are performed at night on weekends, preferably Saturday evening, in the home of the Choctaw family sponsoring the dance. Since the fiddle and guitar players are reimbursed financially, they may be regarded as professional musicians.

This purely instrumental repertory for fiddle and guitar contains versions of the fiddle repertory that have diffused from Appalachia and other regions. Titles include "Sally Gooden," "Orange Blossom Special," "Old Joe Clark," to cite a few of the more familiar pieces. Although some pieces do not have specific titles, no research has been initiated on whether or not they are original compositions of Choctaw speakers. Most probably the titles of the borrowed songs have simply been forgotten.

Other Acculturated Musical Forms.

Radio and television have expanded the listening genres for the Choctaw. In the vicinity of Philadelphia, Mississippi, Country and Western musical styles predominate in public broadcasting programs. This influence is being felt by the Choctaw and is evidenced by the recent formation of similar, electrically amplified bands. Since 1969 there seems to have been at least one active band in existence, although the personnel has changed periodically. A few Choctaw occasionally do participate in the established White Country/Western ensembles that practice and perform in the area.

In the Protestant churches on the reservation, the denominational hymnals, the Broadman Hymnal, and the Methodist Hymnal, are now used extensively in the church services. Most often accompanied by piano or pump-organ, the melody of the hymn is sung monophonically. 'Hymn-Sings' are featured in the Protestant churches on Sunday afternoons when a fifth Sunday occurs in the course of a month. (For further discussion of musical acculturation, see Draper 1971; 1977.)

The *Hitla Tuluwa* Repertory.

The Mississippi Choctaw refer to the *hitla tuluwa* as 'social dances.' The term 'social' should be understood to mean 'communal,' as opposed to 'individual.' It would be inappropriate to convey the sense of secular in the Western European parlance to this repertory of music in this context. The Mississippi Choctaw do not divide reality into sacred/secular dichotomies, underscoring a philosophy that is reflected in other North American Indian tribes. It is proposed that these songs represent what remains of the ritual music of the Choctaw; existing evidence tends to support this thesis.

Animal dances figure prominently in this musical category. Field experiences have determined that animal symbols played a critical role in the aboriginal ideology, including ritual, curing, and cosmology. Further, the Choctaw drum is closely associated with these pieces. The drum is reported to have occupied a role of importance in critical ceremonial observances, including the stick-ball game. Statements made by older informants indicate that the drum was traditionally associated with shamanistic activities. As will be examined below, the drum serves the important function of maintaining continuity in the performances of dance songs. These selected examples support my thesis that the *hitla tuluwa* formed the core of the communal ceremonial repertory prior to contact. A growing literature on the subject suggests that ritual (or religious) music is highly retentive cross-culturally.

A large number of 'hitla tuluwa' songs are remembered by older singers. The performance of these pieces, however, no longer plays a major role in Choctaw life. Examples are performed for the public at the annual fair each summer. Occasions for performance of this music continue to exist in the more conservative Choctaw communities. Performances seem to be focussed around the homes of the respected singers and appear to be impromptu gatherings of individuals rather than planned events.

When field research on this music was initiated in 1969, only a few older individuals (native speakers) remembered and were able to perform the dance songs; the repertory was in danger of becoming extinct. During the last decade, the *hitla tuluwa* have been introduced into the curriculum of the Choctaw schools, at both elementary and secondary levels. Given the renewed interest in preserving Choctaw identity on the reservation, one may hope that this repertory will indeed survive.

Instruments.

The instruments used to accompany performance of the *hitla tuluwa* are striking sticks known as *etiboli*. Approximately half of the existing *hitla tuluwa* repertory employs this instrumental support. Striking sticks appear only with the song leader, who normally does not participate in the dancing. Undoubtedly, the primary reason that only one set of striking sticks has been observed is that the dance formations rarely free the hands for manipulating instruments.

Etiboli are usually constructed from hickory trees, which are reported to offer the 'ideal' sound. The length of the sticks varies, although the majority of examples were approximately eighteen inches long. For practice sessions or recording sessions held for the author, informants used whatever wooden materials were available.

Drums are intimately linked with the *hitla tuluwa* repertory, but they do not function in the role of accompaniment. The drum is played between songs within the song cycle. That is, the drummer begins to play at the termination of a piece and continues until the song leader initiates a new song. Only one rhythmic pattern is exhibited in this context: ♪♫♪♫ , etc.

The drum, *ha the pa chitto*, is preferably constructed from black gum wood, although cyprus, hard pine, poplar, and sweet gum may be used. Drum makers search for a tree trunk that is already hollow and scrape the interior to achieve the desired thickness, approximately one-fourth to one-half inch. The height of the drum depends on the diameter of the tree trunk and its thickness. Examples of drums that were measured were about ten inches high and twelve inches in diameter. The drum head, *aspumon*, is preferably goat skin, although sheep hides are also employed. The skin is attached to the drum by a hickory rim, approximately one-half inch in width. The two sticks used as beaters (*ishit boli*) are constructed from hickory.

In current public performances of the *hitla tuluwa*, the dancers wear small metal jingle bells that are purchased locally. A number of these bells are attached in a cluster through a belt loop on the left side of the body. It is unclear whether the jingle bells are a new addition or a substitution for an earlier, native idiophone. The bells appear to have been used within the time span covered by the memory of present informants; older informants do not recall any item preceding the bells. It is likely, however, that jingle bells offer a new representation of an older sound. Given the prominence of idiophonic instruments among other tribes in North America, including the Southeastern Culture area, one may assume that originally a similar sound was produced by natural instruments, for instance, turtle shell, horn, or hoof rattles. Since jingle bells are not used in the musical practice sessions, or in sessions arranged for recording purposes, it is questionable whether they are to be considered part of the musical system or regarded simply as an aspect of costuming.

Musical Occasions.

In the pre-contact period, performances of the *hitla tuluwa* appear to have been held only at night and to have continued until dawn. The frequency of these occasions is not reported in the early literature on the Choctaw. Today, these performances are led exclusively by male song leaders, referred to as *entuluwa*. Both males and females participate in the dancing group, and the performers may alternate throughout the evening. The only restrictions for participants concern some songs in which relatives, i.e., clan members, of the opposite sex, are not permitted to perform.

There remains a large repertory of songs in the *hitla tuluwa* category that presumably date from pre-contact times. The following list contains the titles of pieces recorded by the author:

Jump Dance	Turtle Dance
Walk Dance	Coon Dance
Changing Partners Dance	Bird Dance
Wedding Dance	Snake Dance
Drunk Dance	Turkey Dance
War Dance	Tick Dance
Muskogie Dance	Duck Dance
Falama (Backward and Forward)	Quail Dance
Stump Dance	Bear Dance
	Gnat Dance.

Certain titles, for example, "Jump Dance," "Walk Dance," "Drunk Dance," and "War Dance," serve as cover terms for a large number of specific pieces. To cite one example, fifteen different Walk Dances were collected. At present, each animal dance is represented only by one specific song. The pieces that are currently retained in the repertory basically consist of strophes. This form may indeed be a simplification or reduction of earlier versions of these pieces. The leader-chorus, or call and response, style is typical of this repertory. The female chorus part doubles the male vocal line at the octave, thus producing a monophonic texture.

The results of my research on the Choctaw *hitla tuluwa* have provided additional information about the structure of the musical occasion for the performance of this repertory, with several hypotheses concerning the nature of this musical event. I was fortunate in finding an elderly informant whose father, many decades ago, served as a song leader for the Bogue Chitto community. My informant asserts that the occasions for performing *hitla tuluwa* were always begun with the singing of a special song, the *amona tuluwa*. This informant remembered the song which was recorded subsequently; a second recording was made to validate the first, and proved to be successful. A transcription of the *amona tuluwa* can be found in the section on musical analysis.

In his monograph on the Choctaw of Bayou Lacomb, Bushnell states that this group has "one dance ceremony, which is in reality a series of seven distinct dances, performed in rotation and always in the same order" (Bushnell 1909: 20). This series is cited here, as follows:

1. *Nanena hitkla* (Man dance)
2. *Shatene hitkla* (Tick dance)
3. *Kwishco hitkla* (Drunken-man dance)

4. *Tinsanale hitkla*
5. *Fuchuse hitkla* (Duck dance)
6. *Hitkla Falama* (Dance Go-and-come)
7. *Siente hitkla* (Snake dance).

There is no *nanena*, or 'man,' dance currently remembered by Choctaw singers. The accompanying description of the dance movements in Bushnell's article corresponds with that of the current *tolobli hitla*, or Jump Dance.[3]

Given the large number of *hitla tuluwa* retained in this category, I propose that Bushnell's report is incorrect, stemming from either lack of knowledge on the part of his informants, or the limited time he spent with the Bayou Lacombe Choctaw. Present informants do assert that the *hitla tuluwa* are to be performed in cycles of seven songs. Consequently, since my initial field research on Choctaw music, I have attempted to determine the sequential ordering within the cycle. Older informants have provided conflicting reports. One characteristic feature of the listings obtained was the appearance of the Jump Dance, *tolobli hitla*, as the initial song; thereafter, the order invariably changed. I have therefore concluded that the Jump Dance was a marker, or an indicator of significance, signalling the beginning of the cycle. This is reinforced by its position as the initial dance in Bushnell's ordering.

There would appear to be additional evidence in support of this thesis. The Jump Dance is the only dance, aside from some versions of the War Dance, in which only men sing. The absence of the female part, then, would make the appearance of this song within the cycle a noteworthy occurrence. Exclusive of the Jump Dance, it is possible that the internal ordering of songs within the cycle was arbitrary and left to the discretion of the song leader. Densmore (1943) provides no additional information; she cites Bushnell's description, yet apparently makes no effort to expand the available information.[4]

Musical Analysis.

In the following section, both the *amona tuluwa* and the available versions of the Jump Dance will be discussed. This section is not intended to provide an exhaustive analysis; rather, what appear to be the salient, unique features will be examined.

Note that when the chorus part is not represented in the transcriptions, the associated vocables have been inserted in the leader's text and placed within parentheses, thus providing continuity between the discrete parts.

Amona Tuluwa.

This song differs from the other *hitla tuluwa* transcribed and analyzed in that there is no recurrent phrase pattern indicating a response from the singing group. One would therefore conclude that this opening song for the musical occasion was sung exclusively by the song leader, *entuluwa*. The term *amona* means "first," indicating that this piece precedes the performance of the song cycles.

One of the significant features of the *amona tuluwa* is the obvious formal division into sections. This is marked by the repeated expression "yo yo!," as illustrated in the accompanying transcription. This division, rarely found in other examples, is underscored by the complementary distribution of vocables. The phoneme /æ/, which is quite prominent in the initial section, does not appear in the second section.

The marker for the end of the piece, "we! ya!," is one of a limited number of ending patterns in this repertory. "Yo! yo!" never appears in the final position, thus forming complementary sets of markers for the *hitla tuluwa*. A unique feature of this piece is the tessitura of the vocal part. Covering an octave plus a fourth, it exhibits the widest range of any of the *hitla tuluwa* examples. The pitches of this piece reflect a minor modal outline, with G natural as the pitch center. There is heavy emphasis on this one tone, with some extended, sustained singing. In the second section, all phrases terminate on this pitch.

In the second section there is an obvious formal pattern. The phrases that appear in brackets are almost exact repetitions, whereas the phrases preceding such segments do not correspond to each other. These three subdivisions form a major portion of the second section. A concluding statement repeats some of the preceding phrases, yet without the requisite pattern.

Rhythmic patterns also serve to distinguish the two sections of this piece. The initial section is non-metrical; after the section markers, the song continues with a purely metrical pattern. The seemingly triple meter is interesting because the Choctaw cultural numbers are four and seven. However, this metrical pattern would distinguish the *amona tuluwa* from the predominantly duple meter of the dance songs.

Jump Dance I.

All dance songs are open-ended; they are repeated until terminated by the song leader. Thus, the ending signal occurs at the discretion of the song leader. In dances featuring a circle formation, the song is repeated until the dancers, usually a variable number of individuals, complete the circle. In the Jump Dances, circle formations do not occur, and therefore the length of the song is entirely dependent on the leader.[5]

The transcriptions appended to this paper were recorded out of context. I have taken the liberty of including the chorus part as it would appear in a performance context.

Jump Dance I contains repetition on two different levels. First, there is the obvious repetition of phrases, as if the leader were pairing the phrases in his part. That is, the immediate repetition of a phrase in the leader's part appears to be a model from which the piece is generated. Second, there is a repetition of sections, or the appearance of repetition, with some minor interpolated variations. These sections are indicated by brackets over the musical staff. The second bracketed section appears to be the model from which the other sections derive. Whether or not, in the past, the sections were to be repeated precisely is speculative. If indeed these songs were bound to a ritual context, one might expect a more rigid internal ordering of phrases.

The pitch system in the Jump Dances varies, if measured by scientific instruments sensitive to minute variations in frequency. This lack of stability may be attributable to the age of the leader, since he is an elderly singer. At present, information on the remainder of the repertory is insufficient to form pertinent conclusions.

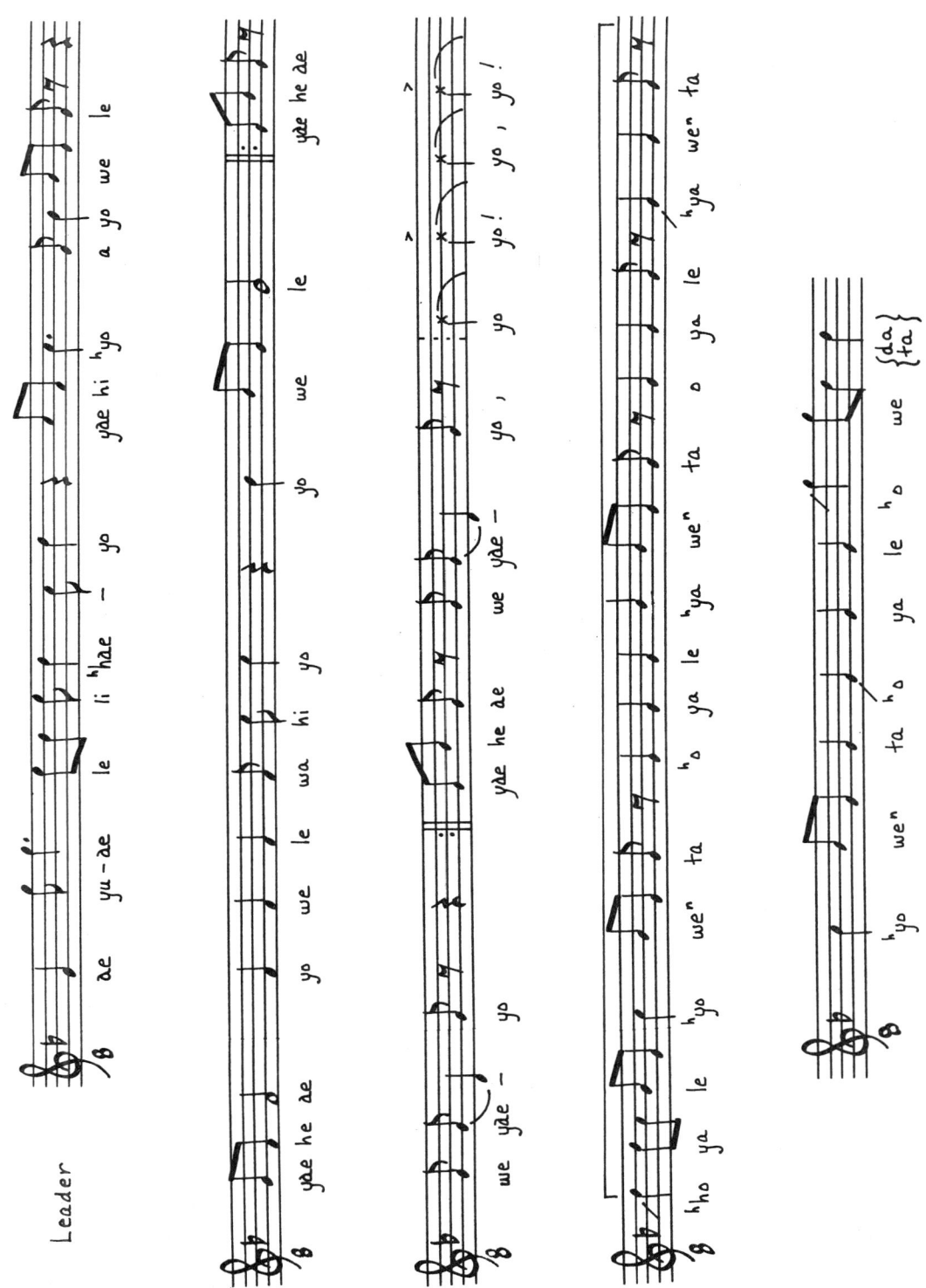

Amona Tuluwa.

Amona Tuluwa (continued):

The melodic outline is built around the minor triad (E-G-B), although Jump Dance I is not exclusively anhemitonic, as might be anticipated. The whole-tone pattern is broken only at the beginning of phrases sung by the leader, thus producing a more "ornamental" effect.

Musical phrases are defined by both an up-glide and aspiration. These I shall refer to as "markers" or "indicators of significance" on the level /phrase/. Both markers are found in the leader and chorus parts. The final marker on the level /piece/ is "ya ho! yo!," the most common in the category of Jump Dances and frequently observed in other pieces of the repertory.

This song is the only Jump Dance in which one rhythmic pattern is maintained throughout in both leader and chorus phrases. Examples I and V are the only Jump Dances that are metrical in the Western European sense.

The syllabic pattern of the vocables is significant because leader and chorus have four-syllable phrases:

yo   ha   le   na
we   hi   yo   we.

The vowel pattern is important in that the leader's part features mid and high vowels; the chorus response exhibits mid and low vowels. The contrast in vowel sounds is a notable organizing factor for this piece, and it may be found in other examples of the *hitla tuluwa*. The number *four* is an important cultural gestalt for the Choctaw, as well as for most other North American Indian tribes.

Jump Dance II.

On a formal level, this piece is organized by the appearance of one musical phrase that recurs throughout the leader's part. This phrase, noted in brackets over the musical staff in the accompanying transcription, serves as a type of refrain for the piece. Further, it appears as the opening and closing phrase sung by the leader. Internally, the appearance of this refrain phrase is characterized by its immediate repetition. The final statement is not repeated, which reflects a pattern observed in the first Jump Dance.

Related to this refrain pattern is the appearance of an intermediary phrase indicated by the letter "A" in the transcription. It is questionable whether or not this phrase is to be included as part of the refrain concept. Since the concept of paired phrases appears in other Jump Dances, this may indeed be the over-riding pattern in the present example. The problem is complicated by the repetition of these refrain phrases. What is troublesome is that without repetitions, the Refrain-A-Refrain pattern forms a total of three phrases, a number inconsistent with Choctaw ideology; the pattern formed with repetitions (Refrain-Refrain-A-Refrain-Refrain) would also be inconsistent with traditional Choctaw gestalts. Between appearances of these refrain phrases are variable numbers of additional phrases in the leader's part. Hence, there is no overall formal pattern that is consistent.

The response phrases of this example are distinctive for the Jump Dance. There is a change in melodic pitches, although the vocables remain unaltered. This new melodic outline appears after the fourth solo phrase in the transcription. The occurence of these changes is patterned: they appear immediately following the Refrain-

Jump Dance I.

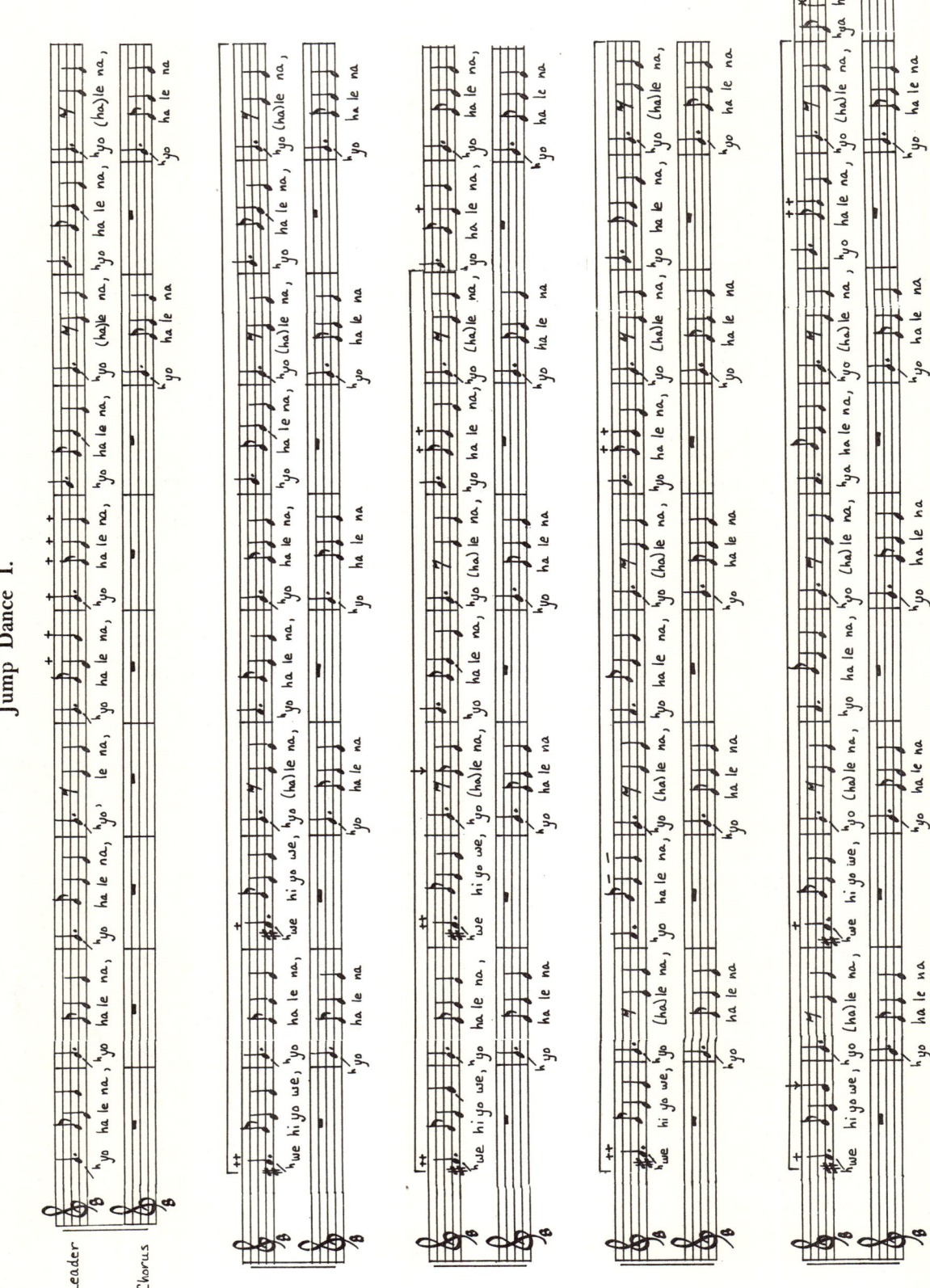

A-Refrain section. Yet the solo phrases immediately preceding the changes are not identical. Such change must ultimately be effected by listening to the leader.

The indicators of significance defining the phrase in the response part include aspiration on both the initial pitch/vocable and the final pitch/vocable. This pattern is retained in the solo phrases with few exceptions.

Textually, this dance song is reminiscent of the *amona tuluwa*, with the appearance of the phoneme /æ/ at the beginning of the piece. This phoneme occurs in the first three leader-chorus phrases and then it ceases to appear. Thus, in both pieces it serves as an introductory pattern.

The leader, especially in refrain phrases, appears to take the chorus response as a model, which he extends to twice its length and manipulates both melodically and rhythmically. It is interesting that the leader's phrases derive textually from the syllabic pattern of the chorus, for example:

> chorus: hi   ya ha
> leader: hi yo hi yo hi ya ha.

The melodic outline is anhemitonic, with G natural serving as the pitch center. This tone is prominent in the response. The solo phrases terminate either on G natural or a third below, E natural.

A certain rhythmic flow is achieved in the longer solo phrases by manipulating the rhythmic structure. The syncopation observed occurs only internally, within the phrase; rhythmic stability marks the beginning and ending of the phrase.

Jump Dance III.

The formal organization of the leader's part features a set of paired (repeated) phrases, which recur throughout the piece. These are the first two phrases of the leader in the accompanying transcription, with the following vocable pattern: "o he ya yo he." Statements of this "refrain" set are separated either by one or two differing phrases. These interpolated phrases follow two basic melodic outlines, yet none is identical in pitch outline or textual underlay. The most important feature of the interpolated phrases is the change in syllabic pattern. The refrain vocables "o he ya yo he" become "wa {he/hi} o yo we." Another interesting linguistic feature is the phoneme /æ/, which the leader sings in the first two chorus responses. Thereafter, the phoneme changes to /a/.

Both up-glides and aspiration serve as phrase markers for the response phrases. The solo phrases contrast with other examples in the category of Jump Dances in that aspiration and/or up-glides are not used as indicators at the beginning of the phrase. Since the leader invariably overlaps with the initial response pitch, the up-glide and aspiration which operate as beginning markers for the chorus also serve as final phrase markers for the leader's phrases. The ending pattern, "ya ho! yo!,' is the most frequently used signal for the repertory.

The pitch outline exhibits a whole tone system, with no additional tones. The pitch center and ending tone are F natural. In rhythmic structure, both the leader and chorus parts form a pattern of seven beats. The overlapping of phrases in the solo line produces an unbroken rhythmic flow.

Jump Dance II.

Jump Dance II (continued):

Jump Dance III (continued):

Jump Dance IV.

The form of this dance song is more highly organized than that observed in previous examples. There are only four differing phrases sung by the leader, and these four are used interchangeably. The solo part may be illustrated as follows:

$$A\ B\ A\ B\ \underbrace{C\ D\ B}\ \underbrace{C\ D\ B}\ \underbrace{A\ B\ B}\ C\ B$$

What is of interest is the apparent grouping of three phrases. Given the general pattern of repeating or pairing phrases in the repertory, the initial pattern, established with the AB AB phrases, may continue with a cognitive grouping of two phrases on the part of the singer. Unfortunately, we do not have a recording of this song made in context, the length of which might determine the form precisely. Informants are reluctant to verbalize about such matters.

The call-and-response pattern is not overlapping, as in previous examples. The lead singer breathes at the termination of his phrases, before joining with the choral response. These two adjacent phrases then become a discrete unit, producing distinct sub-sections within the piece. Both leader and chorus parts are of equal length, the equivalent of six beats in Western terms. This rhythm is broken by the leader's "C" phrases, which contain four beats and produce a heterometric pattern.

It seems that the phrase marker in this piece is the heavy aspiration indicating the beginning of a phrase. This occurs for both solo and response parts. However, this indicator of the phrase occurs twice in each of the parts. The heavily stressed pitch at the beginning of the vocable pattern "he ya" supports this view, and creates an additional phrase. The musical phrase "he ya" becomes a marker itself, designating the completion of the leader's part as well as the chorus part. A glottal stop terminates the solo phrases, thus forming a complex of features which indicate the phrase unit.

The pitch outline is predominantly a whole-tone system. The pitch center is G natural, with all phrases terminating on this pitch. The "C" phrases in the solo part contain the half-step below G natural, and are the only deviations from the anhemitonic mode. There is an interesting pattern in the distribution of pitches: the chorus utilizes the principal tone and a fourth below; the leader sings mainly pitches above the pitch center. Both parts emphasize the pitch center, yet there is an obvious complementary distribution of the remaining tones utilized.

Jump Dance V.

This Jump Dance has two different versions; they are cognitively recognized as being variants of the same song. The subsequent example is designated as "second version."

There is a symmetrical balance between the leader and chorus parts in the first version. Both comprise four beats in rhythmic duration. Again, the discrete parts do not overlap, yet the phrases are sufficiently short that the leader needs only to take a breath at the termination of his phrase. This parallelism continues with the repetition of the response vocable pattern in the leader's text.

The pitch system is basically a whole-tone outline featuring the triad D F# A. A hint of major tonality appears in the fourth solo phrase and recurs in the eighth

Jump Dance IV.

Jump Dance IV (continued):

phrase, which suggests that this version may be of later origin than the succeeding one, and may show an influence of Western tonality. Since there is no formal ending pattern in the recording, it is assumed that the pitch center is D natural.

The formal organization of the leader's phrases may be clearly diagrammed:

$$A\ A\ B\ C\ D\ A\ A\ C\ B\ A\ A\ A\ B'\ B'\ A$$

The A phrase serves as a type of refrain, given its immediate repetition.

Up-glides invariably mark the beginning of the choral phrases. They often function in this manner for the leader. Aspiration is used concomitantly with the up-glides to designate the beginning of the phrase in both parts. The parallel use of the initial vocable (yo) might also be considered an indicator.

There is little rhythmic variety in this piece, which may be described as isometric. Both pitches and vocables appear on the beats. This rhythmic approach places this variant in sharp contrast to the second version.

Jump Dance V: Second Version.

A number of factors suggest that this version dates from an earlier period than the song described above. This example follows the whole-tone pitch outline exclusively, like the remainder of the repertory. The rhythmic complexity, featuring what might be defined as syncopated, off-beat phrasing of accents, is more common to the *hitla tuluwa* songs. The extension, melodically and textually, of the choral pattern by the leader is also typical. Since the first version simply appears to be an abbreviated rendition of this song, I conclude that the present song is older.

On a formal level, there is no consistent pattern in the solo phrases. What is consistent is the ending phrase in the leader's part: "hi ya" always appears on the same pitch, coinciding with the initial pitch of the following choral response. The phrase markers remain the same, as discussed in the preceding version.

The leader appears to extend response phrases both textually and musically, as observed in previous examples. Comparison of the vocable patterns may be illustrated:

```
chorus:                        yo bi he ya
leader: hi yo hi yo hi yo bi hi ya, (or)
        hi yo hi yo bi hi ya.
```

In rhythmic duration the solo phrases may be extended (from 4 beats) to either 6 or 8 beats, producing a heterometric pattern.

Thus, the parallelism between leader and chorus parts in the preceding song is not found in this piece, and the solo parts contain two phrases. The stress, aspiration, and up-glide at the beginning of the leader's "hi ya" imply that it is a distinct phrase.

Jump Dance V.

Jump Dance V: Second Version.

Conclusion.

In the preceding section, it is clear that the *amona tuluwa* and Jump Dance represent two different musical styles, or categories of style. The leader-chorus pattern is the most prominent distinguishing feature, although the lack of metrical orientation in the *amona tuluwa* is indeed a critical factor separating it from the remainder of the repertory. This factor tends to support my informant's contention that the latter song was used as a marker for the musical occasion. As such, this information provides an important contribution to our knowledge of the structure of the occasion.

Some summary statements deriving from a comparison of the individual Jump Dances would appear to be in order. The following points provide an overview of the significant features of this category:

1. No consistent pattern is observed to determine whether or not overlapping occurs between leader and chorus phrases.
2. The predominant orientation in the solo phrases provides for an 'extension,' or elongation, of the response phrases. This normally involves doubling the length of the response phrases.
3. Choral responses never extend beyond the interval of a fifth, with a wider tessitura observed in the solo phrases; the leader often employs the range of an octave.
4. The whole-tone, or anhemitonic, pitch outline is emphasized. Deviations from this pattern are primarily incidental tones. The resulting modal systems are both major and minor, according to the Western notion of tonality.
5. Chorus phrases terminate on the pitch center, yet the solo part is not restricted to ending with this pitch.
6. Phrase markers are consistent in these dances and include either up-glides, aspiration, dynamic stress, glottal stops, or a combination of these features.
7. There is a limited number of final markers on the level /piece/, and these are consistent with the remainder of the repertory.
8. In rhythmic structure, the responses tend to be metrically patterned. Considerably more freedom is exhibited in the solo phrases, characterized by syncopation or off-beat phrasing of melodic accents. The chorus, then, maintains a stable rhythmic foundation for the dancers; the leader is allowed the freedom of rhythmic manipulation. When the leader's phrases exhibit deviations from the metrical pattern, these invariably occur *internally*, within the phrase.
9. Examples I and V are isometric in rhythmic organization; the remaining examples are heterometric.

In comparing linguistic components, the length of the syllable form in leader phrases contains 4, 5, 7, or 9 units; the choral part contains 3, 4, or 6 units. No consistent pattern emerges in comparing leader-chorus phrase lengths within a single piece. A pattern does emerge in the number of vowels used in corresponding call and response phrases. In Jump Dance I, for example, the leader employs three vowel sounds (o, a, e) and the chorus utilizes these three vowels. In Jump Dance III, the leader sings differing vowels (o, e, a), but their number corresponds with that observed in the choral part (o, i, a). All choral phrases terminate with the vowel /a/;

the majority of solo phrases also end with this vowel, the substitution of the vowel /e/ being the only departure from this pattern (*cf.* Jump Dances I and III). In all but one dance, the first syllable in the response part is "yo." If this syllable does not appear in the initial position in solo phrases, it normally occurs within the vocable pattern. The only change in this context occurs in example IV, which introduces a new vocable pattern.

The sum of vowels in both parts is four: a, e, i, o. Comparison of the leader and chorus syllables including these vowels may be diagrammed as follows:

```
leader:   ha na ya he le we bi hi li o ho yo
chorus:   ha na ya he le    bi hi li       yo.
```

Thus, there is a close correspondence between the vocables found in each part.

This brief examination of some specific Choctaw songs infers that meaning appears to be ascribed at the level /piece/, rather than at the level /phrase/ (in Euro-American terms). The lack of meaningful text leads one to look at gross levels of meaning, in contrast to the level /phrase/. The *amona tuluwa* is obviously an indicator of importance; if my theory is correct, the Jump Dances are also significant markers for the beginning of a cycle. If these pieces serve as 'indicators,' then the question arises: are they something more?

One is dealing with abstractions, both in the *amona tuluwa* and in the Jump Dance. There is no counterpart in the phenomenal world, no metaphorical correspondencies to real life. Hence, any semantic attribution becomes meaningless. No Choctaw informant or singer has been able to verbalize about the meaning of these pieces. It is possible that a semantic component, once existent, has been forgotten, or was initially hidden and subsequently forgotten. This argument, however, seems to be specious.

In Choctaw ideology, and apparently in other Native American societies, animal symbols reflect non-tangible, non-phenomenal energies. The Choctaw, especially individuals in the role of shaman, seem to be aware of types of energy that normally escape the human sensory receivers. For the most part, animal dances are abstract statements about this 'other' reality or concept of reality. Animal dances, then, do not function in metaphorical relationships with their earthly counterparts. The latter are simply a means of rendering the world of spirits, or spirit energies, understandable. Given this background, we may assume that the songs under consideration in this article may be functioning in the same manner.

Most ethnomusicologists, and other Western scholars, have traditionally given little credence to the mystical, metaphysical domains of American Indian thought. Yet it is indeed in this sphere of proposed 'reality' that we must examine these pieces if we are to establish their semantic level. This is also true for Native American music in general.

Occasions for the performance of Indian music are indeed transcendent in nature. Outsiders should be aware of this phenomenon in performance contexts. One feels compelled to ask why Western scholars have not pursued research in this area. I expect that we shall determine the semantic component when we have adequate methodologies to examine the metaphysical aspects of this music.

NOTES

1. Field work among the Mississippi Choctaw was initiated in 1969, with the aid of an NDEA Fellowship through Tulane University. Faculty grants from the California State College Foundation at Bakersfield, the Institute of American Cultures, and the American Indian Studies Center at UCLA, have enabled me to continue with this research.

2. Choctaw terms follow, when relevant, the orthography observed in existing works. This is primarily for the convenience of readers referring to earlier publications. The translations of Choctaw terms were provided by my informants.

3. The dance formation of the *tinsanale hitkla* corresponds with the current Wedding Dance, although the Choctaw title has changed. I have been unable to obtain a recording of a *tinsanale hitkla*, and therefore am persuaded to conclude that these dances are the same.

4. The dance movements of the Jump Dance follow the description of Densmore's Stomp Dance (1943). The latter term is one that the older Choctaw singers do not recognize; thus it implies Densmore's designation.

5. In the semi-circular dance formation, males precede females, and participants interlock arms. The dance step comprises a jumping movement on both feet, with the group moving counter-clockwise.

REFERENCES CITED

Bushnell, David
    1909   *The Choctaw of Bayou Lacomb, St. Tammany Parish, Louisiana.* Bulletin 48. The Smithsonian Institution, Bureau of American Ethnology. Washington, D.C.: United States Government Printing Office.

Densmore, Frances
    1943   *Choctaw Music.* Anthropological Paper No. 28. Bulletin 136. Bureau of American Ethnology.

Draper, David E.
    1971   "Acculturation in Choctaw Indian Music." Paper presented at the Annual Meeting of the Society for Ethnomusicology, Chapel Hill, North Carolina.
    1975   "Folk Categories, Contexts, and Musical Performance." Paper presented at the Annual Meeting of the American Folklore Society, New Orleans.

Peterson, John
    1970   "The Mississippi Band of Choctaw Indians: Their recent history and current social relations." Unpublished Ph.D. dissertation, University of Georgia.

Stevenson, George W.
    1977   "The Hymnody of the Choctaw Indians of Oklahoma." Unpublished Ph.D. dissertation, Southern Baptist Theological Seminary.

Swanton, John R.
- 1911 *Indian Tribes of the Lower Mississippi Valley.* Bulletin 43. Bureau of American Ethnology.
- 1931 *Source Material for the Social and Ceremonial Life of the Choctaw Indians.* Bulletin 103. Bureau of American Ethnology.

FOX, OWL, AND RAVEN[1]

Marcia Herndon

Those students of ethnomusicology who study among American Indians continually deal with the problems of music as a holy object and the secrecy this entails. There are several areas of Eastern Cherokee music which would create a logical, contextual segment; however, some of these materials are presently restricted from publication.

One of my major informants, Tahquett Wallace, allowed some of his information to be released after his death. Tahquett and I discussed the context of Fox, Owl, and Raven at great length, and this material represents the essence of our student-teacher relationship. Thus, I decided to make these data public in honor of Tahquett, for he was a very special man. Not only was he gentle and giving to a fledgling ethnomusicologist, but also to the people of the community in which he lived. He was a healer of the first rank and a humble man, who gave freely of his time and ability to help his people.

Ethnographic Background. Running throughout mythology and the world view of the Eastern Cherokee is a strong belief in spirit beings. In the general cosmology, animal spirits loom large, although there are other kinds as well. In many of the myths, tales, and stories reference is made to the special relationship of the Cherokee to particular animals and their spirits in specific contexts. The Cherokee belief in spirit beings thus shares much with the Guardian Spirit complex of the central United States, where real animals have spiritual counterparts.

For a number of years I have been conducting an ethno-scientific study of animal categories and the relationship between real animals and animals of the spirit world. Living animals vary in the number of spirits and souls they possess, and are divided into categories by the number of their legs and their general habitat. The means of division within the animal world (living animals) tends to be mirrored in the spirit world. Those animals having special characteristics will exhibit similar characteristics in the spirit world. There is some difference between the animal and its spirit counterpart, but the principle exhibited by both animal and Spirit Animal is identical in most cases.

Spirit Animals discussed in this paper are all messengers, who come to warn of impending difficulties. When a fox, owl, or raven appears to a Cherokee, three questions arise. First, is this a real animal or not? Second, if it is not, is it a Spirit Animal,[2] or an evil conjurer masquerading as a spirit being? And third, if it is a Spirit Animal, what message does it bring?

The nature of both message and messengers depends partly on context. The first question is whether the animal who has appeared in one's environment is a real animal or a Spirit Animal. A good deal is known about the behavior of the common animals in the areas, and if a fox, an owl, or a raven appears to be normal in its behavior and time of appearance, it is probably a real animal. In the case of Spirit Animals, there is something different about their behavior in each case. If the animal appears to be a Spirit Animal, the next problem is the determination of its authenticity. Evil conjurers (*ski li*) are said to have the ability to change form. They masquerade as messenger spirits because they are frequently connected with difficulty or danger. To explain this type of transformation, we must discuss the kinds of ritual specialist found among the Cherokee.

Ritual Specialists. Power in the Cherokee universe is good, evil, or impersonal. I will not attempt to determine whether or not the idea that there are good and evil forces came from Christian influence. This distinction, however, is very clear within the type of ritual specialists extant today in the idealized statements made by curers. All curing and divination is said to come from Stoneman. There are various statements of this origin myth; basically, the story of the myth is as follows:

> In the beginning of things, there was a Stoneman, just like a human, but with flesh of rock. He had a stone walking stick, and lived in the cliffs in the mountains. Stoneman was an evil man, or not a very good man, anyway. Every hunter who ever went out in the region in which Stoneman lived never returned. Stoneman had a sharp point in the middle finger of his hand. He would come up behind a hunter, strike him with his walking stick, and point that finger into the man's neck, and then drink his blood. Stoneman had to have blood to drink because he could eat nothing. Like other people, though, he had seven hearts, or souls.
>
> In time, the Cherokee got very tired of losing all their brave hunters to the Stoneman, and wanted to use the whole area for themselves. They wanted to be able to travel freely, without worrying about being killed for their blood. They thought and thought, and finally figured out how to catch him.
>
> The first thing they tried was sending out bands of brave warriors. This didn't work, though, because Stoneman had such thick skin that their arrows just bounced off him. Then he would turn on the hunters and kill them.
>
> Then another tactic was tried. Four young girls, virgins, were chosen, who were having their very first menses at the time of the new moon. They were taken out to the Stoneman's favorite trails because when he walked there, there were holes in the ground. The girls were told to lie down in the trail, across it. A group of warriors hid nearby. After a while, Stoneman came

walking up the trail. He stopped dead still when he saw the girls. He said, "Well, grandchildren, what makes you want to do this to me? You have taken away all my power with the pure power of the moon." At this, he sat down in the trail. The girls got up and circled round him four times. Each time they circled, Stoneman vomited up great quantities of blood. At the fourth time, he fell over, saying, "Granddaughters, you do me wrong. Now I must be no more." At this, the young men who had been waiting in the bushes came out. Stoneman instructed them to gather wood and build a fire, and send for representatives from each of the seven clans. When the representatives came, they were told that they must sit up all night, first having put him over a fire on a spit to roast. They did as he said.

All through the night, Stoneman sang to them. These songs were his final gift in reparation to the Cherokee. They were to be remembered for centuries to come. Stoneman sang and sang as he turned on the spit. He sang all the animal songs and all the other songs. He also told them that those who stayed awake all night would remember all the songs better and longer than those who did not. At dawn, all that was left were ashes.

The songs had come from Stoneman's heart. Everyone knows, however, that his heart would not burn. Five of the seven representatives managed to stay awake all night. They sifted through the warm ashes and found an egg, which was Stoneman's main heart. They broke the egg and found his spirits, which look like tiny grubworms, about four to five inches long. Each was a crystal, with a ruby at one end. Those who had stayed awake, each got one. Whoever keeps the hearts will never forget the songs and ceremonies Stoneman gave, as long as the heart is properly cared for.

A Stoneman's heart must be wrapped in a moccasin or a piece of thin leather, and in the old days it was kept in a rock box in a rock cliff. The spirit of the heart must be fed blood once a week, either from oneself or from a bird or animal. The blood must be rubbed in a corn shuck and then given to Stoneman's heart to eat.

The myth of Stoneman describes the origin of Cherokee curing. Stoneman's heart, of which I have seen several examples, is a rutile quartz crystal, red on one end. Kept with this divining crystal are black, red, yellow, and white strings, which are used in various curing ceremonies. Much of the usage of the crystals, which are also signs of office, is closely related to crystal divination elsewhere among Northern American Indians.

While all curing is said to come from Stoneman, there are at least two curing ceremonies for each disease and for each kind of divination. One set comes from the Stoneman tradition, and another from elsewhere. Both are used for good purposes. However, not all ritual specialists perform only good ceremonies. In addition to the two good systems, there are hints of a third system devoted entirely to evil, whose origin is unknown. The existence of this latter system is in question, but its posited existence is a reality in the minds of the Eastern Cherokee.

For purposes of this paper, the idealized statements of good versus evil cures will be used. Several informants have told me that it is possible for anyone who has been trained to be a curer to go bad. This is dependent upon the personality and inclinations of the individual curer. Although great care is taken through divination and other means to make sure that a trainee has the correct personality characteristics (humility, steadfastness, dedication, and kindness), it is possible for mistakes to be made. Even "good" curing will be regarded ambivalently. What is good for one person or group is bad for another. If, for example, a curer does a ceremony to break the bones of an opponent in a game, he is doing his client a favor, although the opponent whose bones are being broken may regard this act as evil.

The good curer is interested only in others. He cannot cure himself, nor can he usually cure members of his immediate family. His interests must be for the general welfare above all, and egotism should be almost totally absent. Each curer trains one apprentice, sometimes a grandson, niece, or granddaughter. An apprentice can learn from more than one curer, but usually has one main sponsor. Curers can be male or female, and at any given time there will be four to seven male curers and four to seven female curers within the Eastern Cherokee tribe.

As far as I know, there are no evil curers (*ski li*). There are accusations of evil, and these may be simply indications of inexplicable difference in personality or behavior on the part of certain individuals within the tribe. The mythology regarding the evil conjurer, or *ski li*,[3] is large and complex. The ski li can turn himself into Spirit Animal form, and his major purpose is to steal the life force from individuals and add it to his own. The ski li is interested only in himself and will do anything to add a number of years to his life span.

Since Fox, Raven, and Owl come to tell of danger or impending disaster, the possibility of death raises the image of the evil ski li, waiting to steal the life force of those who die before their time. When he comes in spirit form, he may be the source of illness, not merely a harbinger of trouble. The procedures differ slightly from spirit to spirit.

The third question raised concerns the nature of the message. Once the messenger is determined to be neither a real animal nor an evil conjurer, its message is defined by its nature. Fox tells of the mildest troubles; Owl's message is graver; and Raven tells of imminent death. As one moves from Fox to Owl to Raven, the time left to an individual to counter danger decreases.

The Role of Music in Curing. When conjurers attempt a cure, they communicate with the spirits, acting as intermediaries between the patient in the real world and the spirit which has the power to forestall, change, or "move" the condition in question. There are four choices for communicating: thinking, whispering, speaking, or singing. Thinking is the least powerful of these; singing the most powerful. The graver the circumstance, the more likely it is that music will be used.

Not all Eastern Cherokee music is ritual in nature. Most music is dance song. The songs discussed in this paper, however, are not dance songs, but ceremonies. As mentioned above, singing is one of four choices in ceremony. As will be seen in the following discussion, not every case calls for the use of music.

FOX

General Description.

Fox, *tsu'la*, is a variety of four-legged (*di da nv sa di*) animal. They may be wild (*ga ya ta hi*) or tame (*ga na sai*); red (*gi ga ge*) or gray (*sa ko ni ge*); real animals or Spirit Animals. Fox is regarded as a messenger and is thought to have a special relationship with the Cherokee.

The fox is not eaten by the Cherokee because it is thought to be bad meat. It is said that the muscles of the fox are full of sweat from running, and even a dog refuses to eat a fox. It is hunted for its bones, for ritual purposes, and for its pelt. The fox is thought to be very smart and related to the dog. Like the wildcat, housecat, mink, otter, wolf, panther, and polecat, it is a round-paw-footed animal within the four-legged category (*di ga sa kwa lv i tsu la ski*).

In the origin myths, the red fox was a later development than the gray fox.[4] The great speed with which the fox moves became its downfall. In the time when animals could do anything, the gray fox ran much faster than it does today. Once, in its haste, it ran near the sun so fast that it was scorched. To this day, the red fox bears the mark of that experience on its fur.

When the gray fox is seen, no one becomes concerned. A red fox is carefully observed; it may be a Spirit Animal, coming to warn the individual or family of sickness or danger. If the fox behaves normally and does not come too close, it is probably a real animal. If it behaves strangely in any way or comes too close, it is probably Fox.

The evil conjurer rarely transforms himself into Fox. He is said, rather, to send sickness to a household, and later to manipulate a real animal instead of a Spirit Animal.[5] He sends a red fox near the house to frighten the sick person to death. At the time, he is said to be lurking nearby, waiting to steal the life force of the newly-dead.

For Fox, then, there are four possible categories: 1) real animal; 2) real animal sent by a conjurer and behaving abnormally; 3) Fox the Spirit Animal; and 4) the rare case of an evil conjurer who has transformed himself into a simulacrum of Fox. Here, the abnormal behavior can signal all three possible alternates to the real animal.

Since both the control over a real fox and the simulacrum of Fox are the work of an evil conjurer, no distinction is made between them. To determine which of the three possibilities (real, Spirit Animal, or conjurer) is true, the Cherokee address the fox in ritual speech, as follows:

> Greetings to you, Fox. Where are you going?
> What are you doing?

A real fox will stop, listen attentively, and then walk away. If the fox is either a real animal under control or a conjurer transformed into Fox, it will not pay attention to the ritual speech. If it is Fox, it will stop and listen, and then speak:

> I come to give warning, but they try to kill me.

The appearance of a ski li-controlled fox is cause for considerable alarm, while Fox is regarded as bringing a friendly warning. When ski li is suspected, the family sends for a conjurer, who performs protection ceremonies for himself and the family, identifies the illness, and moves it away.[6] He then performs ceremonies to block the ski li, thus preventing him from bothering the family.

Fox warns of sickness and death. If Fox appears at the home of a person who is sickly and ill, it is necessary to call for a ritual specialist, who comes and performs ceremonies to remove the sickness. When the sickness is removed, Fox will not come to the area any more. Fox is not the most usual or common of the messengers. Perhaps this is because one sees very few foxes in Eastern Cherokee territories.

The Role of Music.

When the conjurer is called in the case of sickness, particularly if Fox has been in the neighborhood, certain ceremonies are thought, whispered, or said. These ceremonies can be addressed to various spirits. One is specifically for Fox. It is preceded and followed by a fox call, and is done four times, twice each day, for a total of eight repetitions of the ceremony. Like all ritual ceremonies, that for Fox can also be sung; because of the mild danger in Fox's message, however, it is almost never sung. None of my informants has ever sung the song for a patient, although they say that it could be done. The general consensus seems to be that Fox, as one of the weaker messengers, does not require singing in order to depart. It is enough, in most cases, to think the appropriate ritual ceremony for Fox.

OWL

General Description.

Owl (*u gu gu*) is a variety of flying animal (*ga no he li do i*). There are two kinds: hoot owl and screech owl. They are wild (*ga ya ta hi*) animals only. Like Fox, Owl is a messenger. His relationship with the Cherokee is less clear than that of Fox.

The owl is not eaten by the Cherokee because its meat is thought to be tough. The feathers are used in men's hat bands along with those of other birds to impart the qualities of the birds to the wearer. In the case of owl, intelligence and bravery are the qualities stressed. Occasionally, owl is thought of as sly.

There are no origin stories concerning owl. Owl is present as a minor figure in at least two myths. In all collected versions, however, his character is not detailed.

It is easier to distinguish between owl and Owl than between fox and Fox. Usually, an owl is a night animal. If it appears or flies in the daytime, it is probably not a real animal. If it is Spirit of Owl, one then must determine whether it is really Owl, or a ski li who has assumed the shape of Owl. In addition, the ski li sometimes sends an owl.

Again, ritual speech is used to discover whether one is dealing with Owl or a ski li transformed into Owl.

> Let's go. Now many without clans are coming.
> They have long blades in their hands.
> They will cut your head off. Take off!

When this is recited four times, and the owl has remained in the neighborhood, it is probably a ski li, and the services of a conjurer are necessary. If, on the other hand, the owl leaves after the ceremony has been performed, it is probably bringing a message of caution. Owl does not speak to anyone other than a conjurer. A true Owl will return after flying away. In either case, where it is determined to be Owl or a masquerading ski li, a conjurer should be sought.

The first assumption made by the Cherokee when an owl appears during the daytime is that it is the transformation of an evil conjurer. When there is sickness in the house and an owl appears, it is assumed to be a ski li.

Owl is a problem for the conjurer, but recently a young man shot two owls who came in the late afternoon. Several members of his family were watching and saw the bodies fall to earth. When they went to look for the bodies, they were not there. They immediately assumed there was a ski li somewhere, picking buckshots out of his skin.

When the conjurer comes, the ski li transformed will be nearby and true Owl will return. The conjurer addresses it, saying:

> Greetings to you, Owl. Where are you going?
> What are you doing?

If it is true Owl, he will deliver his message in old Cherokee, which is:

> I cry in the daytime, because of death coming.

Then true Owl gives an Owl cry. However, a ski li who has assumed the form of Owl may also give the same message. Should the conjurer remain doubtful, he will use other, more diagnostic ceremonies.

The appearance of Owl causes even greater concern than that of Fox. This is the result of a close association between Owl and evil in the minds of many Eastern Cherokee. Should the conjurer determine that the messenger is truly Owl, he will attempt to define the cause of the illness and its cure. This is done through divination. Owl does not cause sickness in this case; it only indicates the relative gravity of the sickness. Curing is accomplished by using whatever ritual formulae, songs, or herbs are necessary to the diagnosed disease. Usually the forewarned diseases do not require song. Thought, whispering, and speaking are sufficient.

Owl is also propitiated by the conjurer, who thus thanks him for his warning. Once the cure is in progress, Owl no longer need appear in the region and will fly away, his cry being heard from further and further, until he returns no more.

When a ski li sends an owl or appears as Owl, the situation is much more serious. Again, the ski li is the probable source of the illness. He is seeking to add to the length of his own life. What the ski li seeks is the heart of the sick person. He lurks nearby in animal form, awaiting the moment of death. Then he swoops in, nips out the heart, and runs away with it. The heart is roasted and eaten. By this mechanism, the remaining years of the sick person are added to the life of the ski li. The game is a dangerous one: should the ski li fail, some years of his own life are taken away.

The ski li may attack anyone, but infants are favored because they usually have more years of life remaining. Babies must be protected very carefully. This is done by taking them to the water at the time of the new moon. About a third of the Eastern Band of the Cherokee still observe this ritual. The ceremony is performed by the local conjurer, and many adults go to the water every month as well.

A story concerning the sending of an owl by a ski li illustrates how the conjurer works against evil. I was told that not long ago an owl came to tell of death and sickness to a local man. This was taken as an indication of the approach of an evil one. The evil one made seven attempts to approach the sick man. Each time the owl came closer and closer. After the first five times, not one but four conjurers were called. They came and began to work for the man's recovery. At the sixth approach, the evil one could not come any closer than he had gotten on the fifth attempt. At the seventh approach, he was completely blocked out by the weight of the ceremonies of the conjurers. The evil one saw two pine splints with two jack oak splints crossed on top of them lying on the man's chest, and knew that the forces of good were at work and that it was no use. This message was taken back to the ski li. At first the ski li made fun of the sick man and conjurers, but he was clearly overpowered. It was, in the end, the evil ski li who went away unsuccessful. The patient recovered.

The Role of Music.

None of my informants has ever sung the ceremony to Owl for a patient, although all say it could be sung. Owl, as a weaker messenger, does not require singing. It is enough to say the appropriate ceremony.

The ceremony for Owl begins with the animal's customary cry and is accompanied by imitations of its actions. The cry is repeated four times. Then the conjurer says:

> You say, 'I cry in the daytime because of death coming.'
> In the name of your forecasting, I plunge.

The conjurer then goes into the water. Then he cries again four times. This ceremony is performed twice a day, at sunrise and sunset.

RAVEN

General Description.

Raven (*ko la na*) is a flying animal. Like many other animals, they may be wild (*go ya ta hi*) or tame (*ga na sai*). It is thought that Raven was the first bird.

It is said that Raven has seven spirits (*u da te ti*), like man.[7] If you kill a Raven, it will live again. It is said that one never sees a dead raven. Ravens are regarded as being similar to buzzards, who are scavengers. Ravens live among the high rock cliffs in the more inaccessible portions of Cherokee territory. They have great endurance, and are not eaten. Raven feathers are used for contagious magic; when worn, they transmit intelligence and endurance to the wearer.

Of the three messengers, Raven is the most powerful and his message is the strongest. When Raven appears, the danger is imminent. With Fox and even Owl, there is some time to prepare for disaster. Raven's message, however, is urgent.

Raven is also said to guide one to the place where a dead person is to be found. He has protective qualities as well; he guides travellers at night.

When a raven appears, the number of distinctions to be made is far greater than with either Fox or Owl. The first task is to discover whether this is a real animal. A raven, like a fox, will not venture close to a human being. In addition, the real animal will not circle over the head or the house of an individual. The real animal is also a messenger. If he does not cry as he flies, his direction of flight predicts the weather. If he comes from the North, it will be cold; from the South, it will rain. If he comes from the East, there will be heavy wind; from the West, a great storm is coming.

The other choices are multiples of those previously described for Fox and Owl. They are:

1. Spirits of Raven
    a. Red Raven   (Red)
    b. Black Raven   (Black)
    c. Blue Raven   (Blue)
    d. White Raven   (White)

2. Ski li
    a. Ski li appearing in Raven-like form
    b. Raven ski li.

Since Raven is especially powerful, his character is divided into four separate spirits. Red Raven is associated with anger, warmth, and moonrise. In the Cherokee color symbolism, red is a sign of power. The moon, blood, woman, and heat are described as red. Red Raven is associated with lightning, positive power, and is generally regarded as a good spirit.

Black Raven is associated with darkness, death, and warmth. Black Raven is the ruler of night and the underworld. It partakes of the general qualities of evil and mistrust in some aspects. It has bright eyes and can see for long distances even at night. It is Black Raven that can find the lost or the dead.

Blue Raven, like Black Raven, is associated with darkness; in this case, however, darkness is tempered. White Raven is associated with peace, tranquillity, and normal day-to-day life. Neither Blue Raven nor White Raven is talked about very much, except when invoking all four spirits together.

In terms of ski li raven forms, there are two possibilities. In both, there is a Raven-like manifestation. Many ski li can briefly take such an appearance, but particularly strong and evil ski li will take only the Raven-like form. These latter are extremely dangerous.

When dealing with Raven, then, it becomes vital to distinguish among the various possibilities and to identify carefully with what or whom one is dealing. In this process, additional aids are used.

Native tobacco (*cho la*) is important in many Cherokee rituals. Although it may be smoked at any time, the tobacco used in ritual is sanctified through the power of Raven and four other bird spirits. Sanctification is performed by a type of conjurer called *di do ni ski*, who specializes in tobacco. He offers smoke from the *cho la* to Raven and the other Spirits, who, in mingling the smoke with their own power, give qualities of themselves to the tobacco. Raven transmits his ability to see hidden things. The smoke of sanctified tobacco thus can seek out the ski li.

Cho la may be used to determine the presence of a ski li, no matter what form he is taking. It is also used in the cases of Fox and Owl, but is most effective for Raven because of its association with it. Two methods are used. First, the tobacco may be smoked. The smoker requests the tobacco to seek out the ski li. If the smoke drifts in the direction of the raven, Spirit of Raven is ruled out as a possible explanation. If the smoke drifts in a circle, Raven has come.

The second method is to take four small pieces of unsanctified cho la and place them in a square facing the four major directions.[8] Some sanctified cho la is put on top of the square. Again the request is made. If the unsanctified tobacco falls in the direction of the raven, it is a ski li. If it is Raven, the tobacco will not move.

In addition to distinguishing between a true Spirit and a ski li, native tobacco offers some protection against the machinations of the evil one. When it is smoked, it affords the individual four days' grace in which to seek out a conjurer.

A conjurer must be sought as soon as possible, whether Raven or a ski li has come near. When it arrives, he applies an additional test if the client has determined that the apparition is a ski li. He forces the bird to talk. If fire comes from its beak, it is the most dreaded form, the Raven ski li. Only the most powerful and experienced conjurer will face the Raven ski li alone. If he deems himself too weak, he will call in other conjurers to help.

In the case of the Raven ski li, the conjurer(s) must counter the most malevolent and powerful of the evil ones. The usual methods of performing protection ceremonies are insufficient. Here, the conjurer must sing the ceremony, both for himself and for his client. This song, the most powerful counter-medicine of the Cherokee, merges the conjurer with the highest and strongest of the Spirit Beings: the Created Ones, who move Above in Redness.[9]

A successful performance of the ceremony will leave one of two results. Either the ski li will be "knocked away" from the victim and his raven form will be forced to hop or fly away in defeat, or the ceremony will be so powerful that he will be both "knocked away" and transformed back to his human form. The following story illustrates the latter case.

Awhile back, there was an old lady who was sick, and Raven came. She smoked it and found out it was a ski li. The smoke sent it away. Then she called for a conjurer. When the ski li came again, it was quite close. In fact, it flew up and sat on the chimney of her house. It certainly was a Raven ski li. The woman was really sick by this time. The conjurer went out on the porch and used a ceremony that was very successful. It not only knocked the ski li away from the old lady; it also changed him back again! Before his (the conjurer's) very eyes, that ski li changed from a raven to a man. He was embarrassed because there he was, hanging on to the roof and wearing nothing but his undershorts!

If the bird has been determined to be Raven, the conjurer speaks to it, saying:

> Greetings, Raven. Where are you going?
> What are you doing?

Raven answers:

> I forecast death.

The conjurer must then decide whether the Spirit is Red Raven or Black Raven (Blue Raven and White Raven never appear in this context). This is done by asking Raven where it lives. If it looks up to the home of Red power, it is Red Raven. If it looks down to earth, it is Black Raven, lord of the underworld. In either case, the message is very serious. Black Raven's message, however, is the one of most imminent danger: death is almost certain. Even so, the conjurer will attempt to diagnose the disease and give appropriate medicine (usually in herbal form).

Ceremonies are also performed to move the disease away from the client. When Raven is involved, the ceremony unites the power of the four Ravens with that of the Prime Mover of the universe, the Goddess of all, progenitress and unity of all Spirit Beings — the long white shining being, who has no name and who is symbolized by moving water.

The conjurer goes near moving water twice a day. One of two ceremonial cycles is used, each of which is the reverse of the other. In the first, the conjurer speaks to Raven and sings to the nameless Spirit symbolized by water, and plunges into the water. In the second, the conjurer speaks to the nameless Spirit of water, sings to Raven, and plunges in. Either one is done seven times, twice a day.

When the conjurer sings to Raven, he merges with it so that the power of Raven shall move the illness away through the medium of the nameless Spirit symbolized by water. The reverse case is more complex. The conjurer, in singing to the nameless Spirit, merges with infinity, which is whole, complete, and perfect, in order to move the illness into non-being. Raven then has no further reason to stay. As Tahquett says:

> When the spirits of the water hear and are convinced
> by the conjurer, they will cause the sick person to be
> cured so Raven can go away.[10]

Only the most powerful of conjurers would choose the second course.

The ceremony is repeated until the sick person either recovers or dies. Should he die, the conjurer will assemble three other conjurers to hold a purification ceremony in order to prevent himself from becoming the next victim of illness.

The Role of Music.

As mentioned earlier, ritual materials fall into a four-fold continuum of relative power, in which thinking a ritual is the least powerful and singing it is the most powerful. Thus, for less dangerous conditions, a conjurer need only think the ceremony to effect a cure. Should the condition be regarded as slightly more dangerous, the ceremony would be whispered. Yet more dangerous conditions require spoken ceremony. And finally, extremely drastic situations require singing. The major role of music throughout the Cherokee world-view is to demonstrate the closest possible contact with the supernatural. Singing is a medium of the most power a conjurer can achieve.

This continuum can be seen at work in ceremonies concerned with the animal messengers described here. Only the most extreme cases require singing. Fox, Owl, and Raven represent a continuum from least dangerous to most. In terms of performance, Raven ceremonies are always sung; Owl ceremonies are usually said; and Fox ceremonies are thought or whispered. This concept was borne out in my fieldwork. No conjurer had any songs for Fox or Owl, whereas all had songs for Raven.

There are basically two types of songs for Raven, as mentioned above. These are imbedded in two ceremonial cycles, which are the reverse of each other:

I. speak to Raven;
sing to nameless Spirit of water

II. speak to nameless Spirit of water;
sing to Raven.

There is some range of variation in the performance of each type. The nature of the variation depends upon the context of performance. In order to delineate this variation clearly, each song and ceremony will be discussed separately.

Song to Raven. In singing to Raven and speaking to the nameless Spirit of water, the conjurer is appealing directly to Raven by the most powerful means. This produces a spiritual transformation in the conjurer. For that time, he becomes merged with Raven. In this metaphysical state, the impotent weak man takes on the strength of Raven. He then appeals in less strong terms to the total Spirit, the nameless One represented by moving water, and asks that the evil presaged by Raven be 'moved' by the medium of water. The moving of illness is usually expressed metaphorically as moving the illness away from the client and across seven ranges of mountains. This process does not destroy the illness, but simply diverts it from the client. The still-existant illness is let free to land on another person some distance away. Thus, this method of solving dangerous illness can be looked upon as a diversionary one.

In taking on or merging with Raven, the conjurer places himself in some danger. Raven is, indeed, an extremely powerful and dangerous Spirit Animal. How does the conjurer survive this contact? The present ethnographer does not have full detail. There is some evidence, however, that each conjurer is attached to a major Spirit Animal or series of Spirit Animals, and that only those conjurers who have had a previous metaphysical association with Raven would attempt this ceremony. This raises some interesting questions concerning the Raven ski li. Is it a conjurer who has had metaphysical contact with Raven and later has 'gone bad'? After all, Raven represents a very potent source for either good or evil, in its Red and Black forms.

The text of the Raven song indicates this metaphysical connection:

	Cherokee:	English:
a	*ko la na*	Raven
b	*hi ni ye li sgo*	We are mocking them
a	*ko la na*	Raven
b'	*hi ni ye li sgo*	We are mocking them

c	*sge. go hu ski*	See! Nothing
d	*di na da wo la di ski*	Can overcome us
d'	*di na da wo la di ski*	Can overcome us
b'	*i, ye li sgo*	Oh, mocking them
a'	*ko la na*	Raven

In the song, the conjurer expresses his merging with Raven into one metaphysical agency. 'We are mocking them! Nothing can overcome us!' sings the man.

Raven Song.

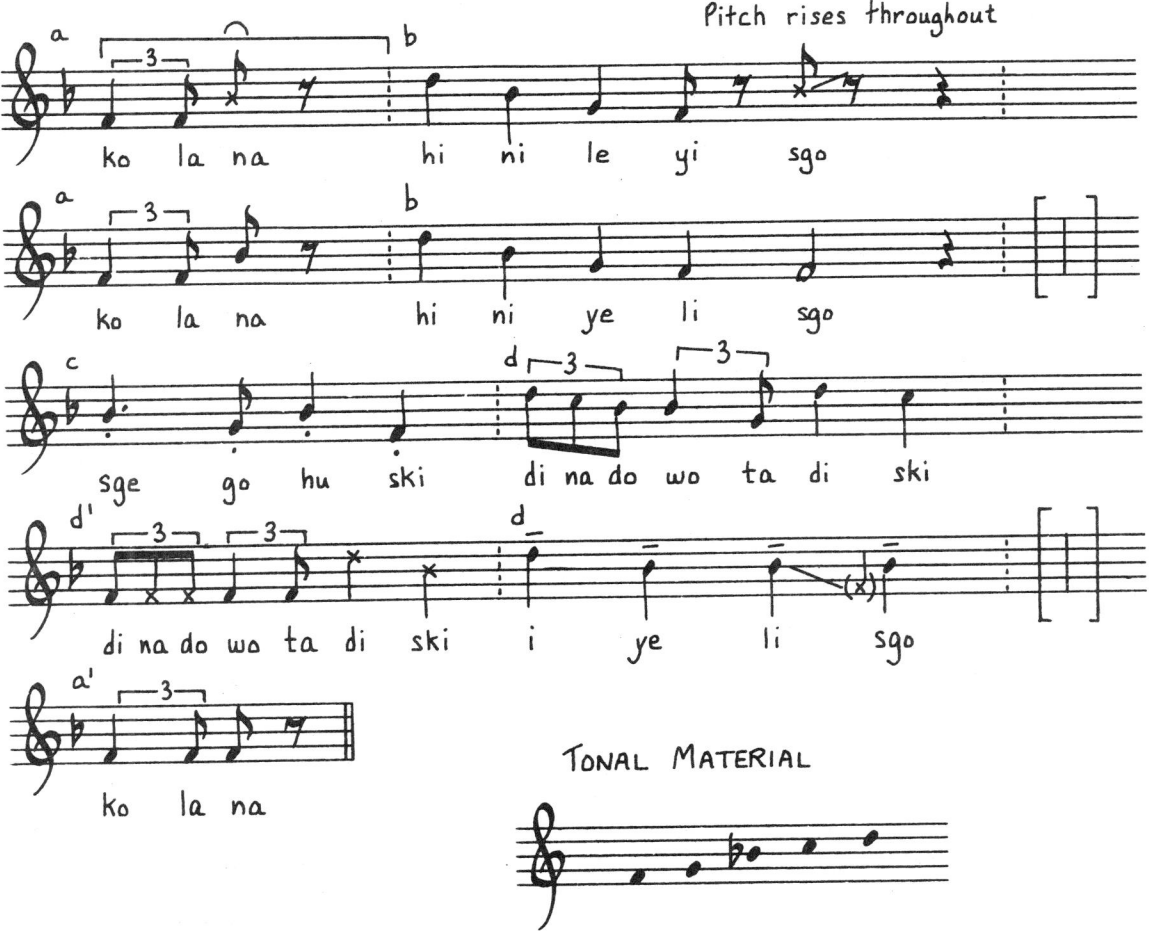

TONAL MATERIAL

The large form of this song is basically two-part song form with the repetition of the first phrase as a coda, as follows:

a b a b'
c d d' b'
a'

Phrases are very short, as is normal in the musical tradition of the Eastern United States. Since the conjurer must of necessity sing alone, however, none of the ceremonial songs have the character of call-and-response found commonly in group singing in this region. It is interesting to note that the second strophe in this example is musically tied to the first by the repetition of the b' phrase at the end of both. The variant of a, here called a' and used as the coda, might also be labelled x. The phrase retains only the verse characteristic, the repetition of *ko la na*, 'Raven,' while the music consists of primes on the lowest tone. This usage of primes to indicate the end of a song or section of a song is fairly common among North American Indians, reaching as far north as the Inuit.

The modal characteristics of this song are pentatonic, with use of five tones anhemitonically. The lowest pitch occurs both at the beginning and the end, and is used sparingly elsewhere. Anhemitonic pentatonic modes are fairly common in the New World.

The presentation of this song to me by my teacher indicates the danger of singing to the spirits out of context. In order to avoid the consequences of bringing Raven upon himself without cause, he sang parts of the Horse Dance at the end of the song, without comment. As a student, it was my duty to unravel the Raven from the Horse.

It should not be assumed from this data that the example given here represents *the* song for Raven. There is good historical evidence to show that both words and music change from conjurer to conjurer through time. Written records of ceremonial chants dating back to the 1870's, kindly shown to me by Lloyd Sequoyah, indicate that each conjurer develops his own ceremonial material in many cases. While some songs and rituals are retained intact from teacher to student, each individual seems to test the validity of each chant for himself. Those that do not work for him are dropped, those that do are kept, and new material is created to fill any void. Thus, the ritual speaking and singing of the Cherokee is a living and developing tradition, in which each conjurer plays his own role as a metaphysical adviser and creator.

Song to the Nameless Spirit of Water. In singing to the nameless Spirit of water and speaking to Raven, the conjurer is basically overpowering the influence of Raven by bringing it into the context of that Spirit without name or form, from whose ideas all forms spring and whose power supercedes all. Little is said of the Nameless one; yet its representative, running water, is contacted every time a ceremony is held. As mentioned earlier, children are placed in the water once a month, and many adults also frequently 'go to the water.' Each repetition of a ceremony requires the conjurer to plunge into moving water. Thus water, as representative of That through which all things live and move and have their being, is the ubiquitous symbol of all spiritual encounters among the Cherokee. To bring any matter into contagious contact with the representative form of this Spirit is somehow to re-form that particle of the universe involved.

The complex act of appealing directly to the Nameless Spirit is not done by all conjurers. For to sing to It is to merge with It; and that merging with the Universal, the Whole, Complete and Perfect, is not to be undertaken lightly. This act reflects either awesome egotism or great humility of spirit. The one is dangerous in the extreme; the other, very rare.

While the act of merging with Raven will only 'move' an illness, the act of merging with the Infinite will take the illness into nothingness. This basic difference implies, again, the relative level of power involved. In all cases except that of the Nameless Spirit, appeal to any Spirit will only 'move' conditions or beings. Only a conjurer of sufficient sweetness of spirit to appeal to the Nameless Spirit can effect a 'cure.'

The act of merging with Totality is once again a dangerous one. How a conjurer may survive such contact is not explained. However, there exists a vast qualitative difference in personality between those conjurers who have chosen lesser and those who have chosen greater means. This difference can only be defined in poetic terms. Such men re-form the world with their minds and praise all existence with every act, word, and thought.

The translation of this song text will be suppressed here. In outline, the words bring together the spirit of the conjurer, Raven, and the Nameless Spirit into one harmony. Raven is first spoken to and then requested to merge with totality as the conjurer merges with it.

The form of the song differs completely from the one presented above. It resembles chant more than music in that it is a simple repetition of a melodic outline with extreme variation. The variant nature of the melody seems to derive from the text. The form, basically, is as follows:

a

a'

x

a^2

a^3

a^4

x'

a^5

a^6

This form falls into the system of magic numbers of the Cherokee. The phrase is repeated, with variations, six times, making seven presentations in all. The magic numbers of the Cherokee are four and seven, each occurring in different contexts. Four is a powerful number; in its contexts, however, it seems to concern ongoing phenomena which have come to a resting place but which are not totally finished.

Here, the form of the song for Raven is basically a strophe with the repetition of two form phrases. This song is not designed to destroy an illness, but only to move it somewhere else. The song to the Nameless Spirit consists of seven phrases. Seven is regarded as more powerful, more fulfilled than four. In its contexts it is always concerned with either the end of a series, or the completion of something, or the fulfillment of something. Here, a seven-step form is found in the context of belief in the absolute destruction of an illness.

The two x-phrases again consist of primes. Their internal placement in the song, however, abruptly disallows a presentation of the ritual material in a group of four. Thus, they prevent the use of four, the unfinished quality.

The pitch material of this song is so atypical of Cherokee music that in itself it suggests the primacy of text and the assumption that this is not music, but chant. Transposed to the area with the least accidentals, the mode is a seven-tone mode, with two half-steps and a minor third in the interval sequence. If we accept this as chant, the mode is unplanned. To force it into the usual pentatonic mode would require the use of 'passing tones,' a practice with which the present author cannot agree.

A third possibility is that the tonal material is planned and represents a deliberate use of seven pitches with the reproduction of an octave, or of seven intervals. This would further emphasize the magic number seven. However, this concept represents the problematical assumption that Cherokee conjurers have two modes of singing: one for songs connected with the magic number four, and one connected with seven, in which all details are performed. As yet, my data show no evidence for this assumption.

Conclusion. This paper presents three messenger spirits and the ceremonial activities with which each is associated. In the ritual context, a continuum of expressive forms may be observed to parallel the continuum of seriousness represented by Fox, Owl, and Raven.

Viewed as a whole, the messenger spirit complex suggests a very real connection between music and other expressive forms, and between expressive forms and aspects of social organization.

NOTES

1. Research for this paper was conducted among the Eastern Band of the Cherokee between 1967 and 1977. The orthography has retained the format used by the Cherokee people who helped me.

My thanks extend to the Cherokee Tribal Council, the Cherokee people, and to those special men and women who minister to the physical and spiritual needs of the community. Without them, this research would not have been possible.

2. To avoid confusion, the names of real animals shall be uncapitalized; those of Spirit Animals capitalized.

3. *Ski li* is a Cherokee word for "owl." "Owl" is a common surname among the Cherokee, but does not imply any association with evil.

4. In the origin myths for modern fauna, the characteristics of the real animal often merge with those of the Spirit Animal. The story of grey fox running near the sun is an example.

5. All conjurers have special affinities with those real animals having spirit counterparts. They have the ability to send animals where they wish. Apprentice conjurers frequently find themselves facing an animal whose ritual formulae they have just learned.

6. Illness cannot be destroyed by ceremony; it can only be 'moved.' A conjurer abjures the illness to go "beyond seven hills," thus taking it out of Cherokee territory.

7. Animals can be classified according to the number of spirits they have. In this system, those with seven spirits constitute the highest order and include man, bear, eagle, and raven.

8. The seven principle directions are North, South, East, West, Up Above, Down Below, and Here.

9. Both song and text are restricted. My mentors have stated specifically that this material cannot be published.

10. The Spirit symbolized by moving water is progenitress of all Spirits and contains all being. She is, therefore, frequently mentioned in the plural when the unity of all existence, both transcendant and non-transcendant, is invoked.

SELECTED BIBLIOGRAPHY

Bibliographies.

Andrews, J. A., *et. al.* "Bibliography of Franz Boas." *American Anthropologist N. S.* 45, no. 3, part 2 (July-September, 1943).

Cardin, Clarisse. "Bio-bibliographie de Marius Barbeau." *Les Archives de Folklore* 2 (1947).

Cavanagh, Beverly. "Annotated Bibliography: Eskimo Music." *Ethnomusicology* 16, no. 3 (September, 1972).

"Frances Densmore: Bibliography." *Ethnomusicology Newsletter* 1, no. 10 (May, 1957); *Ethnomusicology* 1, no. 1 (January, 1958); *Ethnomusicology* 2, no. 3 (September, 1958).

Frisbie, Charlotte J. *Music and Dance Research of Southwestern United States Indians.* Detroit Studies in Music Bibliography, 36. Detroit: Information Coordinators, Inc., 1977.

Guédon, Marie-Françoise. "Canadian Indian Ethnomusicology: Selected Bibliography and Discography." *Ethnomusicology* 16, no. 3 (September, 1972).

Haywood, Charles. *A Bibliography of North American Folklore and Folksong.* 2 vols. New York: Greenberg, 1951; revised ed., New York: Dover Publications, 1961.

Hickerson, Joseph. "Annotated Bibliography of North American Indian Music North of Mexico." Unpublished M.A. thesis, Indiana University, 1961.

Katz, Israel J. "Marius Barbeau 1883-1969." *Ethnomusicology* 14, no. 1 (January, 1970).

Kealiinohomoko, Joan W. and Gillis, Frank J. "Special Bibliography: Gertrude Prokosch Kurath." *Ethnomusicology* 14, no. 1 (January, 1970).

Korson, Rae and Hickerson, Joseph C. "The Willard Rhodes Collection of American Indian Music in the Archive of Folk Song." *Ethnomusicology* 13, no. 2 (May, 1969).

Krader, Barbara, comp. "George Herzog: Bibliography." *Ethnomusicology Newsletter* 1, no. 6 (January, 1956). For additions, see *Ethnomusicology Newsletter* 1, no. 8 (September, 1956) and *Ethnomusicology* 8, no. 3 (September, 1964).

Lee, Dorothy Sara. *Native North American Music and Oral Data, A Catalogue of Sound Recordings, 1893-1976.* Bloomington: Indiana University Press, 1979.

Rhodes, Willard. "Special Bibliography: Helen Heffron Roberts." *Ethnomusicology* 11, no. 2 (May, 1967).

"Special Bibliography: Willard Rhodes." *Ethnomusicology* 13, no. 2 (May, 1969).

Stevenson, Robert. "Written Sources for Indian Music until 1882." *Ethnomusicology* 17, no. 1 (January, 1973).

"English Sources for Indian Music until 1882." *Ethnomusicology* 17, no. 3 (September, 1973).

Books and Articles for the General Reader.

Bahti, Tom. *Southwestern Indian Ceremonials.* Flagstaff, Arizona: KC Publications, 1970.
Ballard, Louis W. "Put American Indian Music in the Classroom." *Music Educators Journal.* March, 1970.
Burlin, Natalie Curtis. *The Indians' Book.* New York: Dover Publications, 1968. (Reprint of 2nd ed., 1923).
Collaer, Paul, ed. *Music of the Americas.* New York: Praeger, 1973.
Curtis, Edward S. *The North American Indian.* 20 vols. Norwood, Massachusetts: Edward S. Curtis, 1907-1930. Reprint ed., New York and London: Johnson Reprint Corp., 1970.
Goodman, Linda. *Music and Dance in Northwest Coast Indian Life.* Tsaile, Arizona: Navajo Community College Press, 1977.
Haefer, Richard. *Papago Music and Dance.* Tsaile, Arizona: Navajo Community College Press, 1977.
McAllester, David P. *Indian Music in the Southwest.* Taylor Museum of the Colorado Springs Fine Arts Center, 1961. Reprinted in *Readings in Ethnomusicology.* Edited by David. P. McAllester. New York: Johnson Reprint Corp., 1971.
McGrath, James, ed. *My Music Reaches to the Sky: Native American Musical Instruments.* Washington, D. C.: Center for the Arts of Indian America, 1973.
Parthun, Paul. "Tribal Music in North America." *Music Educators Journal.* January, 1976.
Rhodes, Robert. *Hopi Music and Dance.* Tsaile: Navajo Community College Press, 1977.
Underhill, Ruth Murray. *Singing for Power: The Song Magic of the Papago Indians of Southern Arizona.* Berkeley and Los Angeles: University of California Press, 1968. (Reprint of 1938 edition).

Books and Articles for the Specialist.

Asch, Michael I. "Social Context and the Musical Analysis of Slavey Drum Dance Songs." *Ethnomusicology* 19, no. 2 (May, 1975).
Baker, Theodore. *Über die Musik der Nordamerikanischen Wilden.* Leipzig: Breitkopf und Hartel, 1882. New edition, with translation by Ann Buckley, the Netherlands: Frits Knuf, 1976.
Black Bear, Ben, Sr. and Theisz, R. D. *Songs and Dances of the Lakota.* Aberdeen, South Dakota: North Plains Press, 1976.
Densmore, Frances. *Chippewa Music.* 2 vols. Bulletins 45 and 53. The Smithsonian Institution, Bureau of American Ethnology. Washington, D. C.: United States Government Printing Office, 1910; 1913.
Teton Sioux Music. Bulletin 61. Bureau of American Ethnology. 1918.
Northern Ute Music. Bulletin 75. Bureau of American Ethnology. 1922.

Densmore, Frances. *Mandan and Hidatsa Music.* Bulletin 80. The Smithsonian Institution, Bureau of American Ethnology. Washington, D. C., 1923.

Papago Music. Bulletin 90. Bureau of American Ethnology. 1929.

Pawnee Music. Bulletin 93. Bureau of American Ethnology. 1929.

Menominee Music. Bulletin 102. Bureau of American Ethnology. 1932.

Yuman and Yaqui Music. Bulletin 110 Bureau of American Ethnology. 1932.

The American Indians and Their Music. New York: The Womans Press, 1936.

Cheyenne and Arapaho Music. Southwest Museum Papers, No. 10. Pasadena, California, 1936.

Music of the Santo Domingo Pueblo, New Mexico. Southwest Museum Papers, No. 12. Pasadena, 1938.

Seminole Music. Bulletin 141. The Smithsonian Institution, Bureau of American Ethnology. Washington, D. C., 1958.

Evans, Bessie and May, G. *American Indian Dance Steps.* New York: A. S. Barnes, 1931.

Fletcher, Alice Cunningham. *The Hako: A Pawnee Ceremony.* The Smithsonian Institution, Bureau of American Ethnology Annual Report, 1900-1901. Vol. 22, part 2. Washington, D. C., 1904.

Garfield, Viola E., Wingert, Paul, and Barbeau, Marius. *The Tsimshian: Their Arts and Music.* Publications of the American Ethnological Society, No. 18. Edited by Marian W. Smith. New York: J. J. Augustin, n.d. New edition, Seattle: University of Washington Press, 1966.

Gilman, Benjamin Ives. "Hopi Songs." *Journal of American Ethnology and Archaeology* 5 (1908).

Hatton, O. Thomas. "Performance Practices of Northern Plains Powwow Singing Groups." *Yearbook for Inter-American Musical Research* 10. Austin: University of Texas Press, 1974.

Herzog, George. "The Yuman Musical Style." *Journal of American Folklore* 41, no. 160 (April-June, 1928).

"Plains Ghost Dance and Great Basin Music." *American Anthropologist* 36 (1933).

Research in Primitive and Folk Music in the United States. Bulletin 24. American Council of Learned Societies. Washington, D. C., 1936.

"A Comparison of Pueblo and Pima Musical Styles." *Journal of American Folklore* 49, no. 194 (October-December, 1936).

Hofmann, Charles, ed. *Frances Densmore and American Indian Music: A Memorial Volume.* Contributions from the Museum of the American Indian, Heye Foundation, 23. New York: Museum of the American Indian, 1968.

Howard, James. *The Southeastern Ceremonial Complex and Its Interpretation.* Memoir: Missouri Archaeological Society, No. 6 (December, 1968).

Johnston, Thomas F. *Eskimo Music by Region: A Comparative Circumpolar Study.* Canadian Ethnology Service Paper, no. 32. National Museum of Man Mercury Series. Ottawa, 1976.

Jorgensen, Joseph G. *The Sun Dance Religion: Power for the Powerless.* Chicago: University of Chicago Press, 1972.

Kolinski, Mieczyslaw. "An Apache Rabbit Dance Song Cycle as Sung by the Iroquois." *Ethnomusicology* 16, no. 3 (September, 1972).

Kurath, Gertrude Prokosch. "Local Diversity in Iroquois Music and Dance." In *Symposium on Local Diversity in Iroquois Culture.* Edited by William N. Fenton. Bulletin 149. The Smithsonian Institution, Bureau of American Ethnology. Washington, D. C., 1951.

"An Analysis of the Iroquois Eagle Dance and Songs." In *The Iroquois Eagle Dance: An Offshoot of the Calumet Dance,* by William N. Fenton and Gertrude P. Kurath. Bulletin 156. The Smithsonian Institution, Bureau of American Ethnology. Washington, D. C., 1953.

Iroquois Music and Dance: Ceremonial Arts of Two Seneca Longhouses. Bulletin 187. Bureau of American Ethnology. Washington, D. C., 1964.

LaFlesche, Francis. *The Osage Tribe: The Rite of Vigil.* The Smithsonian Institution, Bureau of American Ethnology Annual Report, 1917-1918. Vol. 39. Washington, D. C., 1929.

Lesser, Alexander. *The Pawnee Ghost Dance Hand Game.* (c.1933) Madison: University of Wisconsin Press, 1978.

McAllester, David P. *Peyote Music.* Viking Fund Publications in Anthropology, Vol. 13. (c.1949) New York: Johnson Reprint Corp., 1971.

Enemy Way Music: A Study of Social and Esthetic Values as Seen in Navajo Music. Harvard University, Papers of the Peabody Museum of American Archaeology and Ethnology, Vol. 41, No. 3. Cambridge, Massachusetts, 1954.

McClintock, Walter. "Dances of the Blackfoot Indians." Southwest Museum Leaflet. Pasadena, 1937.

The Old North Trail or Life, Legends and Religion of the Blackfoot Indians. (c.1910) Lincoln: University of Nebraska Press, 1968.

Mails, Thomas E. *Sundancing at Rosebud and Pine Ridge.* Sioux Falls, South Dakota: The Center for Western Studies, 1978.

Merriam, Alan P. *Ethnomusicology of the Flathead Indians.* Viking Fund Publications in Anthropology, Vol. 44. Chicago: Aldine Publishing Company, 1967.

Mooney, James. *The Ghost-Dance Religion and the Sioux Outbreak of 1890.* Abridged, with an introduction by Anthony F. C. Wallace. Chicago: University of Chicago Press, 1965. Originally published in Bureau of American Ethnology 14th Annual Report, Washington, D. C., 1896.

Nettl, Bruno. *North American Indian Musical Styles.* Memoirs of the American Folklore Society, 45. Philadelphia, 1954.

"Studies in Blackfoot Indian Musical Culture." *Ethnomusicology* 11, no. 2 (May, 1967); 11, no. 3 (September, 1967); 12, no. 1 (January, 1968); 12, no. 2 (May, 1968).

Parker, Arthur C. *Parker on the Iroquois.* Edited by William N. Fenton. Syracuse: Syracuse University Press, 1968. (Reprint of 1913 ed.)

Roberts, Helen Heffron. *Form in Primitive Music: An Analytical and Comparative Study of the Melodic Form of some Ancient Southern California Indian Songs.* New York: American Library of Musicology, 1933.
  Musical Areas in Aboriginal North America. Yale University Publications in Anthropology, Vol. 12. New Haven, 1936.
Roberts, Helen Heffron and Swadesh, Morris. *Songs of the Nootka Indians of Western Vancouver Island.* Transactions of the American Philosophical Society, Vol. 45, Part 3. Philadelphia: American Philosophical Society, 1955.
Speck, Frank Gouldsmith. *Ceremonial Songs of the Creek and Yuchi Indians.* University of Pennsylvania University Museum, Anthropological Publications, Vol. 50, No. 2. Philadelphia, 1911.
Speck, Frank Gouldsmith and Broom, Leonard. *Cherokee Dance and Drama.* Berkeley: University of California Press, 1951.
Spier, Leslie, ed. *The Sun Dance of the Plains Indians: Its development and diffusion.* American Museum of Natural History. Anthropological Papers, Vol. 16. New York: The Trustees, 1921.
Stevenson, George William. *The Hymnody of the Choctaw Indians of Oklahoma.* Unpublished D.M.A. Dissertation, Music, Southern Baptist Theological Seminary. Louisville, Kentucky, 1977.
Tooker, Elizabeth. *The Iroquois Ceremonial of Midwinter.* Syracuse: Syracuse University Press, 1970.
Underhill, Ruth M. *Papago Indian Religion.* Columbia University Contributions to Anthropology 33, 1946. Reprint ed., New York: AMS Press, 1969.
Wissler, Clark, ed. *Societies of Plains Indians.* American Museum of Natural History. Anthropological Papers, Vol. 11. New York: The Trustees, 1916.
Witmer, Robert. "Recent Change in the Musical Culture of the Blood Indians of Alberta, Canada." *Yearbook for Inter-American Musical Research* 9. Austin: University of Texas Press, 1973.

SELECTED DISCOGRAPHY

Note: All citations refer to 12", 33 1/3 rpm discs unless otherwise specified.

Anthologies.

1973   Asch, Michael, ed. *An Anthology of North American Indian and Eskimo Music.* Folkways FE 4541.
  Ballard, Louis W. *American Indian Music for the Classroom.* Canyon C 3001-3004.
1976   Heth, Charlotte. *Songs of Earth, Water, Fire, and Sky: Music of the American Indian.* New World Records NW 246.

Arctic.

    1954   Boulton, Laura. *The Eskimos of Hudson Bay and Alaska.* Folkways FE 4444.

    1979   *Inuit Games and Songs.* Unesco 6586 036.

Subarctic.

    1972   Jones, Owen R. *Music of the Algonkians; Woodland Indians: Cree, Montagnais, Naskapi.* Folkways FE 4253.

    1974   Mishler, Craig. *Music of the Kutchin Indians of Alaska.* Folkways FE 4070.

Plains.

    1969   *Comanche Peyote Songs.* Indian House IH 2401-2402.

                Kiowa 49; War Expedition Songs. Indian House IH 2505.

    1969, 1974   *Handgame of the Kiowa, Kiowa Apache and Comanche, vols. 1-2.* Indian House IH 2501-2502.

    1971   *Songs of the Arapaho Sun Dance.* Canyon 6080.

    1972   *Arapaho War Dance Songs and Round Dance Songs.* Canyon 6092.

    1973   *Ponca War Dance Songs.* Indian Records IR 1000.

                Sioux Favorites. Canyon ARP 6059.

    1975   *Kiowa Gourd Dance, vols. 1-2.* Indian House IH 2503-2504.

    1976   *Indian Flute Songs from Comanche Land.* Native American Music 401C, cassette.

                Gros Ventre and Assiniboine. Indian Records IR 490.

    1979   Nettl, Bruno. *An Historical Album of Blackfoot Indian Music.* Folkways FE 34001.

Northeast.

    1969   *Iroquois Social Dance Songs.* Iroqraft Q.C. 727, Q.C. 728, Q.C. 729.

    1971   *Chippewa: War Dance Songs for Powwow.* Canyon C 6082.

    1973   *Chippewa Grass Dance Songs.* Canyon C 6106.

    1974   *Winnebago Songs.* Canyon 6118.

Southeast.

    1970   *Songs of the Muskogee Creek, pts. 1-2.* Indian House IH 3001, IH 3002.

    1971, 1974 ?   *American Indian Music of the Mississippi Choctaws, vols. 1-2.* United Sound Recorders USR 3519, USR 7133.

    1976   *Songs of the Caddo, vol. 1.* Canyon C 6146.

    1976-77   *Choctaw-Chickasaw Dance Songs, vols. 1-2.* Choctaw-Chickasaw Heritage Committee, Mannsville, Oklahoma.

    1978   *Stomp Dance, vols. 1-2.* Indian House IH 3003, IH 3004.

Southwest.

- 1968 *Night and Daylight Yeibichei* [Navajo]. Indian House IH 1503.
- 1970 *Navajo Squaw Dance Songs.* Canyon ARP 6067.
  Pueblo Songs of the Southwest. Indian House IH 9502.
  Traditional Apache Songs. Canyon ARP 6071.
- 1972 *Turtle Dance Songs of San Juan Pueblo.* Indian House IH 1101.
  Haefer, J. Richard. *An Anthology of Papago Traditional Music, vol. 1.* Canyon 6084.
- 1973 Haefer, J. Richard. *Papago Dance Songs: An Anthology of Papago Traditional Music, vol. 2.* Canyon 6098.
  Hopi Social Dance Songs, vol. 1. Canyon 6107.
  Yaqui Music of the Pascola and Deer Dance. Canyon 6099.
- 1974 *Dine' Ba'aliil of Navajoland, U.S.A.* Canyon 6117.
- 1979 Heth, Charlotte and Ortiz, Alfonso. *Oku Shareh: Turtle Dance Songs of San Juan Pueblo.* New World Records NW 301.

Great Basin.

- 1972 D'Azevedo, Warren and Merriam, Alan P. *Washo-Peyote Songs; Songs of the American Indian Native Church.* Folkways FE 4384.

Plateau.

- 1953 Merriam, Alan P. *Songs and Dances of the Flathead Indians.* Folkways FE 4445.
- 1973 *Stick Game Songs* [Salish and Kootenai]. Canyon C 6105.
- 1975 *Stick Game Songs by Joe Washington* [Lummi]. Canyon C 6124.
  Yakima Nation Singers of Status Longhouse. Canyon C 6126.

California.

- 1975 *Songs of the California Indians, vol. 1. Concow, Nisenan, Mountain Maidu.* Archaic American Church.
- 1977 Heth, Charlotte. *Songs of Love, Luck, Animals, and Magic: Music of the Yurok and Tolowa Indians.* New World Records NW 297.

Northwest Coast.

- 1967 Halpern, Ida. *Indian Music of the Pacific Northwest Coast.* Folkways FE 4523.
- 1974 Halpern, Ida. *Nootka Indian Music of the Pacific North West Coast.* Folkways FE 4524.

Innovations.

- 1970? *Traditional Indian Hymns.* Witt Memorial Indian Methodist Church Choir, Turley, Oklahoma.
- n.d. St. Marie, Buffy. *Native North American Child: An Odyssey.* Vanguard.
- 1971 Pepper, Jim. *Jim Pepper's Powwow.* Embryo Records SD 731.
- n.d. *Native American Expression.* Brigham Young University Intertribal Choir, Salt Lake City, Utah.
- 1972? Westerman, Floyd. *Custer Died for Your Sins.* Perception Records PLP 5.
- 1974 Ortega, A. Paul. *Two Worlds.* Waltiska.
  Ortega, A. Paul. *Three Worlds.* Waltiska 003.
  Hamana, Bruce. *Hamana.* Canyon Records 7111.
  American Indians Play Chicken Scratch. Canyon C 6120.
- n.d. *Redbone.* Epic EGP 501.
- 1976 *Walk in Beauty My Children.* Bala-Sinem Choir, Fort Lewis College, Durango, Colorado. Canyon C 6149.
- 1977 Chavez, Jose A. *Indian Cowboy.* Apache Spirit AS 666.

Note: The bibliography and discography list representative recordings from all major style areas along with some contemporary innovations. In a few areas, the articles or recordings cited are all that are available and may not reflect a choice on the Editor's part.

Contributors

DAVID P. McALLESTER, a co-founder of the Society for Ethnomusicology and a former editor of its journal, began his studies in Native American music in 1938. He is Professor of Anthropology and Music at Wesleyan University.

WILLIAM K. POWERS is Assistant Professor of Anthropology at Livingston College, Rutgers University. He is author of *Oglala Religion* (University of Nebraska Press, 1977) and numerous books and articles on Native American music, dance, language, and religion. In collaboration with Marla N. Powers, he has recently completed a research project on Oglala food and culture, under the auspices of the Russell Sage Foundation.

THOMAS VENNUM, JR., is an ethnomusicologist with the Folklife Program of the Smithsonian Institution and general editor of the *Smithsonian Folklife Studies*, a monograph and film series. He is currently directing the Federal Cylinder Project at the Library of Congress, a preservation/research/dissemination effort involving more than three thousand early wax cylinder recordings of American Indian music.

MARIA LA VIGNA is a doctoral candidate in the Program in Ethnomusicology at the University of California, Los Angeles, and has recently completed two years of research among the Tewa Indians of San Juan Pueblo. She is currently at the Library of Congress as a researcher for the Federal Cylinder Project.

NORA YEH is the Assistant Ethnomusicology Archivist at University of California, Los Angeles. In addition, she is completing her doctoral dissertation at UCLA on Nan Kuan, a Chinese chamber music tradition. She has taught at Chapman College and for the Semester at Sea Program of the University of Colorado, Boulder.

DAVID E. DRAPER, an interdisciplinary scholar in Anthropology and Music, is presently on the faculty of the Program in Ethnomusicology, University of California, Los Angeles. His research has thus far focused on American Indian and Afro-American societies. Dr. Draper is a Trustee of the American Folklife Center, Library of Congress.

MARCIA HERNDON teaches in the Native American Studies Program, Ethnic Studies Department, at the University of California, Berkeley. Her primary interests are in theory and methodology, especially as expressed in Native American cultures. She is currently completing a book on Southeastern United States Indian music with the assistance of an N.E.H. fellowship.